A Traveler's Guide to the Black Hills

~ John English ~

Crow Peak (photo by author)

Things change constantly.
We do our best to stay current.

To include, delete or update a listing
please email **updates@bhsw.org**

Before booking accommodation, we strongly suggest that you
pop the address into Google Maps™ and
take a look at it in the street-view.

There is no fee for inclusion. The Publisher is not responsible for errors or omissions.

This book was created and printed in the good old USA.
All of the photos in this book are by the author, unless otherwise noted.
Copyright © 2016 John English
All rights reserved.
Pronghorn Publishing/BHSW Inc.
606 6th Avenue, Belle Fourche SD 57717

ISBN 13: 978-0-9635669-2-8

Other Books From BHSW

Fiction:

Murder on the Missouri (Pronghorn)
Waves - Short Stories (Pronghorn)

How-To:

The Gout Book (Pronghorn)
The Building Buddy (Pronghorn)
Woodworker's Guide to Sharpening (Fox Chapel)
Bench Planes & Scrapers (Linden)
Turning Wood with Carbide Tools (Linden)
Harvest Your Own Lumber (Linden)

History:

The Black Hills, A History in Photographs (Pronghorn)
The Cowboy Story, A History in Photographs (Pronghorn)
A Photographic History of Colorado (Pronghorn)

*All titles are available from the BHSW physical store at
518 Grant Street, Belle Fourche 57717 or online at bhsw.org*

There's a Quick Navigation Guide
at the back of the book (page 171).

Old Dodge pickup near Bear Butte (photo by author).

West River – a Short Introduction

The half of South Dakota that is left of the Missouri River on a map is known to the state's residents as 'West River'. It's astounding how different the two halves are. The eastern portion is flat, fertile farmland, while the west is rugged ranches, rivers, rocks and ancient worn-down mountains – the Black Hills.

The river is where the Old West began.

In 1776, the year of American independence, the Lakota conquered the Cheyenne here. They had gradually been moving west from Minnesota, and wild horses on the plains eventually transformed the way they lived. From woodland hunters they became dependent on bison for food, shelter, clothing and a host of personal items. The center of the Lakota world became Ȟe Sápa, the Black Hills (Mo'ȯhta-vo'honáaeva in Cheyenne).

Europeans followed the same migration pattern, relentlessly moving west in search of fertile land and the allure of gold. They soon discovered that the Lakota's Achilles heel was bison. Wipe out the animals and you can destroy the culture.

About halfway between the river and the Wyoming border, just below the North Dakota line, is the modern town of Lemmon. Ten minutes south of downtown is the Grand River National Grassland, which surrounds Shadehill Reservoir. In 1823 a trapper named Hugh Glass was abandoned without supplies or weapons here, and left for dead by his companions after being attacked by a grizzly. He set his own broken leg and spent the next six weeks crawling and stumbling across the plains back to the river. He eventually reached the safety of Fort Kiowa (present day Chamberlain, SD). His story was told in the 2015 movie *The Revenant*, starring Leonardo DiCaprio, who won an Oscar for his portrayal.

That wasn't the only movie that attempted to portray West River life in the nineteenth century. Halfway up Spearfish Canyon, in the heart of the northern Black Hills, is the village of Savoy. Take the gravel road to the right of the hotel and drive a few minutes past Roughlock Falls: you'll then be where the winter scenes in Kevin Costner's epic *Dances With Wolves* were shot.

John Lopez is from Lemmon. An amazing artist whose work is celebrated around the globe, he is first and foremost a horseman. He breeds and gentles colts, and somewhere along the way he began to transform that love into another, sculpture. John does something spectacular with the remnants of West River 'civilization'. In his own words, he chooses among "the elements of the past—the actual implements that plowed the soil or cut the grain or dug the dinosaur—and creates the curve of a jaw, the twitch of a tail, the power of a shoulder." His creations are simply jaw-dropping: you can see several around the Black Hills.

John Lopez's hybrid metal sculpture of the grizzly bear attack on Hugh Glass in 1823 is on view at the Grand River Museum in Lemmon. For more information, visit johnlopezstudio.com.

Photo courtesy of John Lopez

John's horse, **Iron Star**, is on the Main Street in Hill City. His **Sand Hill Crane** is at the Rapid City airport, and the work **Dakotah**, a magnificent bison bull, is at the Dakota Steak House at 1325 North Elk Vale Road in Rapid City.

John Lopez may be a national treasure, but his heart belongs here. And in the same way that he combines those manufactured artifacts with his love of nature, the Black Hills are blessed with breathtaking natural scenery and a lot of manmade attractions. Those two factors combine to provide visitors with an awful lot to do on a vacation. So, getting the most out of your days requires a little planning.

Why this book?

In 2013, we published *The Black Hills – A History in Photographs*. While doing the research for that book, we discovered that there were some commercial guides to the Hills, but in most cases just sorting through their ads was a chore (especially online). And unfortunately, many sites only included destinations that paid for those ads. We realized that there was a genuine need for a comprehensive, family-friendly way to plan a vacation – one that included all the free stuff, too. There aren't any commercials in the body of this book. At some stage, we plan on including some coupons in the back to help visitors recoup the cost of the book., but we promise it will never become just another volume of ads.

Even a vacation needs a little organizing, and by dividing the Black Hills into zones we realized that a visitor can organize days geographically, and avoid a lot of backtracking. We also provide maps at **TheBlackHills.info**, where you can zoom in on a town and then click on everything interesting in and around it. Each of the entries in this book is numbered, and those numbers correspond to a tag on the map. Sometimes you'll need to zoom WAY in to see all the tags. Note that the numbers jump a few at the end of each section in the book, and that's just designed to accommodate future changes. The map gives you a pretty good idea of what's close by, and doable in the time allowed.

We don't want to make decisions for you. But we do want you to be able to make well-informed choices. So, the intention is not to review everything for you, but rather to let you see everything that's available, and then add a few helpful notes (such as directions, accessibility, etc.). We've provided phone numbers for just about everything: if you're looking for more info online, we've found that popping the phone number into a search engine seems to yield better and faster results than words, so we included them.

Speaking of going online, be sure to visit the **Black Hills National Forest** website at fs.usda.gov/main/blackhills/home. It's your forest, and the incredible folks who care for it have provided an invaluable resource for finding everything from hiking trails to campsites in the BHNF. There is no entrance fee: the Forest is open year-round for a variety of recreational activities and uses. However, there are fees at most campgrounds and day use areas. We strongly suggest that you include some quiet time enjoying the forests, canyons, lakes and streams in between visiting the major attractions. Those small charms (most of which cost nothing) can make the difference between a frantic push to get everything done, and an intimate experience that will invite you to return again and again to these ancient Hills.

John

Table Of Contents

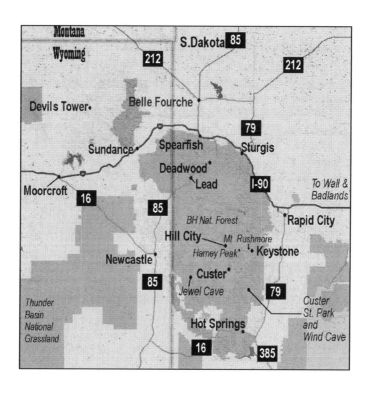

Zone 1: The Northern Hills

The most striking aspect of this zone is the completely different personalities of the communities within it. **Belle Fourche** (with listings beginning on page 10) is a commercial center that serves a vast area geographical area. It's the shopping hub for ranches and small communities in four states (both Dakotas, Montana and Wyoming). For fifty years, more cows and sheep were shipped from the Belle Fourche train depot than from anywhere else in the entire country, and there are still big sales every week. Here you'll find Western clothing, tack shops and one of the best annual rodeos in America. (The image at right is the author's oldest son, Tyler, riding a bareback bronc.)

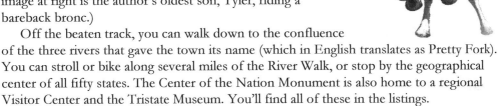

Off the beaten track, you can walk down to the confluence of the three rivers that gave the town its name (which in English translates as Pretty Fork). You can stroll or bike along several miles of the River Walk, or stop by the geographical center of all fifty states. The Center of the Nation Monument is also home to a regional Visitor Center and the Tristate Museum. You'll find all of these in the listings.

Deadwood (page 20) played host to the likes of Wild Bill Hickok, Seth Bullock and Calamity Jane, and is still a rocking place. Many of the original building are beautifully preserved, and the town has an impressive rodeo grounds. Now also home to a vibrant casino industry, among the town's crown jewels are the Adams House Museum and the new Days of 76 Museum.

Lead (page 39) was once home to the world's largest open pit goldmine, which you can visit. Built on steep hillsides, it's a historic town with a very bright future: the mile-and-a-half deep shafts and tunnels of the old mine are now being used for scientific research.

Spearfish (page 46) is known for a university and a sawmill, and it has become a haven for retirees, too. Blessed with great restaurants and coffee shops, it's also the gateway to the magnificent Spearfish Canyon.

And while **Sturgis** (page 56) will always be thought of first as the home of the annual motorcycle rally, the town also has an incredibly rich history – much of it connected to Fort Meade. It's also on the doorstep of one of the most unusual mountains out West, the solitary peak of Bear Butte (at left), which is a deeply spiritual site for the Lakota and Northern Cheyenne people. By the way, if you hike to the top, please respect any prayer offerings you see tied to branches.

Belle Fourche

ZIP: 57717

Things to See and Do – Belle Fourche

The Tristate Museum (001)

- *415 5th Avenue.*
- *Free admission, donations accepted.*
- *thetristatemuseum.com*
- *(605) 723-1200*

This is an exceptional regional museum. Among the subjects covered by the collections are cattle and sheep operations, sugar beet and railroads, dinosaurs, music, military displays, and the lives of cowboys, ranchers and settlers. There's a nice saddle collection, too.

Johnny Spaulding Cabin (002)

- *415 5th Avenue.*
- *Free admission, donations accepted.*
- *thetristatemuseum.com*

Here's a wonderful example of a restored, hand-hewn log, two-story cabin built in 1876 during the gold rush. Visitors can climb the tiny staircase to the bedrooms, or see how people cooked and lived out West 140 years ago. Located on the Tristate Museum campus.

Center of the Nation Monument and Visitor Center (003)

- *415 5th Avenue.*
- *Free admission, donations accepted.*
- *thetristatemuseum.com*
- *(605) 723-2010*

The city of Belle Fourche is the closest settlement to the geographical center of the United States (including Hawaii and Alaska). In 2007, a 21-foot diameter monument of etched South Dakota granite was installed behind the Museum, on the south bank of the river, to house a bronze National Geodetic Survey marker. It's a great photo opportunity with a large flag display, and the adjacent Visitor Center can answer a lot of tourism questions. Great spot for a picnic lunch, too…

The River Walk/Bike Path (004)
- *Two good places to start are at Hermann Park or the Museum*
- *Free.*
- *bellefourche.org (to download a map of the path, go to Site Map, then Parks, and then Belle Fourche River Walk Map. Or pick up a printed copy at the Visitor Center.)*
- *(605) 723-2010*

The Walk is a five-mile circular trail that wanders along the river, visits neighborhoods and the downtown area, and wanders through some of the city's parks. Parents with antsy children will appreciate this opportunity to burn off some energy. Bring your Frisbee™, as there is a disc golf course along the river near the Visitor Center.

Community Center and Indoor Pool (005)
- *1111 National Street*
- *Very modest fee*
- *bellefourche.org (click on 'Site Map')*
- *(605) 892-2467*

A city-owned complex that centers on a 25-meter indoor swimming pool, it also has a wading pool, hot tub, water slide, huge gymnasium with racquetball courts, a cardio room, weight room, a walk/run track, and even WiFi. Daily rates are available, and are very reasonable. Just what a family needs if the weather turns wet…

Belle Fourche Country Club (006)
- *10941 SD Highway 34*
- *9 holes with cart $26 to $39 (2015)*
- *bellefourchecountryclub.com*
- *(605) 892-3472*

It's a scenic nine-hole course, very well maintained with a couple of quite challenging holes. There's a good bar and restaurant (the menu is on their website). You can book a tee time online from March to October, and you can rent clubs if you didn't bring yours.

The Center of the Nation AMC Car Collection (007)
- *709 State Street*
- *Free (year round)*
- *(605) 641-9941*

This is a remarkable private collection of AMC automobiles housed in a building on the main street (State Street). The owner, Ellis Tripp, is a gracious host who will meet fellow enthusiasts on site if they phone for an appointment.

Please note that this isn't a place for kids to run off some energy: it's a privilege to be allowed access to this private resource.

Rocky Point Recreation Area (008)
- *18513 Fisherman's Road*
- *State Park, $6 per vehicle daily rate (2015)*
- *gfp.sd.gov/state-parks/directory/rocky-point*
- *(605) 641-0023 (reservations advised)*

Located on the 8,000-acre Belle Fourche Reservoir (about 5 minutes east of town on Highway 212), the State Parks facility offers beaches, boat ramps, campgrounds, cabins, fish cleaning stations, a dump station, potable water fill, playgrounds, and even game checkouts. Fish species are walleye, yellow perch, channel catfish, black crappie, smallmouth bass, white bass and tiger Muskie.

City Parks (009)
- *There are 11 parks in the city limits, several with playground equipment.*
- *bellefourche.org (go to Site Map/Parks/Belle Fourche Parks map)*
- *Free.*
- *(605) 723-2010*

Black Hills Roundup Rodeo (010)
- *At the Rodeo Grounds and downtown*
- *Fee for rodeo events, (July 1-4, 2016)*
- *blackhillsroundup.com*
- *(605) 723-2010*

One of the oldest outdoor rodeos in America, where top ranked cowboys and cowgirls compete in barrel racing, bareback, saddle bronc, steer wrestling, bull riding, team roping and more. There's a weeklong carnival, huge fireworks display, a mile-long parade, a barbecue, ranch rodeo and the Miss Rodeo contest. Wonderful family fun!

The horse in the image is a good three feet off the ground…

SD High School Rodeo Finals (011)
- *At the Rodeo Grounds, mid-June*
- *Fee*
- *sdhsra.com*
- *(605) 529-5868*

High school rodeo is a serious business in cattle country: the skills on display are required daily on the ranch. These young men and women love what they do, and they are very, very good at it. This is a great way for families to enjoy a top quality rodeo on a budget. It's very exciting, especially for kids who like horses. And nothing tastes as good as a rodeo burger!

Belle Fourche Skate Park (012)
- *At Highland Park on National Street*
- *Free*
- *bellefourche.org*
- *(605) 723-2010 – Visitor Center*

If your kids brought along their skateboards, this is a great place for them to burn off some energy. It's located half a block west of the Community Center. If you need boards, Wal-Mart™ in Spearfish (605-642-2460, fifteen minutes away) usually has a few inexpensive ones in stock, and there are several large sporting stores in Rapid City.

Ice Skating/Hockey Rink (015)
- *National Street and 7th. Avenue*
- *Free*
- *facebook.com/Belle-Fourche-Hockey-Rink*

An outdoor rink, it's flooded in winter when the weather is cold enough. It's located less than a block east and south of the Dakotamart supermarket.

Community Theatre (013)
- *At the Belle Fourche Area Community Center.*
- *Fee for tickets (April-October)*
- *facebook.com/BFCTheater*
- *(605) 892-2467*

There are usually about four plays each season.

Center of the Nation Concerts (fall-spring) (018)
- *At the Belle Fourche Area Community Center*
- *Fee for tickets, available by subscription*
- *centerofthenationconcerts.org*
- *(605) 892-3602 or 892-5599*

The Center of the Nation Concert Association is a private, non-profit organization that was established in 1992. Each year, CNCA puts on five concerts in the terraced, indoor auditorium at the Community Center, which has remarkable acoustics. They usually run from October through April. There are also **FREE** outdoor summer concerts at the Band Shell in Herrmann Park, sponsored by the **Belle Fourche Arts Council.** For a schedule, visit *bellefourchearts.com*. The park is two blocks east of Hwy 85 on Jackson St.

Belle Fourche Cowboy Band (014)

- *bfcowboyband.com*
- *(605) 892-4366*

Organized in 1931, the band is a regional treasure. In 1935, it was invited to play at the Stratosphere Bowl when the National Geographic Society and the Army were making their famous balloon flights. And in June of 1953, the band was invited to play for President Eisenhower at Mount Rushmore – where it was designated as the President's official band for the occasion. Summer concerts are held in venues such as the band shell in Herrmann Park, the Ranch Rodeo (4th of July weekend), parades and other events – you can see schedule online at the website above. The music is somewhat eclectic – from patriotic to film themes, and classics such as Ghost Riders in the Sky.

Center of the Nation Marathon (016)

- *Sept 12-17, 2016*
- *Entry fee $30 - $150*
- *mainlymarathons.com*
- *Hanne@mainlymarathons.com*

If you're a runner you may already know about the Center of the Nation low-key marathon, which is scheduled over six days in six adjoining states – MT, ND, SD, WY, NE and CO. There are opportunities for full, half and 5K runs.

The Belle Fourche leg is on September 14th and begins at 6:30 AM on the River Walk behind the Visitor Center. Register online, and earlier is cheaper.

Hometown Thursdays (017)

- *State Street (downtown)*
- *Free*
- *hometownthursdays.com*
- *(605) 645 4078*

This is a mini street festival featuring live music, which takes place downtown on Thursday evenings, June through August. Two blocks are closed to traffic for the event and there's ample parking, food vendors, shopping, kid activities and a street dance.

Where to Eat - Belle Fourche

Note: Many of the eateries listed here are located along Belle's 5th Avenue, which is also known as State Highway 85, the main north-south artery through town.

The Green Bean Coffee Shop (020)

Great sandwiches, gourmet coffee, top notch service, and still surprisingly affordable. Located on the south side of the city's main street, three blocks east of Highway 85.

710 State St
(605) 723-0760
Find it on facebook.com

Patty's Place (021)

Offers a comprehensive menu of standard fare, and is also known for barbecue and Cajun specialties, and baked goods. Gift shop on premises. Check out the hot sauce rack!

1405 5th Avenue (Hwy 85)
At the corner of Hwy 85 and National St.
(605) 723-0099
Find it on facebook™

American West Steakhouse (022)

Burgers – Steaks – Bar
Also does large scale catering and Bar-B-Cue.

1807 5th Ave
(605) 723-0139
Find it on facebook

Jumpin' Jacks (023)

Truck stop, American style family diner.

16 North 5th Street
(605) 892-2270

Belle Inn Restaurant (024)

Family dining with cowboy flair. Not fancy, but good food and great pie.

2511 5th Avenue
(At the south end of town)
(605) 892-4430

China Garden (025)

614 5th Avenue
(605) 892-3888

Luigi's Italian Restaurant (026)
  Pizza restaurant with bar, about three minutes east of town. Excellent!
      11301 US Hwy 212
      (605) 892-9066

Bob's Café (027)
  Old-fashioned, no frills diner. Park in rear.
      610 5th Avenue
      (605) 892-4298

Papa John's Pizza (028)
  This is a take-out facility at the Big D gas station.
      2406 5th Avenue
      (605) 892-2411

Pizza Hut (029)
      1819 5th Avenue
      (605) 892-2671

Hardee's (030)
      2504 5th Avenue
      (605) 892-6170

Subway – North (031)
      10982 US Hwy 212
      (605) 723-7827

Subway – South (032)
      1400 Mill St
      (605) 892-4020

Dairy Queen (033)
      208 Pine St (right on Hwy 85)
      (605) 723-7222

Ski's Pizzeria (034)
  Take and bake, or they'll bake for you.
      1853 5th Ave
      (605) 723-7547

Taco John's (035)
      1401 Mill St
      At the corner of Hwy 85 and National St.
      (605) 892-6436

Outlaw Saloon (036)
      616 5th Avenue
      (605) 892-9072

Cowboy Back Bar (037)

Music, burgers, outdoor dining.
618 5th Avenue
(605) 892-2566

The Branding Iron (038)

About a mile south of town on the west (right) side of the road. Music, good food.
19079 US Hwy 85
(605) 892-2503

Belle Fourche Country Club Bar & Grille (039)

Call ahead or visit online for hours and menu.
bellefourchecountryclub.com/barandgrill
(605) 892-3472

Grap's Burgers & Brews (040)

The newest venue for dining in Belle Fourche.
512 National St
(605) 723-1610

Where to Stay - Belle Fourche

AmericInn Lodge & Suites (050)
This award-winning hotel is a block north of the golf course. There's a pool, breakfast room and family suites. The AmericInn earned a 5.0 ranking on Tripadvisor in 2015.
2312 Dakota Avenue • (605) 892-0900

Sunset Motel (051)
4.5 rating on Tripadvisor in 2015. Located at the south end of town.
19022 US Hwy 85 • (605) 892-2508

Ace Motel (052)
4.5 rating on Tripadvisor in 2015.
109 6th Avenue • (605) 892-2612

Econo Lodge (053)
4.0 rating on Tripadvisor in 2015.
1815 5th Avenue • (605) 892-6663

Super 8 (054)   (605) 892-3361

Bunkhouse Motel (055)   (605) 892-2634

King's Inn (056)   (605) 892-2634

Reid Motel (057)   (605) 892-2521

Scoot Inn B&B (058)   (605) 892-2660

Camping

Riverside Campground (060)   (605) 892-6446

Wyatt's Campground (061)   (605) 892-0600

Rocky Point Recreation Area (008)   (605) 641-0023
gfp.sd.gov/state-parks/directory/rocky-point

Besler's Cadillac Ranch (062)   (605) 390-1078
Horse boarding, RV and tent sites, cabins, barn for weddings etc., little log church.

Where to Shop - Belle Fourche

Gifts and Souvenirs

Black Hills Gifts & Souvenirs (070)	518 Grant Street	(605) 591 2947
The Olive Branch Western Store (071)	501 State St	(605) 723-1111
CON Visitor Info Center's Gift Shop (072)	415 5th Avenue	(605) 723-2010
Office Emporium (073) – also UPS shipper	612 State St	(605) 892-3411
Belle Flowers & Gifts (074)	619 State St	(605) 892-4626
Posy Palace Flowers & Gift Baskets (075)	839 State St	(605) 892-2244
DJ Saddlery Leather Goods (076)	10989 Gilger Ln	(605) 892-4459
Love That Shoppe Antiques (077)	515 State St	(605) 568-0123
Mason's 5th Ave Gas and Gifts (078)	510 5th Avenue	(605) 892-4564
Man Cave Cigar, Tobacco & Knives (079)	617 State St	(605) 346-0177
Tristan's New & Used (080)	607 State St	(605) 892-9191
CBH Travel Center (081)	18765 Hwy 85	(605) 723-9000
Rustic Soul (082)	509 Grant Street	(605) 210-1421

Everyday Needs

Shopko (090)	General store, pharmacy	(605) 892-3393
Runnings (091)	Hardware, gifts and apparel	(605) 892-2588
Dakota Lumber (092)	Hardware and lumber	(605) 892-4041
Roundup Building Center (093)	Hardware and lumber	(605) 892-2094
Family Dollar (094)	General store	(605) 892-0088
West Tire (095)	Tires, auto repair	(605) 892-2001
Southside Garage (096)	Tires, auto repair	(605) 892-9181
Sturdevants (097)	Auto parts	(605) 892-2658
NAPA (098)	Auto parts	(605) 723-6272
E.T. Sports (099)	Motorcycles, ATVs	(605) 892-2945
Carl's Trailers (100)	Trailer sales and service	(605) 892-4032
Mr. Movies (101)	DVD rentals	(605) 723-0034
Strandz (102)	Hair stylist	(605) 723-8644
Hair Country (103)	Hair stylist – men & women	(605) 892-3889
Coop's Barber's (104)	Men's barbershop	611 State St
Stereos & Stuff (105)	Electronics, cellphones	(605) 892-4904
Belle Fourche Liquor (106)	Beer and liquor	(605) 892-4125
Lueder's Food Center, Inc. (107)	Groceries	(605) 892-6375
Lynn's Dakotamart (108)	Groceries	(605) 892-4330
Integrity Meats (109)	Locally raised beef	(605) 892-6215
Belle Fourche Medical (110)	Clinic	(605) 723-8970
Spearfish Hospital (111)	Hospital, ER (911)	(605) 644-4000

Deadwood
ZIP: 57732

Things to See and Do – Deadwood

Days of '76 Museum (120)
- *18 Seventy Six Drive*
- *Adults $6.00, Children 7-13 $3.00, Children 6 & under free (Spring 2016)*
  - *Combo pass for Adams House and Days of '76 Museum $12.00*
- *DeadwoodHistory.com*
- *(605) 578-1657*

This is a breathtaking collection of both pioneer and Native American artifacts, archives and firearms, along with the largest collection of horse-drawn vehicles in the state. The 32,000-square-foot facility is located beside the rodeo grounds at the north end of town. Simply magnificent! The name comes from the founding of the town and the gold rush of 1876. Deadwood – the entire city – is a National Historic Landmark.

The Adams House and Museum, and HARCC (121)
- *House – 22 Van Buren Street*
  - *Adults $8.00, Children 7-13 $4.00, Children 6 & under free*
- *Museum – 54 Sherman Street*
  - *Suggested donation: $5 for adults, $2 for children.*
- *DeadwoodHistory.com*
- *(605) 578-1657*

Founded in 1930, the museum has three floors of exhibits and a renowned Western bookstore. Its goal is to preserve and share the history of the Black Hills. The home of the museum's founder, W.E. Adams, is also open to the public. Built in 1892, it is a wonderful Queen Anne with a round tower, oak woodwork and stained glass windows. According to DeadwoodHistory.com, the home "sat silent for almost 60 years after W.E. Adams' death in 1934, when his second wife Mary Adams closed the doors. Mrs. Adams left everything intact from the sheet music in the piano bench, the books in the library, the china in the pantry, to the patent medicines in the bathroom, the gilded settee in the parlor and even the cookies in a cookie jar."

Visitors, especially those with an interest in Black Hills history including gold mining, might also want to check out another Deadwood History resource. The **Homestake Adams Research and Cultural Center** (HARCC) at 150 Sherman Street is invaluable to researchers, and casual visitors can also "browse through tens of thousands of historic photographs, view rare and unique historic documents, attend a lecture, or take part in a workshop".

Mount Mariah Cemetery (122)
- *From Highway 85, go east on Cemetery Street and take a left on Lincoln.*
- *$2.00*
- *cityofdeadwood.com*
- *(605) 578-2600*

The Mt. Moriah Cemetery Visitor Center offers a fifteen minute interpretative video plus interactive resources that focus on "cemetery history, native and introduced plant species, cemetery symbolism and death statistics within Deadwood from 1875 to 1900.". The main attractions are the graves of **Wild Bill Hickok** and **Calamity Jane**, but this is also "the final resting place of western legends, murderers, madams, and pillars of Deadwood's early economic development". Seth Bullock, a friend of Teddy Roosevelt and the first sheriff of Deadwood, is buried above Mount Mariah on the steep trail to White Rocks, with a view across the gulch to the tower on Mount Roosevelt.. Potato Creek Johnny, who found a huge gold nugget in the creek in 1929, also rests in the cemetery. Note that it is a challenging uphill hike from downtown, and anyone with health issues should drive.

Broken Boot Gold Mine (123)
Enjoy an underground tour of an authentic, century-old gold mine. See where miners revealed ore veins with black powder and candlelight.

brokenbootgoldmine.com   *767 Main Street*   *(605) 578-9997*

Deadwood Mini Golf (124)
Located at the Comfort Inn and Suites, this is an 18-hole course with an arcade on site. Family fun. Seasonal.

deadwoodcomfortinn.com   *225 Cliff Street*   *(605) 578-7550*

Fish' N Fry (125) Also see Entry 294.
Kids or adults can fish for trout without a license. The staff will clean the fish, and they can be taken home or fried on site as part of a full meal. Seasonal.

fishnfrycampground.com   *21390 US Hwy 385*   *(605) 578-2150*

Trial of Jack McCall and Main Street Shootouts (126)
This is a nightly entertainment surrounding the trial of the man who shot Wild Bill Hickok. His capture occurs at 7:30 PM in front of the Saloon #10 on Main Street. The trial is then held at 8:00 PM at the Masonic Building.
Note: The actual murder took place at 622/4 Main Street, the location of the original Nuttal & Mann's saloon.

deadwoodalive.com   *715 Main Street*   *(605) 578-1876*

Northern Hills Railway Society – Model Train Displays (127)
deadwoodmodeltrains.com   *622 Main Street*   *jackanf54@yahoo.com*

Deadwood Stage Coach Tours, LLC (128)

dhermann321@gmail.com   *624 Main Street*   *(605) 280-3025*

Double Key Treasure Hunts (129)

In 1931, James "Deacon" Porter, a member of the exclusive Double Key Treasure Hunt Society, hid a treasure and put together some information so that someday it could be found. Explore Deadwood's historical sites as you solve the clues. Designed for adults, teens and children, with written clues and a hidden treasure. For groups of 2 to 8 people.

doublekeytreasurehunts.com   *(800) 494-3183*

Mind Blown Studio – Watch Glass Being Blown (130)

Toni Gerlach demonstrates her art for spectators. Classes, and one-of-a-kind gifts, also make this studio, deli, and coffee shop well worth a visit.

mindblownstudio.com   *73 Sherman Street*   *(605)571-1071*

1876 Dinner Theater (131)   *624 Main Street*   *(605) 580-5799*

Chinatown Tour (132)

This is a twenty-minute tour of an underground tunnel complex that was used by some 500 Chinese Americans in the late 1800s. It was a conduit to deliver goods and laundry services. There was actually an ordinance that said Chinese people were not allowed on Main Street after dark!

Under the Gold Nugget Trading Post   *673 1/2 Main Street*   *(605) 578-2104*

Saloon #10 (133)

Packed full of historic Deadwood memorabilia – see the chair where Wild Bill was shot will playing poker, or the wall of famous and infamous Deadwood residents. This is not the actual location of the murder, which happened at the old Nuttal and Mann's Saloon at 624 Lower Main Street. But it is definitely worth a visit.

saloon10.com   *657 Main Street*   *(605) 578-3346*

Tatanka: Story of the Bison (134)

This is a hands-on Interpretive Center featuring a Lakota encampment and what founder Kevin Costner described as "a centerpiece for two cultures, one whose very lives depended on the buffalo, and one who saw it as a means to an end."

storyofthebison.com   *100 Tatanka Drive*   *(605) 584-5678*

Gambling...

AG Trucano, Son & Grandsons (140)	155 Sherman Street	(605) 578-2000
Bodega Casino (141)	658 Main Street	(605) 578-1162
Bullock Casino (142)	633 Main Street	(605) 578-1745
Bunkhouse and Gambling Hall (143)	68 Main Street	(605) 578-3476
Cadillac Jack's Gaming Resort (144)	360 Main Street	(605) 578-1500
Celebrity Casinos (145)	629 Main Street	(605) 578-1909
Deadwood Gulch (146)	304 Cliff St/Hwy 85 S.	(605) 578-1294
Deadwood Mountain Grand (147)	1906 Deadwood Mt Dr.	(605) 559-0386
Deadwood Super 8 (148)	196 Cliff Street	(605) 578-2535
First Gold Hotel & Gaming (149)	270 Main Street	(605) 578-9777
Gold Dust Casino (150)	688 Main Street	(605) 578-2100
Hickok's Hotel (151)	685 Main Street	(605) 578-2222
Franklin Hotel/Silverado (152)	700 Main Street	(605) 578-3670
Iron Horse Inn Casino (153)	27 Deadwood Street	(605) 717-7530
Midnight Star (154)	677 Main Street	(605) 578-1555
Mineral Palace Casino (155)	601 Main Street	(605) 578-2036
Mustang Sally's Casino (156)	634 Main Street	(605) 578-2025
Saloon #10 Casino (157)	657 Main Street	(605) 578-3346
The Lodge at Deadwood (158)	100 Pine Crest Lane	(605) 584-4800
Tin Lizzie (159)	555 Main Street	(605) 578-1715
VFW Post 5969 (160) Slots	10 Pine Street	(605) 722-9914
Wooden Nickel Casino (161)	9 Lee Street	(605) 578-1952

Mount Roosevelt Monument (170)

This is a fairly long (about ½ mile) uphill hike, not great for people with health issues. From the Friendship Tower on top, one can see Bear Butte, Terry Peak, Harney Peak and even the Bear Lodge Mountains in Wyoming. Below are the cities of Lead and Deadwood. The tower is actually a monument proposed by Seth Bullock to honor his friend, Teddy Roosevelt. The summit is at 5,690 feet. *North out of town on 85, left and then right on Mount Roosevelt Road at the Lodge at Deadwood, watch for the sign that points to the gravel road on your right.*

Bike Deadwood (171)

Bicycle rentals for the whole family, which can be used to explore the town or travel the Michelson Trail that's built on an old railway bed (nice and flat!). *pumphouseatmindblownstudio.com   73 Sherman Street   (605) 571-1071*

Black Hills Off Road Rentals (172)

Snowmobile and ATV rentals located at the Mystic Hills campground. *NOTE: For off-road maps, go to fs.usda.gov and search for 'Color OHV Maps'. blackhillsoffroadrentals.com   21766 Custer Peak Road   (605) 770-1737*

Mad Mountain Adventures (173)

Snowmobile and ATV rentals.

NOTE: For off-road maps, go to fs.usda.gov and search for 'Color OHV Maps'.

madmountainadventures.com   *21443 US Hwy 385*   *(605) 578-1878*

Deadwood Recreation Center (174)

The rec center (click on Departments on the city website) is open to the public, and day rates are very reasonable – the family fee was just $7 in early 2016. The facility has a water slide, zero entry pool, lap pool, indoor tracks, racquetball and squash court, cardio and weight rooms, saunas, a basketball court and even a function/party room for rent.

cityofdeadwood.com   *105 Sherman Street*   *(605)578-3729*

Boot Hill Tours (175)

One hour narrated open-air bus tour of Deadwood's rich history. Rates were adults $10, children $5, seniors $9 in early 2016.

boothilltours.com   *3 Siever Street*   *(605) 580-5231*

Tomahawk Lake Country Club (176)

Designed by renowned golf course architect Lawrence Hughes in the late 1930s, this is a beautiful, challenging, nine-hole, par 36 course in the Black Hills National Forest. Check online or call for tee times. Daily Green Fees (2016) are 9 holes, $25 and 18 holes $36. Bar, grill, pro shop.

golftomahawk.com   *South 7 miles on Hwy 385*   *(605) 578-2080*

Alkali Ike Tours (177)

Air-conditioned bus tours of downtown Deadwood and Mount Mariah Cemetery. Rates were adults $10, children $5, seniors $9 in early 2016.

Alkaliiketours.com   *657 Main Street*   *(605) 578-3147*

Whitewood Creek and the City Parks (178)

A chain of small parks in the middle of town along Whitewood Creek offer picnic facilities, fishing, biking and walking paths. Very picturesque. There are four city parks in Deadwood – the new Martha E. Bullock Park on Charles Street, which was completed in 2015; the Richard Gordon Memorial Park at 168-234 Sherman Street (Cemetery Street); the Methodist Memorial Park at the corner of Shine and Williams Streets (it mimics "the layout of the original church that stood here, with benches laid out like pews and a giant brick and steel steeple designed to match the original church bell tower"); and Gateway Monument Park. Also, a portion of the Mickelson Trail meanders through the city. For more information, visit the **Deadwood Visitor Center** in the old train depot.

Deadwood Chamber & Visitor Center (179)

Located in the old Railway Depot, this is the best place to start exploring Deadwood. You can usually park in front of the building ($0.25 for 30 minutes), and there are clean bathrooms. The staff and the literature (especially maps such as the self-guided walking tour) are very informative.

deadwood.com   *767 Main Street*   *(605) 578-1876*

White Rocks (180)

At 5,250 feet (just 30 feet shy of being a mile high), this vantage point is a short but tough hike beginning in Mount Mariah Cemetery. Follow the signs to the grave of Seth Bullock and then take the service road for the phone tower and the trail to the top. The view from up there includes Terry Peak, Mount Roosevelt and even Bear Butte in the distance, with the city of Deadwood below.

Days of 76 Rodeo and Arena (181)

The Days of '76, which also includes parades on Deadwood's historic Main Street, has been a staple each summer in Deadwood for just about a hundred years. Usually around the last weekend in July, the magnificent log rodeo arena hosts award-winning competitions in bareback and saddle bronc riding, steer wrestling, roping, barrel racing and bull riding. Even when there's no event scheduled, you can drive right to the arena and kick your toes in the dirt. Then walk across the parking lot to the museum and meet some prospectors, miners, muleskinners and madams...

daysof76.com   *50 Crescent Drive*   *(605) 578-1876*

George S. Mickelson Trailhead (182)

The Deadwood trailhead/entrance to the Michelson trail is near the old railroad depot on Sherman Street in Deadwood. **Trailink.com** describes the trail this way: "Named in honor of the former South Dakota governor who crusaded for the trail before his death in a plane crash in 1993, the George S. Mickelson Trail runs through the heart of the Black Hills, connecting Deadwood with Edgemont 114 miles to the south. The trail incorporates nearly 100 converted railroad bridges and 4 tunnels, and much of it traverses national forest."

For details, visit Game, Fish and Parks at...

gfp.sd.gov/state-parks/directory/mickelson-trail/trailheads.aspx

Deadwood Jam (183)

If you're in the Hills in mid-September, you can enjoy a two-day outdoor Reggae and Blues festival with national acts such as Alison Krauss, Blood Sweat and Tears, and the Nitty Gritty Dirt Band. Get the latest info at *facebook.com/deadwoodjam.*

Deadwood Trolleys (184)

Since 1992, the trolleys have traveled two and a half million miles and carried four million passengers! They run at regular intervals between all the hotels, motels and other key stops throughout Deadwood, and the cost per ride is just $1 per person. In summer they start at 7 AM and run until 1:30 in the morning – and 3 AM on Friday and Saturday nights. Winter weekday hours are a little more restricted (until midnight). A trolley ride is a great way to see the historic old town.

Kool Deadwood Nights (185)

This event in late August "brings car lovers together for four days full of classic cars, classic music and classic fun. It's a '50s and '60s sock hop, Deadwood style. Enjoy parades, show and shines and FREE concerts on Main Street featuring the biggest names in rock 'n roll history". There's also a classic car auction (call 605-348-1369). *deadwood.com/events/kooldeadwoodnites*   *Call the Chamber (605) 578-1876*

Deadweird (186)

In late October (Halloween weekend) the annual Monster Ball features a live band with dancing and prizes. Then the Costume Contest delivers more than $10,000 in cash and prizes for the best costumes on Saturday. Both of these events are FREE, so come in costume or just come to watch - it is quite the sight! Must be 21 to participate. Also take in some of the "spirited tours, offering a view of some of Deadwood's darker stories told in the beautifully-restored Adams House Victorian mansion. These spooky Halloween tours are offered at 6:00, 7:00, 8:00 and 9:00pm throughout October. Call (605) 578-3724 for tour reservations
deadwood.com/events/deadweird   *Call the Chamber (605) 578-1876*

ATV Rentals at Custer Crossing (187)

Go south on US Hwy 385 to Custer Crossing, about 12 miles from Deadwood.
NOTE: For off-road maps, go to fs.usda.gov and search for 'Color OHV Maps'.
blackhillsatvrentals.com   *22036 US Hwy 385*   *(605) 584-1700*

Black Hills Veterans MARCH (188)

Conceived in 2002, the Black Hills Veteran March is a picturesque trek through the mountainous terrain of the beautiful Black Hills. This march/marathon pays tribute to the many sacrifices that this nation's veterans have made in the past, and continue to make today. The 26.2 mile march takes place in the National Forest on the Mickelson Trail, and is held on a weekend at the end of September. Registration begins at $35 and closes when 1,000 marchers register. Participants receive a T-shirt, and finishers also get a commemorative coin. Sponsors are welcome!
blackhillsveteranmarch.com   *benjamin.g.lamp.mil@mail.mil*   *(605) 357-2939*

Deadwood Mickelson Trail Marathon (189)

An annual event held in early June, this is a point to point course, beginning in the hamlet of Rochford, and finishing at the historic Engine House at the Deadwood Trailhead. The host hotel, The Lodge at Deadwood, provides a bus to the start, and will host an expo. The event organizer, Wheeler Event Management, has partnered with the Black Hills Area Habitat for Humanity affiliate.

deadwoodmickelsontrailmarathon.com   *(605) 390-6137*

Historic Black Hills Studios (190)

"Home to the Fassbender Photographic Collection. The collection may rank among the most significant photographic resources for historians of the American West. Potentially, many never before seen images of the early days of the South Dakota cities of Spearfish, Lead and Deadwood in addition to the entire Black Hills region are in the collection. The grand opening of Spearfish Canyon Road, presidential visits and a vast selection of early mining photos are among the many images that will have great interest to the general public."   [Curator: Richard Carlson]

historicblackhillsstudios.org   *150 Sherman St.*   *(605) 941-1964*

Blacktail Horseback Tours (191)

Rides begin at the top of Bessie Gulch with horse assignment and some riding instruction. The trail works uphill through switchbacks to a scenic overlook and includes a history of the Homestake gold mine. The two-hour ride also includes some info about forestry management practices.

blacktailhorsebackandwalkingtours.com   *11432 Blacktail Bench Rd*   *(605) 722-4241*

Trout Haven Resort (192)

Pay to fish pond, cabins, camping.

22485 US Highway 385   *(605) 341-4440*

DeadWheels Bicycle Rentals (193)

Deadwheelsbikerentals.com   *32 Charles*   *(605) 484-6592*

Where to Eat – Deadwood

Best Western Hickok House Restaurant (200)
> 137 Charles Street
> Home style cooking, including Rancher Steak Tips and Breakfast Burritos
> (605) 578-1611

Boondock's Diner & Amusements (201)
> 21559 US HWY 385 (9 miles south)
> Vintage diner, Studebakers, rides, costumed photos.
> (605) 578-1186

Brown Rock Sports Café (202)
> 360 Main Street
> Specialty pizzas, American fare and Starbucks coffee.
> (605) 578-1500

Buffalo Bodega Saloon & Steakhouse (203)
> 658 Main Street
> Full menu including prime rib.
> (605) 578-9993

Bully's Restaurant (204)
> 649 Main Street
> Located in the Bullock Hotel, serves breakfast.
> (605) 578-1745

Creekside Restaurant at Deadwood Gulch Gaming Resort (205)
> 304 Cliff Street (Hwy 85 South)
> Full menu
> (605) 578-1294

Deadwood Dick's Saloon and Eatery (206)
> 51 Sherman Street
> Burgers, chili dogs, salads, etc. Patio.
> (605) 578-3224

Deadwood Grille (207)
> 100 Pine Crest Lane (in the Lodge at Deadwood)
> Best Overall Restaurant in the Black Hills (2014 Reader's Choice Awards).
> Seafood, certified Angus steaks, chef's signature cuisine, extensive wine list.
> (605) 581-2120

Deadwood Legends Steakhouse (208)
709 Main Street (at the Silverado Franklin hotel)
Casual elegance, reasonable prices.
(605) 578-3670

Deadwood Mountain Grand Coffee Kiosk (209)
1906 Deadwood Mountain Drive
Coffee, deli and breakfast items.
(605) 559-0386

Deadwood Social Club (210)
657 Main Street (in the Saloon No. 10)
Northern Italian steakhouse, Tuscan pastas, buffalo. *Wine Spectator*'s Award.
(605) 578-3346

Deadwood Station Bunkhouse & Gambling Hall (211)
68 Main Street
Gourmet coffee shop and Old West saloon
(605) 578-3476

Diamond Lil's Bar & Grill (212)
677 Main Street (in The Midnight Star, upstairs)
Pizza, burgers, sandwiches, salads and Kevin Costner's movie memorabilia.
(605) 578-3550

Gem Steakhouse & Saloon (214)
601 Main Street
Breakfast, lunch and dinner. Hand cut Angus certified steaks.
(605) 578-2036

Gold Country Inn Café (215)
801 Main Street (in the Gold Country Inn)
Diner is open from 6:30am to 1:30pm.
(605) 578-2393

Hickok's Pizza (216)
685 Main Street
Great pizza, eat in or take out (family option, as it's located in a casino).
(605) 578-2222

First Gold Nugget Buffet (217)
270 Main Street
Breakfast, lunch and dinner. Weekend crab and prime rib buffet.
(605) 578-9777

Lee Street Station Cafe (218)
9 Lee Street
Breakfast and lunch – burgers, soups, salads (a local favorite).
(605) 578-1952

Mavericks Steak and Cocktails (219)
> 688 Main Street
> Popular steakhouse.
> (605) 578-2100

Mustang Sally's (220)
> 634 Main Street
> Burgers (including veggie versions), sports bar.
> (605) 578-2025

Mystic Hills Hideaway (221)
> 21766 Custer Peak Road
> Breakfast, lunch and dinner. 10 miles south, deck and patio, resort.
> (605) 584-4794

Oggie's Sports Bar (222)
> 100 Pine Crest Lane (located in the Lodge at Deadwood.)
> Breakfast, lunch and dinner.
> (605) 571-2120

Oyster Bay Bar (223)
> 626- 628 Main Street (located in the historic Fairmont Hotel)
> Pasta, burgers, seafood and fresh oysters.
> (605) 578-2205. Also offers fun 'ghost tours' of this old bordello!

Pump House at Mind Blown Studio (224)
> 73 Sherman Street
> Coffee, deli, art, gifts and glass blowing demonstrations!
> (605) 571-1071

Santana's Sports Bar & Grill (225)
> 1906 Deadwood Mtn. Grand Drive (located in the hotel)
> Pizza, burgers, soup and salads,
> (605) 559-0386

Silverado Franklin's Grand Buffet (226)
> 709 Main Street (located in the hotel)
> 80-foot long buffet, wood-fired pizza, plus crab & prime rib on weekends.
> (605) 578-3670

Stockade (227)
> 658 Main Street (see 203, Buffalo Bodega)
> Outdoors, burger menu, summer only, live music starting at 11:30 am.
> (605) 578-1162

Super 8 Pizzeria (228)
> 196 Cliff Street (located in the Super 8)
> Pizzas made from scratch, burgers, subs, salads and fresh-baked cookies.
> (605) 578-3235

The Grand Grille (229)
> 1906 Deadwood Mtn. Grand Drive (located in the hotel)
> Light lunches to elegant dinners, and outdoor dining above Whitewood Creek.
> (605) 559-0386

The Pour House (230)
> 645 Main Street
> Bar and pizzeria.
> (605) 717-0132

Tin Lizzie Gaming Resort - Restaurant (231)
> 555 Main Street
> Breakfast, lunch or dinner buffets, crab & prime rib on weekends.
> (800) 643-4490

Taco John's (232)
> 86 Charles Street
> (605) 578-3975

Dairy Queen (233)
> 673 Main Street
> (605) 717-0406

Sugar Shack (234)
> 22495 Hwy 385 South
> (605) 341-6772

Deadwood Winery (235)
> 696 Main St
> Craft beers, winery, sandwiches.
> (605) 578-9975

Nugget Saloon (236)
> At the Broken Arrow,
> 604 Main
> (605) 578-1422

Where to Stay – Deadwood

Best Western Hickok House (240)   137 Charles Street   (605) 578-1611
Family owned and operated, casino, restaurant, and 45 rooms.

Black Hills Inn & Suites (241)   206 Mountain Shadow Lane   (605) 578-7791
Creek-side location, indoor pool & hot tub, continental breakfast. Trolley to town.

Bullock Hotel (242)   633 Main Street   (605) 578-1745
19th century elegance (1895) and 21st century amenities, 28 rooms, some haunted!

Butch Cassidy Suites (243)   57 Sherman Street   (605) 343-8126
Three nice air conditioned suites offer an alternative to hotel/motel rooms.

Cadillac Jack's (244)   360 Main Street   (605) 578-1500
Gaming resort, restaurant, business center, exercise room.

Cedar Wood Inn (245)   103 Charles Street   (605) 578-2725
Family owned motel, nice gardens, and 6 block walk along creek to Main Street.
No pets.

Celebrity Hotel (246)   629 Main Street   (605) 578-1909
Restored century-old casino-hotel, heated towels, fine soaps, and lots of atmosphere.
Also see Branch House (264).

Comfort Inn & Suites (247)   225 Cliff Street   (605) 578-7550
Mini-golf, casino, 69 rooms or suites, WiFi, spa, easy parking.

Deadwood Dick's (248)   51 Sherman Street   (605) 578-3224
Nice rooms & suites in a historic warehouse, old gated elevator, some pet rooms.
Antique mall below (25 vendors), souvenirs with risqué logo available, too.

Deadwood Gulch (249)   304 Cliff Street   (605) 578-1294
Some creek-side rooms, hot tub, exercise room, full breakfast, computer, gift shop.

Deadwood Mountain Grand (250)   1906 Deadwood Mtn. Drive   (605) 559-0386
Perched on a hill overlooking the city, the 98-room luxury hotel is next to Deadwood's
largest event facility. Pets OK. Spa, indoor pool, hot tub, three restaurants.

Deadwood Station (251)   68 Main Street   (605) 578-3476
Recently renovated motel, affordable.

First Gold Hotel & Gaming (252)   270 Main Street   (605) 578-9777
Located on the actual site of the first gold discovery in 1875, it has 190 rooms and five suites, plus three daily buffets and 11 casinos. Kids under 12 free. Pets OK.

Franklin Motor Lodge (253)   700 Main Street   (605) 578-3670
Part of the Silverado Franklin.

Gold Country Inn (254)   801 Main Street   (605) 578-2393
Located a few blocks from downtown in a quiet neighborhood, it has a cafe, slot casino, and 53 rooms 'for the budget-minded guest'.

Hampton Inn/Tin Lizzie (255)   531 Main Street   (605) 578-1893
Free hot breakfast. Restaurant, indoor pool, casino, fitness center, easy parking.

Hickok's Hotel & Gaming (256)   685 Main Street   (605) 578-2222
Constructed in 1899, it has been totally renovated with twenty-two rooms and suites, and an award winning pizza pub.

Historic Franklin Hotel/Silverado (257)   700 Main Street   (605) 578-3670
Opened in 1903, it has accommodated Theodore Roosevelt, William Taft, John Wayne, Buffalo Bill Cody, Babe Ruth, Kevin Costner and John L. Sullivan. Buffet restaurant.

Holiday Inn Express (258)   22 Lee Street   (605) 578-3330
24-hour Business Center, 4 out of 5 positive reviews on Tripadvisor.

Hotel by Gold Dust (259)   25 Lee Street   (605) 559-1400
Renovated in 2014, 42 'boutique-style' rooms, casino, restaurant.

Iron Horse Inn (260)   27 Deadwood Street   (605) 717-7531
"Victorian charm at reasonable rates." Casino, on-site parking.

The Lodge at Deadwood (261)   100 Pine Crest Lane   (605) 584-4800
140 rooms and suites, some with fireplaces and private decks. Two restaurants, gift shop. On a hill – magnificent views. Free parking. Water Playland (fun family pool).

Martin Mason Hotel (298)   33 Deadwood Street   (605) 722-3456
Victorian atmosphere, 5 rooms, 3 suites, ballroom, no pets. "Ranked #1 in Deadwood by Trip Advisor." When booking, note says "NO CHILDREN UNDER 16!" (Feb '16)

Mineral Palace Hotel and Gaming (262)   601 Main Street   (605) 578-2036
75 rooms/suites, biggest casino in town, restaurant, liquor and gift stores, free parking.

Springhill Suites/Marriott (263)   322 Main Street   (605) 559-1600
Includes "microwave, mini-fridge, large work desk, free high-speed internet access, and a spa-like bathroom". Complimentary hot breakfast, Infinity pool and hot tub.

Super 8-Deadwood (264)   196 Cliff Street   (605) 578-2535
Indoor pool, hot tub, complimentary continental breakfast (freshly baked caramel and cinnamon rolls), a pizzeria and casino. Sun deck overlooks Whitewood Creek.

The Branch House (299)   633 Main Street   (605) 578-1745
Renovated in 1996, it was once an icehouse. It has eight deluxe rooms (all different floor plans), and is part of the Celebrity Hotel (246). Weight/workout room.

Thunder Cove Inn (265)   311 Cliff Street   (605) 578-3045
Built in 1995, affordable, very good reviews on Tripadvisor, rooms at the back look at the mountains with bunnies and squirrels, and may be quieter.

Maya Jo's B&B (266)   21291 Strawberry Hill Lane   (605) 578-2149
Six cabins, four with plumbing and two use shower house. Beautiful rustic setting, 3 miles south on Hwy 385. Affordable rates.

Tucker Inn B&B (267)   771 Main Street   (605) 641-2843
Six bedrooms with communal rooms and a kitchen and bath on each of the two floors.

1899 Inn (268)   21 Lincoln Avenue   (864) 210-1899
Small bed-and-breakfast in Deadwood's historic Presidential District. Three guest rooms with views of the ponderosa forests. Home to three black cats, laundry facilities, electric vehicle charging, hosts somewhat fluent in American Sign Language, French.

Black Hills Adventure Lodging (269)   (605) 490-9944
A large selection of cabins and vacation, log and luxury rustic homes for rent.

Cole Cabins (270)   21355 US Hwy 385   (605) 245-7335
ATV from the yard, bring the dog and snowmobile, family reunions. Seven larger cabins and six seasonal ones, all surrounded by trees and on a creek.

Executive Lodging of the Black Hills (271)   (605) 578-3555
A large selection of cabins and vacation, log and luxury rustic homes for rent.

First Deadwood Cottages (272)   388 Main Street   (605) 920-8834
Unique small homes in town, each with two or more bedrooms, free off street parking, hot tub, outdoor kitchen and BBQ area. Most have a full kitchen and laundry facilities.

Mystic Hills Hideaway (273)   21766 Custer Peak Road   (605) 584-4794
Cabins in resort with beautiful surroundings and all the modern conveniences.

Twin Pines Lodge (274)   10 Centennial Ave   (605) 621-3431
Downtown, sleeps up to 9 with 4 bedrooms and 3 baths, great views.

Camping...

Days of 76 Campground (290)   50 Crescent Dr.   (605) 578-2872
Located on Whitewood Creek, the park has thirty-nine hook-up sites, a gift shop, newer bathrooms and showers, a dump station, WiFi, and a shuttle on the Deadwood Trolley. Pets are welcome. There are also some tent camping sites, a corral and stalls.

Creekside Campground (291)   (605) 578-2267
6 miles south on Hwy 385, on a creek, easy access for RVs, cabin rentals too.

Custer Crossing Campground (292)   (605) 584-1009
15 miles south on Hwy 385, café, cabins and ATV rentals. See 187.

Deadwood KOA (293)   11484 U.S. Hwy 14A   (605) 578-3830
Nestled among pines and aspens, it has RV sites, tent sites, basic and deluxe cabins, pool, sauna, store, WiFi, cable TV. Max pull thru is 50 feet. Seasonal shuttle to town.

Fish 'N Fry Campground (294)   21390 Hwy 385   (605) 578-2150
RVs, tents, cabins, creek-side camping, store, café, arcade, pool, basketball court, laundry facilities, Wi-Fi. [Also see Entry 125]

Hidden Valley Campground (295)   21423 Hwy 385   (605) 578-1342
Seven acres, six miles south on a creek. Shaded, pine trees, store, WiFi, basketball court, horseshoes, game room, playground, and volleyball. ATV to trails. Cabins, laundry.

Steel Wheel Campground (296)   21399 Hwy 385   (605) 578-9767
Convenience store, restaurant, nice cabins, ATV and snowmobile rentals, very clean, 50 sites – 7 pull-through. Located next to Hidden Valley (295).

Whistlers Gulch Campground (297)   235 Cliff Street   (605) 578-2092
In town convenience with an out-of-town atmosphere. Store, basketball, volleyball, tennis, pool, sun deck, tents to large rigs, cabins, laundry.

Mystic Hills Hideaway (See 172, 221, 273)   (605) 584-4794
Cabins, campground, and restaurant nestled in the forest 10 miles south of Deadwood.

Where to Shop – Deadwood

Gifts and Souvenirs
(This book's publisher has a souvenir store at 518 Grant St in Belle Fourche. Stop in and say hi.)

Berg Jewelry (300) — 650 Main Street — (605) 722-0011
Black Hills gold

BH Gold Jewelry by Coleman (301) — 644 Main Street — (605) 578-1983
Black Hills gold

Black Hills Laser Designs (302) — Call for retailers — (605) 722-1949
Laser engraved gifts and souvenirs

Boothill Emporium (303) — 67 Sherman Street — (605) 717-1020
Souvenirs and gifts

Broken Arrow Trading Co. (304) — 606 Main Street — (605) 578-1394
Souvenirs and gifts

Canyon View Amish (305) — 250 US Hwy 14A — (605) 578-9877
Furniture store with gifts and décor items

Chubby Chipmunk Chocolates (306) — 420 Cliff Street — (605) 722-2447
Homemade truffles and chocolates … mmm…

Comfort Inn Gift Shop (307) — 225 Cliff St — (605) 578-7550
Souvenirs and gifts

Dakota Coin & Collectibles (308) — 620 Main Street — (605) 484-5618
Coins, precious metals.

Days of 76 Museum Gift Shop (309) — 18 Seventy Six Drive — (605) 578-1657
Souvenirs and gifts

Deadwood Dick's Gift Shop (310) — 53 Sherman Street — (605) 578-3224
25 antique dealers, and souvenirs

Deadwood Gift Shoppe (311) — 666 Main Street — (605) 722-4975
Western and SD gifts, pottery, leather, bling

Deadwood Harley-Davidson (312) — 645 Main Street — (605) 722-2675
Clothes, leather, collectibles, accessories.

Deadwood KOA (313)   11484 U S Hwy 14A   (605) 578-3830
Souvenirs and gifts

Deadwood Mtn Grand Co. Store (314) 1906 Deadwood Mtn Drive   (605) 559-1188
Souvenirs and gifts

Old West Trading Post (315)   620 Main Street   (605) 430-0889
Antiques, buy, sell, trade…

Deadwood Tobacco Co. (316)   628 Main Street   (605) 722-1510
Full service tobacconist, gifts, souvenirs

First Deadwood Souvenirs (317)   696-1/2 Main Street   (605) 578-1583
Souvenirs and gifts

Gold Dust C-Store (318)   688 Main Street   (605) 578-2100
Gifts, souvenirs, liquor, convenience goods

Gold Nugget Trading Post (319)   675 Main Street   (605) 578-2104
Souvenirs and gifts

Gunslinger Coffee (320)   669 Main Street   (320) 491-9694
Gifts and coffee

Happy Days Gift Shop (321)   639 Main Street   (605) 578-1888
Classic memorabilia from the 50s to today

Madame Peacock's Accessories (322) 638 Main Street   (605) 559-1002
Clothes, accessories, jewelry, bar on site

Mineral Palace Store (323)   601 Main Street   (800) 847-2522
Gift shop

Miss Kitty's Mercantile (324)   649 Main Street   (605) 559-0599
Local, natural lotions and soaps

Mt. Moriah Cemetery Gift Shop (325) 44.376°N 103.725°W   (605) 578-2600
Souvenirs and gifts

Ponderosa Trading Co. (326)   667 Main Street   (605) 578-3829
Souvenirs and gifts

Roughriders Leather & Gifts (327)   653 Main Street   (605) 578-1626
Leather Apparel, gifts

Saloon #10 Outerwear Shop (328)   657 Main Street   (605) 578-3346
Shirts, caps, gifts

Stagecoach Gifts (329)   651-1/2 Main Street   (605) 578-1344
    Souvenirs and gifts

Steel Wheel Trading Post (330)   21399 Hwy 385   (605) 578-9767
    Souvenirs and gifts

The Pink Door Boutique (331)   643 Main Street   (605) 717-7465
    Clothing, gifts

Woody's Wild West (332)   641 Main Street   (605) 578-3807
    Old West photo studio

Wild Bill's Trading Post (333)   624 Main Street   (605) 430-0889
    Antiques, gifts, souvenirs, Wild Bill Hickok exhibit

Wild Bill Hickok

Lead

ZIP: 57754

Things to See and Do – Lead

Homestake Gold Mine Surface Tour & Visitor Center (340)

Open year round, this facility is at the lower end of the town and is adjacent to the world's largest open pit gold mine. The visitor/interpretive center offers surface tours of the mine (daily from June to September), and a short, really good, free informative film. There is also a mini-museum and a huge gift shop with lots of Black Hills gold. The Observation Deck is open to the public – just walk out back and use the coin viewers to look down into the massive open cut – truly impressive, as is the new interpretive center.

The mine's website describes the tour thus: "[It] includes a trip through historic Lead, and a surface tour of Sanford Lab. In the Yates hoist room, you'll see hoists that have been in operation since 1939, including how they are maintained. You'll also learn about the more-than 5,000 feet of rope that take personnel to the underground. If you're lucky, you may even see the hoists in action! You'll also learn a little bit about the mining process and the state-of-the-art waste water treatment plant designed by Homestake Mining Company and still used today by Sanford Lab and other companies around the world."

Tours last approximately one hour. Adults are $7.50, with discounts for students and seniors, and kids under seven are free. The mine is an absolute must for any visit to the Hills, as impressive as Mount Rushmore and Devils Tower.

sanfordlabhomestake.com   *160 West Main Street*   *(605) 584-3110*

Wells Fargo guards protect a shipment of gold traveling from the Homestake mine in Lead to a bank in Deadwood. Photo by John Grabill, 1890.

Black Hills Mining Museum (341)

Three blocks up the hill from the open pit mine, a not-for-profit educational corporation takes visitors deep into the history of Lead's mining past with several exhibits and activities. You can view many historical items such as machinery that was used to actually mine the gold in the Homestake, and other area mines (gold mining is still happening on a large scale in the Hills). There's an informative tour of a simulated underground gold mine, which is billed as "the only comprehensive look at both early-day and modern underground mining that can be found in the Black Hills". The realistic exhibit was created in the '80s by actual miners to tell the story of the Western Hemisphere's deepest gold mine. There's also hands-on gold panning ($10, it takes place in a special indoor tank and is taught by a professional), and all visitors are guaranteed to take home a sample of real placer gold they pan themselves.

blackhillsminingmuseum.com   *323 West Main Street*   *(605) 584-1605*

Historic Homestake Opera House (342)

Billed as "a theater built by a gold mine", this magnificent facility was dedicated in 1914 and was the social and cultural heart of the northern Black Hills for the next 70 years. It is still in constant use: on the website, click on Events (in the pull-down menu at upper right) for upcoming shows, plays and concerts. Known as the 'Jewel of the Black Hills' for its rich Victorian décor (it was built just after her reign – she died in 1901), the theater survived a fire in the 1980s and has recently been beautifully restored. The complex originally housed a heated swimming pool, library, the 1,000-seat theater, a billiard hall, bowling alley, social hall, game rooms and a smoking lounge. There's a new interpretive center, and an indoor shooting range in the basement (call 722-2172 for info). Tours of the theater run $10 per person (kids under age 6 free), and take 30-45 minutes. The building is wheelchair accessible.

leadoperahouse.org   *313 West Main Street*   *(605) 584-2067*

Black Hills & Ft. Pierre Railroad Roundhouse (343)

Learn how the trains traveled the hills in this spectacular, restored 1901 building that now houses a restaurant. This was where an engine would be put on a turntable and turned around to face another direction. The facility's Living Map Theatre presents a 35-minute program that illuminates the gold rush of 1876. Coffee shop, gift shop, restaurant, lots of atmosphere.

blackhillsftpierrerailroadroundhouse.com   *106 Glendale Drive*   *(605) 722-1901*

Lead Country Club (344)

Established in 1922, Lead Country Club is one of the oldest courses in western South Dakota and is home to some of the first grass greens in the region. At approx. 6200 feet, the 'Mile High Club' is a full service 9 hole course. This is a par 36 and plays 3202 yards from the white tees, and 3331 yards from the blue tees. Five of the six par-4s are over 400 yards. The red tees measure 2733 yards and play to a par 37. The club is located 7 miles south of Lead on Hwy 85, just off the Rochford Road. The course winds through tree-lined meadows and the small greens will challenge even the most gifted player. After a round, enjoy a great burger at the clubhouse and full bar.

leadcountryclub.com   *11208 Ironwood Lane.*   *605-584-1852*

Recreational Springs Resort – ATV and Snowmobile Rental (345)

There are more than 600 miles of trails through the Hills. This resort offers "the wheels, great food, cold beer, fuel and supplies". Full or half day rentals, must be 14 or over, have a valid driver's license, and have a guardian with under 18s. There are 2 and 4 seat ATVs (listed at $225 and $300 in March 2016), and the business had a 4.5 out of 5 Tripadvisor rating. The resort also offers wedding packages.

recreationalspringsresort.com/recreational-rentals   *11201 Hwy 14A*   *(605) 584-1228*

Northern Hills Recreation Association (346)

This is a group that organizes events for families and kids in fields as diverse as gold panning, snowmobiling, snowshoes, cross-country skiing, mountain biking and motocross.

northernhillsrec.org   *515 S Main Street*   *(605) 584-2654*

Andy's Trail Rides – Horseback (347)

Andy has been on horseback since he was old enough to walk, and started leading trail rides at the age of nine. He'll lead you on real trails up secluded elk paths that wind through wooded mountain terrain. As the horses make their way through stands of trees, over fallen logs and across creeks, they head to the mountain peak where a breathtaking 85-mile view awaits. This is not a typical head-to-tail trail ride. Personable and charming, Andy has been awarded the 'Quality Community Service Award' by the State of South Dakota.

andystrailrides.com   *11186 Deer Mt. Rd.*   *(605) 645-2211*

Terry Peak (348)

The downhill ski resorts of Terry Peak and Deer Mountain (349) are both just a short drive southwest of Lead. The summit of Terry Peak is 7,100 feet, and that resort has the highest lift service between the Rockies and the Alps. That means long runs in some of the country's most beautiful settings without worrying about thin air and altitude problems.

"A variety of terrain will keep everyone from the novice to the expert interested. A sizable Terrain Park includes a Half Pipe plus a variety of jumps and rail features. Three high-speed detachable quad chairlifts, one fixed grip triple and the snow carpet offer a smooth ride up the slope. All major lifts meet on the top so finding your family or ski party is easy."

The Stewart Lodge is the main lodge and offers ski lessons, a learning center, ski rental, a retail store, cafeteria and lounge, plus the Dark Horse Saloon. The skiing and snowboarding season generally runs until the final week of March, or the first week of April. Terry Peak Ski Area is open on Christmas, Christmas Eve, New Year's Day, New Year's Eve, Martin Luther King Day and President's Day, from 9am to 4pm. There is an excellent and very informative website that publishes the calendar of events. Two lodges, great restaurants and bars, five lifts and more than two dozen trails covering all skill levels make Terry Peak one of the best vacation experiences in the Black Hills.

2015/16 adult full day rates were $53, 6 to 12 were $39, and over 70s were free.

terrypeak.com   *21120 Stewart Slope Road*   *(605) 584-2165*

Deer Mountain Ski Mystic Resort (349)

Deer Mountain, about two miles southwest of Lead on Highway 85, is home to "the most powder accumulation in the Black Hills", averaging more than 200 inches annually. The resort is very family friendly, and features a Zero Gravity Tube Park (with inner tubes and a 1,000-foot lift… there's a movie of this on the website). It also offers "the most diverse ski terrain" in the Hills, with everything from groomed trails to powder runs, glade runs and un-crowded, wide open slopes. The summit is 6,850 feet, and the mountain offers more than fifty trails. The chairlift is less than 8 minutes, and the Little Fawn learning area offers a tow.

The base lodge is very comfortable and welcoming, and Deer Mountain offers both a Ski Café and a Ski Pub. Instruction is available. Check out the website's photos of the box sled race held in the spring (usually late March).

2015/16 adult full day rates were $42, 12 and Under were $34, and over 70s just $10.

skimystic.com   *11187 Deer Mountain Road*   *(605) 580-1169*

Black Hills Trails Office - The Mickelson Trail (350)

One of the best family activities in the entire Western US, this former rail-bed has been converted to accommodate a diverse range of outdoor experiences where people can ride (horse or bike), run, walk or ski year-round, depending on weather. Most of the route follows the tracks of a branch line that was constructed by the Chicago, Burlington and Quincy Railroad in 1890. The trail is named for former South Dakota two-term Governor (1987-1993), who died in a plane crash with seven others in Iowa on April 19, 1993. Incidentally, his Dad was also Governor in the late '40s.

Here's how the Game, Fish and Parks Department describes it: "Imagine a path where the ghosts of Wild Bill Hickok and Calamity Jane still roam; where bicyclists, hikers and horseback riders can explore spruce and ponderosa pine forests; and the very young, the very old and people of all abilities can enjoy… gentle slopes and easy access to the beauty of the Black Hills."

The trail is about 109 miles long and contains more than a hundred converted railroad bridges and even four rock tunnels. There are several branch trails, too, including one to Custer State Park. The surface is primarily crushed limestone and gravel, and the trail stops by several towns along the way. Cellphone reception can be sketchy between these communities. At the height of the tourist season – especially during the motorcycle rally in August – book your accommodation ahead of time if you plan on walking the entire trail.

There are fifteen trailheads, all of which offer parking, self-sale trail pass stations ($4 a day in 2016, and just $15 for an annual pass), vault toilets, and tables. Most of the trail does not exceed a 4% grade, but a few parts of the trail might be considered strenuous. Dumont is the highest point, and the 19-mile stretch from Deadwood to Dumont is the longest incline. In addition to the official state website listed below, check out the Trail affiliates site, a commercial enterprise that lists a number of support services (from bikes to bunks) that can make planning a trip to the Trail a lot easier: mickelsontrailaffiliates.com

I highly recommend the Mickelson Trail as one of the most intimate, personal ways to fully experience the extraordinary beauty of these Hills.

mickelsontrail.com   *11361 Nevada Gulch Road*   *(605) 584-3896*

Handley Recreation Center (351)

The Lead recreation center offers a walking track, sauna, cardio equipment, Friday Night skate night, boxing, a weight room, racquetball, a climbing wall and various health/sport classes. Daily passes in 2016 were $2.75 for adults, a dollar for kids/students through college, and just $6 for a family.

handleyrecreationcenter.com   *845 Miners Avenue*   *(605) 584-1113*

Spearfish Falls (352)

Located closer to the south end of Spearfish Canyon, the Falls are better known to locals than tourists. In the tiny hamlet of Savoy (the postal address is actually Lead), go to the south end (to your right when looking at the front door) of the Latchstring Restaurant's parking lot and follow the chain-link fence along the highway to a gap. This leads to a bridge over the creek, and if you cross it and follow the trail that winds to your left, it will bring you to the base of the falls. Bring your camera, and a picnic.

Roughlock Falls (353)

In Savoy, a little village in Spearfish Canyon, take the gravel road to the right of the hotel (Spearfish Canyon Lodge) and go about a mile. There is a beautiful park on your left with spots where you can dangle feet in the creek and maybe spot some trout, a dramatic waterfall with easy access, tall canyon cliffs all around, and public restrooms. It's a great photo opportunity, especially in fall when the leaves are turning.

Pathways Spiritual Sanctuary (354)

This is a quiet, safe, sacred 80-acre oasis open to the public free of charge where people can spend time walking, sitting, contemplating, reading, writing, reflecting or healing in the natural landscape of the sacred Black Hills. Walking paths meander through forest and meadow and lead to inspirational bronze sculptures, a meditative labyrinth, hand-hewn benches and bronze plaques with inspiring quotes to contemplate. Pathways' mission is to preserve and maintain the space for all who visit, without regard to their beliefs, race, religion, culture, personal history or life experiences.

pathwaysspiritualsanctuary.org   *21793 Juso Ranch Road*

Where to Eat – Lead

Subway (359)   161 W Main St   (605) 584-3993
Bob's Silver Star Lounge (360)   322 1/2 W. Main St. (Bar)   (605) 584-2740
Cheyenne Crossing (361)   Spearfish Canyon- Hwy 14A & 85 (605) 584-3510
This is a very popular family restaurant at the south end of Spearfish Canyon. David Brueckner, has created a cozy log cabin atmosphere with great food (the breakfasts are wonderful!) and a gift shop. Locals love this place. Cheyenne Crossing is located a few minutes west of Lead on 85.
Dakota Shivers Brewing (362)   717 West Main Street   (605) 415-5352
A micro brewery with a macro heart!
Lewie's Saloon & Eatery (363)   711 S. Main St.   (605) 584-1324
Beer, burgers, family and bikers. 4.5 out of 5 on Tripadvisor in the spring of 2016, and also 4 out of 5 on *The Daily Meal.*
Lotus Up Espresso & Deli (364)   32 Baltimore St.   (605) 722-4670
Nice, inexpensive coffee shop with great baked goods, breakfast and lunch.
Pizza Lab (365)   124 Hwy 14A (Central City)   (605) 578-9933
Pizza, ribs, wings and salads, family-oriented, lunch buffet.
Homestake Chop House (343)   106 Glendale Dr.   (605) 722-1901
Casual fine dining located in the historic railroad roundhouse, the menu includes wild game, beef and seafood.
The Latchstring Inn (366)   Spearfish Canyon (Savoy)   (605) 584-3333
It has been feeding canyon travelers since 1909. Remarkable scenery, full menu, open year-round.
The Sled Haus (367)   443 South Main St.   (605) 639-5322
New York style burgers, sandwiches, domestic import and craft beer. Very good reviews.
Boar's Nest (368)   11275 Highway 14A   (605) 738-6090
Burgers, chicken, pulled pork, micro-brews, plus they have hot rods, rat rods and Harleys on display. OK for families.
Stampmill Restaurant Saloon (369)   305 W Main St.   (605) 717-0554
Formerly known as the Bumpin Buffalo, it received 3/5 good reviews on Yelp and 4/5 on Tripadvisor (spring 2016).
Café 808 (370)   312 W Main St.   (605) 571-0808
New in 2016, good reviews, breakfast, pies and Hawaiian dishes!

Where to Stay – Lead

Barefoot Resort (380)	21111 Barefoot Loop	(605) 584-1577
Black Hills Vacation Cabins (381)	20677 Maitland Rd.	(605) 578-2369
Black Hills Vacation Homes (382)	744 Prospect Ave. Ste. #111	(605) 722-9950
Blackstone Lodge & Suites (383)	395 Glendale	(605) 584-2000
Copper Mountain Resort (384)	900 Miners' Avenue	(605) 584-1800
Dakota Spur Hotel (385)	509 W. Main St.	(605) 559-1120
KDR Unlimited Lodging (386)	503 W. Addie St.	(605) 717-0676
Main Street Manor Hostel (387)	515 W. Main St.	(605) 717-2044
Ponderosa Motor Lodge (388)	705 Glendale Drive	(605) 584-3321
Recreational Springs Resort (389)	11201 Hwy 14A	(605) 584-1228
Spearfish Canyon Lodge (390)	10619 Roughlock Falls Rd	(605) 584-3435
Terry Peak Chalets (391)	21150 Stewart Slope Rd.	(605) 359-5364
Terry Peak Lodge (392)	21117 Stewart Slope Rd.	(605) 584-2723
Town Hall Inn (393)	215 West Main Street	(605) 584-1112
Trailshead Lodge (394)	22075 US Hwy 85 S	(605) 584-3464
West Main Lodge (395)	622 W. Main St.	(605) 584-2369
Whitetail Court Motel (396)	11295 US Hwy 14A	(605) 584-9085

Where to Shop – Lead

Aspire Boutique (410)	603 South Main St.	(605) 591-0600
	Jewelry, accessories, collectibles	
Bloomers Flowers and Gifts (411)	132 Hwy 14A	(605) 578-7737
	In Central City, on the way to Deadwood	
Lynn's Dakotamart (410)	145 Glendale Drive	(605) 584-2905
	Groceries, floral	
JL's Gift Shop (413)	100 S Main St	(605) 584-3478
Lead Deadwood Arts Center (414)	Opera House, 309 W Main	(605) 584-1461
	Art gallery, framing and gift shop	
Homestake Visitor Center (340)	160 West Main St.	(605) 584-3110
Northern Hills Fly Fisher (415)	310 West Main St.	(605) 920-0465
High Mountain Outfitters (416)	308 West Main St.	

Spearfish
ZIP: 57783

Things to See and Do – Spearfish

DC Booth Historic Fish Hatchery and the City Park (425)

An extraordinary resource, the hatchery is one of the best spots in the Hills for a romantic stroll, a family day out, or a sneaky way to educate children! It was built in 1899 to stock trout in the Black Hills area, all the way to Yellowstone. Still functional, the hatchery currently produces about 25,000 rainbow trout annually. The facility offers an underwater viewing area, tours of the Booth house, a museum and a gift shop. There's also a refurbished railway car that was custom built to transport fish, and an ice house. The hatchery offers several short hikes (a little strenuous), opportunities to feed fish and ducks, and a park-like environment complete with bronze outdoor statuary. It is adjacent to the main city park, a beautiful facility along Spearfish Creek that includes a huge playground, picnic tables along the river, restrooms and basketball courts, and a large, quite beautiful campground. Admission to both park and hatchery is free. On the third weekend in July, the park hosts one of the region's largest outdoor festivals, an event that includes art, music, food, kids' activities and vendors. $5 on Friday evening with a concert, free on Saturday and Sunday with performers in the band shell.

dcboothfishhatchery.org   423 Hatchery Circle – a block west of Main   (605) 642-7730

Elkhorn Ridge Golf Club (426)

Elkhorn Ridge Golf Club is a modern Championship course open to the public. Its second nine is scheduled to open in August 2016 (call to confirm). The course features "breathtaking views of the historic Centennial Valley. These challenging 9 holes afford over 285 feet of elevation change, hidden canyons, elevated tees, and broad sloping greens. All levels of players can enjoy five different teeing areas on each of the nine holes. Play 18 holes from the 'Tips' and the course stretches over 7,300 yards and is rated at 74.8 from the Championship Tees. Enjoy Elkhorn's practice facilities featuring double-ended teeing areas, multiple target greens, and a greenside practice bunker allowing for all types of short-game sharpening."

golfelkhorn.com   6845 St. Onge Road - Exit 17 off I-90   (605) 722-4653

Spearfish Canyon Country Club (427)

About as pretty as a golf course can be, it was opened in 1921 and offers 18 holes of spectacular scenery. The original front nine (3138 yards) has challenging small greens and lots of elevation changes. The new back nine (3529 yards) is a links style, with rolling hills and large greens. The 19th hole is the Fairway Junction Bar & Grille, with a full liquor license and an extensive menu.

spearfishcanyoncountryclub.com   120 Spearfish Canyon Road   (605) 717-4653

High Plains Western Heritage Center (428)

It's a little difficult to find, but absolutely worth the effort (directions below). The Center includes a five-state pioneer museum (ND, SD, MT, WY and NE), and has more than 20,000 square feet of exhibits featuring Western art, artifacts and memorabilia - including the original Spearfish to Deadwood stagecoach! There's a turn-of-the-century kitchen, a saddle shop and smithy, and fine representations of forestry, mining, ranching and rodeo. Outside, families can visit the Longhorn cattle, a furnished log cabin, a rural schoolhouse and antique farm equipment. Upstairs, enjoy a three state view from the balcony, or visit the book and gift shop. 2015 rates were $10 for adults, $3 for 6 to 16 year olds, and $22 for a family.

From I-90 take Exit 14, go south to the frontage road (the Pizza Ranch will be in front of you), go left/east to Heritage Drive (past the car dealership), take a right and then go about a mile on Heritage. The Center is on top of the hill, on the right.

westernheritagecenter.com   *825 Heritage Drive*   *(605) 642-9378*

Matthews Opera House (429)

At the heart of Spearfish's arts scene, the facility was originally dedicated in 1906 and completely restored by 2006. It had been built with private funds by a rancher from nearby Wyoming, Thomas Matthews, and over the past century has been home to movies, sports events and dramatic productions. Today, it is home to a very active community theater company with plays, concerts and other entertainments offered year round. For upcoming performances, click on 'Events' on the website.

matthewsopera.com   *612 Main Street*   *(605) 642-7973*

Spearfish Canyon Scenic Byway (430)

One of the best drives/motorcycle rides in America!

Leaving Spearfish, one passes a small segment of original plains grasses on the right, just before the Forest Service parking area. A sharp curve a couple of miles into the canyon indicates that you've reached Split Rock. Pull over for a minute and absorb the atmosphere: cliffs several hundred feet tall all around, and below your feet the creek has gone partially underground as it flows through a series of limestone caverns. The rock was split to make way for the railroad 120 years ago. Visit **Community Caves** (2.7 miles up the Canyon): park and walk toward the stream to find them. Moving along, one can eat lunch at the Botany Bay picnic area on the right, or pass Bridal Veil Falls a little farther along on the left. Here, a small parking area and observation deck let you photograph the 60 foot waterfall, which is a raging torrent in spring and often a mere trickle by late summer.

Devil's Bathtub is next. It's on the left (going south from Spearfish), and the trailhead is at Cleopatra Place. It's about a mile, following the creek, and expect to get your feet wet. The tub itself is a swirling pond with a small waterfall and caves. Be careful swimming. As with most of the canyon, the surroundings are breathtakingly beautiful.

At Mile 20, two **Kissing Rocks** sit in the stream to your left, and to the right is the almost hidden entrance to the **Eleventh Hour Gulch** trail (look for a small waterfall). A favorite among locals, this is an arduous climb over fallen boulders, but worth the effort. You can follow the creek and hike upward through the gulch, all the way to the rim of the canyon 1,000 above, if you have the right stuff. (Continued…)

If you missed lunch at Botany Bay, there are several more breathtakingly beautiful picnic sites along the canyon, including Long Valley at the confluence of Iron Creek and Spearfish Creek. In the little village of Savoy, visit the hidden Spearfish Falls on the east side of the road (a bit of a climb), or the gentle park at Roughlock Falls a mile up the gravel road beside the hotel on the west. Keep going past Roughlock Falls and a couple of miles later you'll arrive at the spot where the winter scenes in *Dances With Wolves* were filmed. There are walking/hiking/horseback trails all over this area, including the two Rimrock Trails (one begins at the Rod & Gun campground, the other at the Timon campground, as does the Little Spearfish trail). Other trails worth checking out online are the 1.2 mile, fairly steep 76 Trail to Buzzard's Roost that begins near the entrance to Roughlock Falls.

Back in Savoy, spend a moment among the plants in the Latchstring parking lot's Native Botanical Garden, all of which are designed to live with low moisture and high altitude. This whole area is especially impressive during fall colors.

There are several other small treasures to stop and explore along the canyon as one heads south from Savoy, including ponds and perches overlooking the stream. At the south end, where Hwy 14 meets Hwy 85, is one of the locals' favorite eateries, Cheyenne Crossing. To complete a loop, go left (east) on 85 and it will bring you to Lead, then Deadwood, and finally back to the Interstate at Exit 17, about five miles east of Spearfish.

Spearfish Art Gallery (431)
Located below the Matthews Opera House on the Main Street, the gallery is small but impressive, featuring the work of about fifty local artists at any one time.

matthewsopera.com   *612 Main Street*   *(605) 642-7973*

Spearfish Waterpark (432)
Located in the old Walmart store, the Spearfish Recreation & Aquatics Center features cardio equipment, weight machines, a walking and running track, two basketball courts, billiard tables and batting cages, but its centerpiece is an outdoor waterpark. It has a 'Bubble Vortex Pit', a lazy river, double flume slides, a drop slide, a climbing wall and a three-lane pool. Impressive. In early 2016, rates for the waterpark were $8 for adults, $6 for kids, and free for 3 and under. They charge $3 for 'spectators': adults who like to be poolside on the sun chairs, supervising kids or grandkids.

spearfishreccenter.com   *122 Recreation Lane*   *(605) 722-1430*

Spirit of the Hills Wildlife Sanctuary (433)
Open in spring and summer to the public, the sanctuary is not a zoo but a non-profit animal rescue effort that was founded in 1999. It is home to over 320 animals from more than 40 species – big cats (African lions, tigers, leopards, mountain lions, lynxes and even a serval, which is a medium-sized African wild cat native to sub-Saharan Africa.), bears (Syrian brown bears and American black

bears), wild canines (wolf-hybrid dogs and coyotes), birds, and even some farm animals. Now one of the most diverse animal rescues in America, Spirit of the Hills relies on donations to keep going.

Adults are $15, kids (4-11) are $10, Seniors/Student/Military are $12 and ages 3 and under are free. Cash or checks only, and call ahead to confirm. To get there, take Exit 8 and go south toward the hills on McGuigan Road, which turns to gravel and becomes Tinton Road after 4 miles. At the Y, veer right and look for signs on your left.

spiritofthehillssanctuary.org   *500 Tinton Rd.*   *(605) 642-2907*

Termesphere Gallery (434)

While Dick Termes has been a Spearfish treasure for decades, the rest of the world is also familiar with his work. Celebrated from Tokyo to New York, his 'Termespheres' adorn homes and public spaces around the globe, and are part of many prestigious collections. They hang in space, powered by electric motors, and rotate slowly.

"What you are seeing when you look at a Termesphere painting is an optical illusion" his website says. "It's an inside-out view of the total physical world around you on the outside surface of a hanging and rotating sphere. If you were on the inside of this sphere, this painted image around you would seem normal, but it is read from the outside. From any point when you look at the spherical paintings, the image reads correctly. Termespheres capture the up, down and all around visual world from one revolving point in space."

Mixing geometry and fine art, the gallery is a visual feast that plays with the intellect as much as the senses. It's located on a gravel road a couple of miles southeast of town. If you have an art student in the family, it will be difficult to get them to leave. Call for an appointment, and directions.

termespheres.com   *1920 Christensen Drive*   *(605) 642-4805*

McNenny State Fish Hatchery (435)

Located off the I-90 frontage road near the Wyoming border, the hatchery is a beautiful spot to bring kids to learn. It provides trout and salmon for stocking in the Black Hills, Missouri River reservoirs and eastern South Dakota's lakes and streams. There are 8 covered raceways outdoors, along with 3 spring-fed production ponds and a natural sinkhole display pond that's 121 feet deep! Interpretive signs provide a self-guided tour, and most kids go a little nuts over all the fish. After visiting the hatchery, there are a number of small lakes and fishing ponds next door to the west, and these are a wonderful spot for fishing and picnics. Please note that nonresidents under age 16 do not need a South Dakota fishing license as long as they are fishing with an adult who has a valid South Dakota fishing license. (The kid's fish must be included in the daily and possession limit of the parent or guardian.) Youth wishing to take their own limit of fish may purchase a nonresident fishing license. And if there's still time, just a few minutes west of the hatchery on the frontage road is the Vore Buffalo Jump (see the Wyoming section of this Guide). Within the site are the butchered remnants of as many as 10,000 bison as well as thousands of chipped stone arrow points, knives, and other tools. To find the hatchery, from Exit 2 follow the service road on the north side of the interstate back toward Spearfish for a few hundred yards until you see the signs.

gfp.sd.gov/fishing-boating/hatcheries/mcnenny-hatchery.aspx
          19619 Trout Loop   *(605) 642-6920*

The Thoen Stone (436)

The Lakota successfully kept gold fever at bay in the Black Hills until Custer's expedition of 1874. Forty years prior to that, a group of seven prospectors was dispatched by the tribes after discovering gold. The last of them, Ezra Kind, scratched his tale onto soft sandstone on Lookout Mountain (it's on display at the Adams Museum in Deadwood) before the Indians got him. At a site on the other side of the valley, with a great view of Lookout, a group of history enthusiasts have erected a replica of the Thoen stone (so named in honor of Louis Thoen who discovered it in 1887), and a small monument. From Jackson Street, take St. Joe and walk up the hill. There are markers, and it's a short, easy hike.

Hike Lookout Mountain (437)

Lookout Mountain Park, on the east side of the Interstate in Spearfish, is 750 acres reserved for hiking and mountain biking, and some of the trails are kept up. To climb the mountain from the east, go south on the Main Street which becomes Colorado Boulevard. Just past the golf course, take a left on Sandstone Hills Drive and go under the Interstate. Veer left on Sandstone to Branding Iron Drive and take a right. Go three blocks to Pony Express Lane and find a spot to park that won't annoy the residents. The trailhead here leads to the top of Lookout Mountain. To climb from the west, go up Jackson Street to 10th (a block shy of the Interstate), take a left and go four blocks to Nevada, and find a parking spot. Then walk under the Interstate and up the trails to the top. It's a serious hike, not for the infirm but well within the scope of kids. It's about 1.5 to 2 miles long, depending on your route, and the steepest part comes first. Bring your camera!

Hike Crow Peak (438)

This adventure takes most of a day. It's 3.5 miles each way (vertically only 1,500 feet), and the views from the top at 5,750 feet are astonishing. Hiking, biking and horseback are allowed: no motorized vehicles. At the Burger King in Spearfish, head west on Hillsview Road to Higgins Gulch Road (Forest Service Road 214) and take that for 7 miles to the trailhead. Pack food and water!

Iron Creek Lake Campground (439)

Another gem known to the locals, this mountain lake is open to the public for swimming and canoes, but difficult to find. It was created in the 1930s as a WPA project, and is a beautiful spot to bring the kids for an afternoon, or a full day. The store stocks most necessary supplies for camping and picnicking, as well as fishing licenses, lures and bait. It also registers campers, rents paddle boats and serves short order meals and snacks. Camping sites and cabins are available: call for reservations, especially in August.

From Exit 8, take McGuigan Road south toward the hills until it turns into Tinton Road, and follow this for 13 miles after it turns to gravel. On your right, a sign says Beaver Creek Road. Follow this for half a mile to the Iron Creek Lake sign on your left.

ironcreeklake.com   *20912 Iron Creek Lake Road*   *(605) 642-5851*

Big Hill X-Country Skiing (440)

This is a well maintained trail network in Black Hills National Forest, about 7 miles southwest of Spearfish on route 134. From Exit 8, take McGuigan Road south toward the hills until it turns into Tinton   Road, and follow this to the parking lot at Big Hill (signposted). There are 17 total miles of dressed trails, mostly rated moderate with a few difficult. There is a Black Hills Nordic Ski Club, with a facebook page:
facebook.com/BHNSC
The Black Hills National Forest has a page on cross-country skiing...
fs.usda.gov/activity/blackhills/recreation/wintersports (click on XC Skiing)
You can also download a PDF brochure on Big Hill, with maps, at...
fs.usda.gov/Internet/FSE_DOCUMENTS/stelprdb5194538.pdf

Black Hills State University Theater (441)

The Summer Stage program offers great plays at great prices on campus.
On the homepage click on...
    ACADEMICS
    ART/ART EDUCATION
    THEATER PROGRAM (left-hand column)
    SUMMER STAGE (left-hand column)
bhsu.edu   *1200 University St., Unit 9539*   *(605) 642-6268*

Where to Eat – Spearfish

Coffee Shops & Drive-Throughs

Blackbird Espresso (450)	503 N. Main Street	(605) 717-0022
Common Grounds Restaurant (451)	135 E. Hudson St	(605) 642-9066
The Green Bean Restaurant (452)	304 Main St	(605) 717-3636
Mountain Brew Espresso (453)	2537 E. Colorado Blvd	(307) 290-2665
Queen City Coffee (454)	231 W Jackson Blvd	(605) 559-1025
Starbucks in Safeway (455)	1606 North Ave	(605) 642-5728
Soul Food Bistro (456)	2728 1st Ave	(605) 717-0693

Dessert

CherryBerry (460)	1420 North Ave.	(605) 559-5300
Leones' Creamery (461)	722 1/2 Main St.	(605) 644-6461

Ethnic & Specialty

Barbacoa's Burritos & Wraps (470)	305 West Jackson Blvd.	(605) 722-1774
Golden Dragon - Chinese (471)	1850 North Ave.	(605) 642-2641
Flanagan's Irish Pub (472)	729 N. 7th St.	(605) 722-3526
Roma's Ristorante - Italian (473)	2281 E Colorado Blvd.	(605) 722-0715
Guadalajara's – Mexican (474)	83 U.S. Highway 14	(605) 642-4765
Jade Palace China Buffet (475)	715 Main St.	(605) 642-2588
Bay Leaf Café - Mediterranean (476)	126 W Hudson St	(605) 642-5462
Sunshine Café – Healthy! (477)	638 Main St.	(605) 642-7639
Qdoba Mexican Grill (478)	130 Ryan Rd	(605) 559-0542

Family Dining

Cafe 608 (479)	608 N. Main St.	(605) 717-0077
Killian's Tavern & Steakhouse(480)	539 W Jackson Blvd.	(605) 717-1255
Lucky's 13 (481)	305 North 27th St	(605) 642-1582
Millstone Family Restaurant (482)	620 East Jackson Blvd.	(605) 642-4200
Perkins Restaurant (483)	2301 East Colorado Blvd.	(605) 642-8535
Sanford's Grub & Pub (484)	545 W Jackson Blvd	(605) 642-3204
Steerfish (485)	701 N. 5th St.	(605) 717-2485

Fast Food

Arby's (490)	333 West Jackson Blvd.	(605) 642-0109
Burger King (491)	123 E. Utah Blvd.	(605) 642-4332
Culver's (492)	2423 Platinum Dr.	(605) 722-4868
Dairy Queen (493)	907 East Colorado Blvd.	(605) 642-7455
KFC/Long John Silver's (494)	2405 East Colorado Blvd.	(605) 642-4044
Jimmy John's (495)	1420 North Ave, Suite 500	(605) 717-2459
McDonald's (496)	131 Ryan Rd	(605) 642-8279
Philly Ted's Cheezsteaks (497)	134 Ryan Road, Suite B	(605) 559-0344

Subway downtown (498)	1712 North Ave	(605) 642-5205
Subway by Walmart (499)	3025 1st Ave #1	(605) 722-4500
Taco Bell (500)	1705 North Ave.	(605) 644-8805
Taco John's (501)	504 W Jackson Blvd.	(605) 642-4620

Pizza

Domino's Pizza (510)	741 North Main St #1	(605) 642-0288
Dough Trader (511)	543 West Jackson Blvd.	(605) 642-2175
Papa Murphy's Pizza (512)	310 W Jackson Blvd	(605) 642-3663
Pizza Hut (514)	435 West Jackson Blvd.	(605) 642-7717
Pizza Ranch (515)	2625 E Colorado Blvd.	(605) 642-4422
Little Caesars (516)	1420 N. Ave #3	(605) 642-3355

Sports Bars

Applebee's (520)	301 North 27th St	(605) 642-9480
Spearfish Canyon CC (521)	120 Spearfish Canyon Rd	(605) 722-7020
Stadium Sports Grill (522)	744 North Main St.	(605) 642-9521

Pubs & Breweries

Crow Peak Brewing Company (530)	125 W. Highway 14	(605) 717-0006
B & B Lounge (531)	703 N. Main St.	(605) 642-2134
False Bottom Bar (532)	645 Main St.	(605) 559-0700
Level Wine Bar (533)	604 N. Main St.	(605) 645-6046
Spearfish Creek Wine Bar (534)	127 W. Grant St.	(605) 722-7027
Z Bar & Nightclub (535)	529 N. Main St.	(605) 642-3600

Where to Stay – Spearfish

Bed & Breakfast

Apple Blossom B&B (540)   214 E Jackson Blvd   (605) 717-1457
  Historic home in a residential district close to downtown.
Diamond M Ranch B&B (541)   20041 Crow Peak Bench Rd   (605) 642-2399
  5 miles west of Spearfish on 40 acres, fire pit, no smoke, no pets.
Secret Garden B&B (542)   938 N Ames St   (605) 642-4859
  Brick home (1892), on Nat. Register, gardens, hot tub, veggie garden.
Spearfish B&B (543)   4220 Airport Road   (605) 642-2485
  Close to town but quiet, renovated historic property, good walking.

Campgrounds

Camp Harley (545)   555 Winterville Drive   (605) 642-7500
  Small campground solely for the Sturgis Motorcycle Rally.
Chris' Camp (546)   701 Christensen Drive   (605) 642-2239
  Petting zoo, heated pool, rec room, basketball, playground with no mosquitoes!
Elkhorn Ridge RV Park (547)   20189 US Hwy 85   (605) 722-1800
  Cabins, RV, tent, pets ok, pool, playground, courts, disc golf, large store.
Iron Creek Lake Campground (548) 20912 Iron Creek Lake Rd   (605) 642-5851
  RV, tent, rustic cabins on lake, store and café, 12 miles SW on USFS 134.
KOA (549)   41 West Hwy 14, I-90 frontage road, west of Exit 10   (605) 642-4633
  Pool, WiFi/cable, large store, easy access, 50/30 Amps, pull-throughs, pets ok.
Spearfish City Campground (550)   Exit 12 to Canyon, left   (605) 642-1340
  One of the prettiest municipal campgrounds in the West! Has everything…

Hotels/Motels

All Star Travelers Inn (560)	517 West Jackson Blvd.	(605) 642-5753
Bell's Motor Lodge (561)	230 N. Main Street	(605) 642-3812
Crow Peak Lodge (562)	346 West Kansas Street	(605) 559-3333
Orchard Creek Cottages (563)	514 W Mason St	(605) 642-4234
Rimrock Lodge Rustic Cabins (564)	10900 Rimrock Place	(605) 642-3192
Sherwood Lodge (565)	231 West Jackson Blvd.	(605) 642-5753
Spearfish Creek Inn (566)	925 North 3rd Street	(605) 642-9941
Best Western (567)	540 East Jackson Blvd	(605) 642-7795
Days Inn (568)	240 Ryan Rd.	(605) 642-7101
Fairfield Inn by Marriott (569)	2720 1st Ave E.	(605) 642-3500
Hampton Inn (570)	240 N 27th St	(605) 642-3003
Holiday Inn (571)	305 N 27th St	(605) 642-4683
Baymont Inn & Suites (572)	323 S 27th St	(605) 642-8105
Quality Inn (573)	2725 First Avenue	(605) 642-2337
Rodeway Inn and Suites (574)	2275 E Colorado Blvd.	(605) 642-2350
Super 8 (575)	440 Heritage Drive	(605) 642-4721

Where to Shop – Spearfish

Wild Rose Gifts (580)	Gifts	616 N Main St	(605) 644-0166
Sunflower Cottage (581)	Gifts	640 N. 7th St.	(605) 559-2525
Maurice's (582)	Ladies' Fashion	2735 1st Ave	(605) 642-2760
The Knothole (583)	Crafts	947 E. Colorado	(605) 717-5668
Flying E (585)	Floral	521 N. Main St.	(605) 642-2253
David Harding (586)	Wildlife Art	2 Dd Dr.	(605) 645-1725
Frogworks (587)	SD photography	frogworksimages.com	(605)581-2706
UPS Store (588)	Shipping	810 N. Main St.	(605) 717-8771
JacketZone (589)	BHSU apparel	617 Main Street	(605) 642-6636
BHSU Bookstore (590)	Books	On campus	(605) 642-6636
The Junk Drawer (591)	Antiques	611 N Main St	(605) 641-5766
Visit Spearfish (592)	Tourism Info	603 N Main St	(800) 344-6181

Spearfish Regional Hospital
(593)
1440 North Main Street
(605) 644-4000
Call 911 in an emergency.

Sturgis

ZIP: 57785

Things to See and Do – Sturgis

Much more than the spectacular motorcycle rally in August, Sturgis is a vibrant city with strong historic roots. Its early years were centered on Fort Meade, which is still an active base with a Veteran's hospital and a great Cavalry museum.

Sturgis Community Center (600)

There's a cardio room, weight room, racquetball courts, an indoor running track, an indoor pool with a 72-foot waterslide plus hot tub and sauna, a gym with basketball and volleyball courts, and even a performing arts theater. 2016 daily rates were $5 for adults, $4 for seniors and $3 for students.

Sturgis-sd.gov   *1401 Lazelle Street*   *(605) 347-6153*

Harley Davidson Plaza (601)

An 11,000 square foot open air 'town square', the new plaza is more than just a place for Harley-Davidson to host special events during the rally. It is open all year to the public and features seating areas, a stage for entertainment, two fireplaces and a spot for taking photos with the iconic 'Sturgis" emblazoned on the hillside in the distance. The Plaza hosts festivals, street dances, markets, art exhibits, vehicle shows and other public gatherings.

At the corner of Second and Main Street.   *(605) 720-0800*

Sturgis Motorcycle Rally™ (602)

Hosting hundreds of thousands of motorcycle enthusiasts each year, the Rally is a truly American experience. The crowds are generally well-behaved, and it's fairly G-rated downtown in the middle of the day and perfectly safe, if you want to experience the spectacle. The entire city center is wall-to-wall motorcycles, and many of them are works of art. The worst thing you'll see is an occasional pair of breasts with pasties, or a rude T-shirt. It's not a child-appropriate environment, in large part because the crowds can be very dense. The campgrounds are, in general, more adult in nature. Driving in the Hills during Rally week – and in the week before and following – can be intimidating, as there are tens of thousands of bikers on the roads. Getting a hotel or a restaurant reservation can be a big challenge, too, as can visiting venues such as Devil's Tower or Mount Rushmore. One thing really worth noting: in all the years we've witnessed the Rally, we've never met a rude or threatening biker.

sturgismotorcyclerally.com   *040 Harley-Davidson Way*   *(605) 720-0800*

Gypsy Vintage Cycle (603)

This business specializes in "vintage motorcycles of all makes and models with an emphasis on American, English and Japanese manufacturers of the '50s and '60s. Our showroom features restored and near new motorcycles. Additionally, we maintain a large inventory of original and complete 'project bikes'."

Gypsievintagecycle.com   *2007 Junction Ave.*   *(605) 347-6488*

Indian Motorcycle Sturgis (604)

"Founded in 1901, Indian Motorcycle eventually made its way back to Sturgis in 1936 courtesy of C.F. "Pappy" Hoel, a founding father of the influential motorcycle club the Jackpine Gypsies. Not only did Pappy Hoel's Indian Motorcycle dealership introduce this legendary brand to the Black Hills of South Dakota, he and the Jackpine Gypsies founded the greatest motorcycle riding event in America."

indianmotorcyclesturgis.com   *2106 Lazelle St.*   *(605) 206-7830*

Bear Butte State Park (605)

Sacred to several tribes, Bear Butte is seen by many Native Americans as a place where the creator has chosen to communicate with them through visions and prayer. If you visit the park and/or hike to the summit (just under two miles), you'll notice colorful pieces of cloth and small bundles or pouches hanging from trees. These prayer cloths and tobacco ties represent the prayers offered by individuals during their worship. Please respect these and leave them undisturbed. The mountain is an igneous (fire, as in volcano) eruption. The Bear Butte Education Center highlights the mountain's geology, history and the cultural beliefs of the Northern Plains Indians. An on-site interpreter is available during the summer months. There is a fishing lake with crappies and northerns that has a dock, a campground, a horse camp and a picnic shelter. A bison (buffalo) herd roams the base of the butte, and visitors should not get close as these are dangerous wild animals. Alcohol is illegal in the park, as are uncased firearms and bows. Bear Butte was added to the National Register of Historic Places in 1973. Daily fees are $4 per person or $6 per vehicle, or a SD State Park sticker. Campsites (23 of them) are non-electric and run $11 ($13 for horse sites).

gfp.sd.gov/state-parks/directory/bear-butte   *20250 Hwy 79 N*   *(605) 347-5240*

Sturgis Motorcycle Museum (606)

Located in an old Post Office building, the museum has some really old bikes in its Early days exhibit, and an entire display dedicated to British motorcycles. Anybody with even a mild interest in motorcycles will enjoy the full showcase of vintage bikes and memorabilia.

sturgismuseum.com
999 Main Street   *(605) 347-2001*

Old Fort Meade Museum (607)

Fort Meade was established during the winter of 1878 by Phil Sheridan and was eventually named in honor of General George Meade. It outlived all the other frontier posts nearby, and in 1944 became a VA Hospital and now a National Guard camp. The museum, which concentrates on Cavalry history in the West and offers three floors of exhibits, is open all summer, seven days a week. It's located 1-1/2 miles east of Sturgis on Hwy 34/79. It's a bit of a shock to see historical racism on display, but a necessary reminder. Included are references to 'bringing religion to the Indians' and similar concepts. Overall, it's a very informative collection, and the staff are extremely helpful.

fortmeademuseum.org   *Building 55, Fort Meade* *(605) 347-9822*

Black Hill National Cemetery (608)

Located about three miles east of Sturgis along I-90, the cemetery is administered by the Department of Veterans' Affairs and contains approximately 20,000 graves on 106 acres. It was officially established in 1948, but there are internments here from the late nineteenth century. Sergeant Charles Windolph, a Medal of Honor recipient who survived the Little Bighorn in 1876, is buried here. Born in Germany in 1851, he was 25 when he served with Custer, and 98 when he passed in March of 1950. Senator Francis Case lies here, too: Lake Francis Case, a large reservoir behind Fort Randall Dam on the Missouri River, is named after him for his efforts to expand practical, responsible use of the river. In 1954, Case served on a committee that was formed to put the brakes on Senator Joseph McCarthy. Brigadier General Richard E. Ellsworth, Commander of Rapid City Air Force Base (which was renamed Ellsworth Air Force Base in his honor), is also interred here.

cem.va.gov/CEMs/nchp/blackhills.asp *20901 Pleasant Valley Drive* *(605) 347-3830*

Boulder Canyon Country Club (609)

A 9-hole course just a few minutes south of Sturgis, this par 36 is 3,231 yards from the blue tees and 3,430 from the blacks. Soft or non-spiked shoes are required. Rental carts are available, and the Boulder Canyon Grille offers a full menu. Open to the public. As of spring 2016, green fees M-W were 9 Holes: $26.00 and 18 Holes: $36.40, with carts $10 and $15. Fees on weekends were slightly higher. Call for tee times. Lovely course.

bouldercanyoncountryclub.com   *(605) 347.5108*

T&M Trail Rides (610)

Horseback trail rides in the Nemo area – 1, 2, 4 hour and all day rides. Now, what's the point in coming to the West if you don't saddle up?

facebook.com/TM-Trail-Rides *12737 Guest Ranch Loop, Nemo* *(605) 280-7934*

Sturgis Strikers Bowling Alley (611)

This seasonal alley opens in late August, a week after the Rally. It has 12 bowling lanes, a bar and grill, pool tables, darts and a pro shop.

sturgisstrikers.com   *910 First Street*   *605-720-2695*

Wonderland Cave (612)

In 1929 a search for a lost dog led two loggers to the upper room of this immense cavern that has the largest variety of crystal formation in the Hills. The first commercial tours began during the summer of 1930, and today more than two dozen rooms are featured in Wonderland Cave. Formations include Stalactites, Stalagmites, Dogtooth Spar Crystals, Column Formations, Helictites, Lobulites (better known as Popcorn Crystal), Calcite Lily Pads, Ribbon Stalactites, Boxwork Crystals, Flowstone and many more. To get there from Sturgis, take exit 32 from I-90 and go south on the very scenic Vanocker Canyon Road. Open May through October, weather permitting.

wonderlandcavesouthdakota.com   *12634 Alpine Road, Nemo*   *(605) 578-1728*

Black Hills 100 Endurance Race (613)

This is an annual 100 mile, 50 mile and 30 kilometer race held on the Centennial Trail in June. It's "more difficult than entry-level races such as Lean Horse or Rocky Raccoon and is certainly less difficult than a graduate level race such as Hardrock." The 100 mile begins and ends at the City Park in Sturgis, and goes to Silver City. There are aid stations along the way, and runners may leave drop bags at three trailheads. The 100 mile course has a cumulative vertical gain of 16,231 feet of climb and 16,231 feet of descent for a total elevation change of 32,462 feet, and takes place at an average elevation of about 4,627 feet. The 100 mile cutoff time is 32 hrs.

blackhills100.com

Where To Eat (and Drink!) – Sturgis

Bars & Restaurants

Beaver Bar (625)	12998 Hwy 34	(844) 692-3283
Belle Joli Winery (626) *Winery*	3951 Vanocker Canyon Rd	(605) 347-9463
Bobs Family Restaurant (627)	1039 Main Street	(605) 720-2930
Broken Spoke Saloon (628)	19942 N Highway 79	(617) 562-1300
Dungeon Bar (629)	1031 Main St	(605) 920-9266
Easyriders Saloon & Steakhouse (630)	888 Junction Avenue	(605) 561-2400

Full Throttle Saloon (631)

This business suffered a major fire in 2015 when a power cord shorted, but owner Michael Ballard is rebuilding "the world's largest biker bar".

	12997 State Highway 34	(605) 423-4584
Gold Pan Pizza (632)	1133 Main St	(605) 720-5221
Iron Horse Saloon (633)	888 Junction Ave	(605) 561-2400
JJ Davenport's (634)	1020 Junction Ave	(605) 720-1150
Jambonz Grill & Pub (635)	2214 Junction Ave	(605) 561-1100
Kang San – Korean (636)	2715 Lazelle St	(605) 561-0404
Loud American Roadhouse (637)	1305 Main St	(605) 720-1500
Oasis Bar & Fireside Lounge (638)	1145 Main St	(605) 347-4609
One-Eyed Jack's Saloon (639)	1304 Main St	(605) 423-4120
Roscoz Bar (640)	976 Lazelle St	(605) 720-7608
Shanghai Garden (641)	1541 Lazelle St	(605) 720-0701
Side Hack Saloon & Grill (642)	1027 Lazelle St	(605) 347-2828
Sturgis Coffee Company (643)	2275 Lazelle St	(605) 720-1480
Sturgis Wine Co. (644) *Wine bar*	1117 Main St	(605) 720-9596
The Knuckle (645)	931 1st Street	(605) 347-0106

Brewery/museum/excellent family dining (adult during the Rally).

Weimer's Diner & Donuts (646)	1120 Main St	(605) 347-3892

Fast Food & Chains

Arby's (660)	2882 Dickson Dr.	(605) 720-4859
Burger King (661)	2610 Lazelle St	(605) 347-3700
Dairy Queen (662)	2703 Lazelle St	(605) 720-0963
Domino's Pizza (663)	1057 Main St	(605) 561-0555
McDonald's (664)	2351 Lazelle St	(605) 347-2798
Pizza Hut (665)	2249 W. Lazelle	(605) 347-4573
Pizza Ranch (667)	2711 Lazelle St	(605) 347-3400
Subway (668)	2715 Lazelle St	(605) 347-9250
Taco John's (669)	2314 Junction Ave	(605) 347-3556

Where To Stay – Sturgis

Hotels/Motels

Best Western Sturgis Inn (680)	2431 S Junction Ave	(605) 347-3604
Day's Inn (687)	Exit 30 off I-90	(605) 347-3027
Holiday Inn Express (681)	2721 Lazelle St	(605) 347-4140
Iron Horse Inn, Whitewood (682)	600 Service Rd	(605) 722-7574
Lantern Motel (683)	1706 Junction Ave	(605) 347-4511
Star-Lite Motel/Knight's Inn (684)	2426 Junction Ave	(605) 347-2506
Super 8 Motel (685)	2600 Whitewood Rd	(605) 347-4447
South Pine Motel (686)	1051 Park St	(605) 390-2520

Campgrounds

Bear Butte Creek Campground (695)	13174 Hwy 34	(605) 347-3023
Big Rig RV Park (696)	2551 Dolan Creek Rd	(605) 347-1510
Buffalo Chip Campground (697)	20622 131st Ave	(605) 347-9000
Creekside Campground (698)	20538 Hwy 79	(605) 347-9061
Days End Campground (699)	2501 Avalanche Rd	(605) 347-2331
Eagles Landing Campground (700)	2881 Avalanche Rd	(800) 488-9809
Iron Horse Campground (701)	20446 Hwy 79	(877) 700-4766
Lamphere Ranch Campground (702)	13010 Lamphere Ranch Rd	(605) 347-5858
No Name City Cabins & RV (703)	20899 Pleasant Valley Dr.	(605) 347-8891
Ride N Rest Campground (704)	20494 State Highway 79	(605) 490-8292
Rush-No-More RV Resort (705)	21137 Brimstone Place	(605) 347-2916
Shade Valley Camp Resort (706)	20158 137th Pl Hwy 34	(605) 347-5556
Sturgis RV Park (707)	1175 W Woodland St	(605) 720-1501
Sturgis View Campground (708)	20497 Avalanche Rd	(715) 222-9285
Suzie's Camp (709)	20983 Pleasant Valley Dr.	(605) 347-2677

Where To Shop – Sturgis

Black Hills Rally And Gold (720)	Gifts	1101 Main St	(605) 347-3564
Chamber of Commerce (721)	Gifts	2040 Junction Ave	(605) 347-2556
Fabric Junction Quilt Shop (722)	Gifts	1609 Junction Ave	(605) 347-2235
Howdy's Whitewood Plaza (723)	Gifts	1319 Laurel, Whitewood	(605) 269-2648
Just For Looks (724)	Gifts	1006 Main St	(605) 720-4247
Kick Start Travel Center (725)	Gifts	12998 Highway 34	(605) 423-5000
Newell Conoco (726)	Gifts	Hwy 212, Newell	(605) 456-2112
Rocking Tree Floral (727)	Gifts	1340 Lazelle St	(605) 347-4432
Sturgis Harley-Davidson (728)	H-D	1040 Junction Ave	(605) 347-2056
Sturgis Photo & Gifts (729)	Gifts	1081 Main St	(605) 347-6570
Sturgis T-Shirt and Gifts (730)	Gifts	1861 Lazelle St	(605) 206-2015
The Knuckle Trading Post (731)	Gifts	931 1st Street	(605) 347-0106

Zone 2: The Southern Hills

Sure, the biggest tourist attraction in the southern Black Hills is Mount Rushmore. But that's just the icing on the cake: the rest of this dessert is just as sweet and infinitely diverse. There are the towns – Custer, Hill City, Hot Springs and Keystone – and then there's nature's bounty: Wind Cave National Park, Jewel Cave National Monument, Custer State Park, Pactola Lake and the Needles Highway (above), to name a few.

Pactola is a reservoir, created by a dam that was built across a steep valley. At the bottom of the lake is the old mining town of Pactola, The water that runs through it is Rapid Creek, which eventually ends up making its way through Rapid City at the base of the Hills, and then on into the Missouri and the Gulf. The dam is, in part, a flood control mechanism. Back in 1972, it was a lot smaller. On June 9th that year, 238 people lost their lives in the state's largest flood, and more than 3,000 were injured. There was about one billion dollars worth of property damage in 2016 terms ($160m in 1972).

South of Pactola another reservoir, Angostura, offers thirty-six miles of shoreline near the town of Hot Springs. That's also home to a mammoth site and some natural mineral springs where a road-weary tourist can soak in 87° comfort. From steam trains to artist communities and wineries, the southern Black Hills have more than enough surprises to fill any vacation calendar.

Custer
ZIP: 57730

Things to See and Do – Custer

Custer State Park (750)
- *13329 US Hwy 16A*
- *1-7 consecutive days pass is $20 for a vehicle or $10 for a motorcycle (2016). Camping fees extra.*
- *Download the brochure at gfp.sd.gov/state-parks/directory/custer/docs/tatanka.pdf*
- *(605) 255-4515*

Arguably the greatest treasure in the Hills, this breathtakingly beautiful State Park encompasses 71,000 acres and is home to about 1,500 buffalo (American bison) plus mountain lions, coyotes, pronghorn antelope, mule and whitetail deer, elk, bighorn sheep, mountain goats, burros, prairie dogs and a huge array of other mammals, as well as large populations of fish and birds (birdwatchers can pick up a checklist at the visitor center). A spectacular annual buffalo roundup takes place around the last weekend in September (call to confirm actual dates), and the Park has had a long tradition of inviting private citizens on horseback to help. Those without mounts can start the day with a pancake feed, watch the entire event from high ground, and then attend an arts festival with 150 or so booths near the new visitor center.

Families visiting the Park can take Jeep tours to view buffalo up close, be part of a hayride and chuck wagon cookout, go horseback riding, rent watercraft, go rock climbing, or follow any of the numerous hike/bike/horseback trails. There are lots of organized programs, too – Junior Naturalist, Story of the Buffalo, Hook & Cook Fishing, and Canoeing Basics, to name a few. There are guided nature hikes, birding for kids, and even a Wildlife Loop Road Caravan several times a day.

The Park also offers "family-friendly patio talks on topics ranging from Lakota uses of bison, pine-needle basket making, horns and antlers, geology, animal tracks and more. Patio talks are designed as a hands-on, come-and-go, informal presentation allowing visitors to interact with a park naturalist on the patio of the Peter Norbeck Outdoor Education Center". And for those interested in geocaching, the Park offers eight locations with lists available at the visitor center.

If you get there in April, there's usually a bluebird house workshop on Earth day, and throughout the summer there are special activities designed to let kids and campers of all ages learn about this exquisite resource. There are two lakes (Legion and Sylvan), four resorts, and lots of accommodation within the park in lodges and campgrounds. A one-day state fishing license is $16 for non-residents ($67 for a family annual), and fishing is allowed in any of the streams or lakes. Trout limits are 5 daily and 10 possession. If you have physical restrictions, just driving through the park is a feast for the eyes – with tunnels, Needles (rock formations), and abundant wildlife.

State Game Lodge (751)
- *13389 US Hwy 16A*
- *(605) 255-4772 (Custer State Park Resort)*

A magnificent native rock and pine structure built in the early 1920s, the lodge was the summer White House for President Coolidge in 1927, and Dwight Eisenhower stayed here in 1953. It's the largest resort in Custer State Park (see Where To Stay in Custer below), and if you book a room here you may see buffalo from the front porch.

The town, county and state park are named for Lt. Col. George Armstrong Custer, who led an expedition here in search of gold in 1874. A discovery of ore in French Creek led to the 1876 Gold Rush that begat the towns of Lead and Deadwood farther north. There was a treaty in place with the Lakota nations (the Sioux) at the time, forbidding European settlement in the Black Hills. Greed, better weapons and larger numbers led the miners and settlers to believe they could take the prize by force, which indeed they eventually did. But not without a price. Custer and 267 of his men were dispatched in the Battle of the Greasy Grass at the Little Bighorn creek on June 26, 1876. The battlefield is now a National Monument, located about three hours drive northwest of the Black Hills. Interestingly, it is named Little Bighorn Battlefield by the National Park Service. Though the government lost the battle, it won the war and thereby earned the naming rights. Custer's Last Stand was against a combined force of primarily Lakota, but also Northern Cheyenne and Arapaho tribes.

The State Game Lodge is a beautiful place to stay, but if you're budget conscious there are several other options within the park, including cabins and camping. For accommodations with a roof, call 888-875-0001 for details, or visit custerresorts.com. If you're bringing your own bedroom (RV or tenting), visit the Game, Fish & Parks website at gfp.sd.gov/state-parks/directory/custer/campgrounds or call 800-710-2267. You can also book sites at campsd.com

The Gordon Stockade (752)
- *13329 US Hwy 16A*
- *(605) 255-4515*

In violation of the 1868 Treaty of Fort Laramie, which had ceded the Black Hills in perpetuity to the Lakota and banned white settlement, a group of prospectors from Sioux City, Iowa followed on Custer's heels and settled on French Creek in the winter of 1874/5. The first thing they did was build a log fort, which has been recreated in the state park and is a free attraction now. The original stockade was only used for a few months before the US Cavalry evicted Mr. Gordon and his party. But over the next eighteen months a flood of prospectors overwhelmed the limited resources of the army, and by 1876 the white population the Hills exceeded ten thousand. The current stockade is actually the third reconstruction. Locals built the first one in 1925, right after the State Game Lodge was constructed (above). Then, a CCC crew rebuilt that in 1941, and that lasted until the new millennium. A visit to the site gives one a feeling for what life was like just before the Black Hills changed hands. Well worth a stop.

Mount Coolidge Fire Tower (753)

- *13329 US Hwy 16A (Park Headquarters)*
- *(605) 255-4515*

Mount Coolidge is about three miles south of Hwy 16A, on state road 87. Originally known as Sheep Mountain and then Lookout Mountain, it was finally renamed for Calvin Coolidge in 1927. He was a Vermont lawyer, Governor of Massachusetts, and the 30th President of the United States (1923-1929). He enjoyed the outdoors and set up his summer White House in this part of the southern Black Hills in 1927. Known as Silent Cal, he spoke little but had a good sense of humor. Most historians agree that he was a relatively successful chief executive, leaving the country in better shape than he found it, and he was a strong advocate of racial equality. But the Wall Street Crash quickly followed his term, and this has affected his reputation: some analysts believe his small government policies and lack of federal oversight helped in part to create the Great Depression. In 1932, he actively campaigned for the re-election of his successor, Herbert Hoover, who was soundly defeated by FDR.

The fire tower atop the mountain named after Coolidge sits at 6,023 feet and the air is a little thin at this elevation. You'll need a smaller vehicle if you want to drive all the way to the top. The 1.2 mile gravel road leading to the summit is closed to RVs, and is open to cars, pickups and SUVs from about Memorial Day through late September, depending on the weather. The winding unpaved road is a bit of an adventure on a motorcycle (road bike), especially coming down.

At the top, the tower and caretaker's accommodation are of native stone and were constructed by the CCC in the late 1930s. The architectural style will be familiar to patrons of the national parks. The view is astonishing – one can see all the way to the Badlands some sixty miles to the east (if the day is clear), and the entire southern Hills are at your feet. Being a fire tower (still active), there is an emphasis on its function: plaques along the observation deck recount the 1988 Galena Fire that destroyed some 17,000 acres of the park.

Peter Norbeck Outdoor Education Center (754)

- *13329 US Hwy 16A (Park Headquarters)*
- *(605) 255-4515*

In addition to the Coolidge tower and the Gordon Stockade, the Civilian Conservation Corp (CCC) was quite active in the Hills during the 1930s. These young men, facing unemployment during the Depression, chose to become part of a dignified and rewarding effort to rebuild some of the country's infrastructure. Throughout the Black Hills you will come across examples of their work, such as several bridges and roads in Custer State Park, plus the park's Peter Norbeck Outdoor Education Center, the Wildlife Station visitor center and the dams that created many of the reservoirs in the Hills, including Stockade Lakes and Legion Lake. Families sometimes make a game of finding as many CCC commemorative plaques as they can while on vacation, which is also a nice way to inform children of their heritage. Governor Peter Norbeck was the force behind the establishment of Custer State Park back in 1919. The center has animal mounts, exhibits, info, interpretive programs and a bookstore.

Black Hills Playhouse (755)

- *24834 S. Playhouse Rd*
- *(605) 255-4141*
- *blackhillsplayhouse.com*

This is the home of a professional theater company, Dakota Players, that delivers 'top-quality plays at friendly South Dakota prices' every summer (June through August) in the heart of Custer State Park. The Playhouse began as a dream of Dr. Warren Lee of the University of South Dakota, back in 1946. It sits on the site of the old Camp Lodge CCC camp, and in its early days the audiences braved fire trails and dirt roads to watch great theater in the middle of the forest. The University of South Dakota's theater department has been a long-time supporter of the project, as has the South Dakota Department of Game, Fish & Parks, and Custer State Park. In 1998, the BHP was awarded a National Endowment for the Arts grant to form the Children's Theatre Company of South Dakota (CTCSD). Today, Dakota Players serves children and adults in South Dakota, Nebraska, Iowa and Minnesota through touring theatre programs, camps and workshops. Show times are Tuesday through Saturday at 7:30pm with matinees on Wednesday and Sunday at 2:00pm. To reserve tickets, call the number above or visit the website. Prices for adults (as of spring 2016) are $34.00, and children eighteen and under are $16.00. There are discounts for adult students, as well as for seniors and members of the military. As the Playhouse is actually within the Park, a state park pass is required (available at any Park entrance). This is professional theater, and most productions are not recommended for small children.

Crazy Horse Memorial (756)

- *12151 Avenue of the Chiefs, Crazy Horse SD 57730*
- *(605) 673-4681*
- *crazyhorsememorial.org*

Located about five minute's drive from the town of Custer, this is self- billed as 'the world's largest ongoing mountain carving'. It's a tourist attraction that was begun in the 1940s by a Bostonian of Polish descent, Korczak Ziolkowski, and it is only partially finished – the first blast occurred in 1948, almost seventy years ago. According to the Memorial's website, "Henry Standing Bear, a Lakota chief, conceived the idea of a portrait likeness of the Lakota leader, Crazy Horse, carved out of the lasting granite of his Paha Sapa." The site goes on to say that "the mission of Crazy Horse Memorial Foundation is to protect and preserve the culture, tradition and living heritage of the North American Indians". The site is certainly worth visiting as an engineering feat, and there is also a museum, a gift shop and even a restaurant. About a million people visit the sculpture every year.

For information on Lakota culture, see the section on interpretive centers near the end of this book.

Custer Area Arts Council (757)

This group's website, CusterAreaArts.com. has a calendar that lists what's happening in the arts in the Custer area – local musicians, artwork, dance, theater and so on. Just click on the Calendar link at the top of their home page.

1881 Courthouse Museum (758)

- *411 Mount Rushmore Road*
- *(605) 673-2443*
- *1881courthousemuseum.com*

Constructed of local bricks, the Italianate building was dedicated in 1881 when this was still a Territory and it served as an active courthouse and government center until 1974. It's on the National Register, and became a museum in the centennial year of the Gold Rush, 1976. There are Lakota cultural exhibits; natural science displays; a room dedicated to the Custer expedition which includes photographs taken on the excursion plus one of his guns and some campsite artifacts; mining and mineral exhibits including gold ore and a replica of a mine; a look into Victorian life and an interactive dollhouse where children can arrange the furniture; a ranch room with everything from barbed wire to saddles and branding irons; the original courtroom and judge's chambers; a one-room schoolhouse replica; military and forestry exhibits; and outside a carriage house, outhouse and log cabin. Visitors can also tour a general store, two jail cells, and some antique guns and knives. Across the street is the oldest building in the Black Hills: the Flick cabin was constructed in 1875 and is furnished as a pioneer home. The museum is open seasonally: call first. It is also on facebook™. Handicap accessible.

National Museum of Woodcarving (759)

- *12111 Us Highway 16*
- *(605) 673-4404*
- *woodcarving.blackhills.com*

Open from the beginning of May through mid-October, this attraction is popular with woodworkers, Disney aficionados and art enthusiasts. The museum includes more than thirty hand-carved and animated scenes (many of life in the Old West), which were created by one of the original animators from Disneyland, Harvey Niblack. There are displays of work by nationally known carvers, and the facility also offers whittling and carving classes. There is a really well-stocked souvenir shop that carries carved items such as the exquisite work by Jeff Phares shown here (*Walks on Sacred Ground*), and lots of locally made gifts. But the heart and soul of the place is the Niblack collection, which kids find very entertaining and adults find completely engrossing. Well worth a visit.

Helicopter Tours (760)

- *24564 Hwy 16*
- *(605) 673-2163*
- *coptertours.com*

About a mile and a half north of the Crazy Horse Memorial on Highway 16/385, you'll find **Black Hills Aerial Adventures**. From early May through the end of October, the company provides tours around Crazy Horse, Harney Peak, Mount Rushmore, or the historic towns of Lead, Deadwood, Keystone and Custer. View the Wharf and Ingersoll mines and the largest and deepest gold mine in North America – the Homestake Open-Pit. One tour includes views of a portion of Spearfish Canyon including Roughlock Falls, the mountain lakes – Pactola, Sheridan and Sylvan – and the granite formations of the Cathedral Spires, Needles, Little Devils Tower and Harney Peak. Tours start at just $49 per person. Two other heliports at Mount Rushmore and the Badlands offer further choices. Reservations are welcome, but not required.

Black Hills Balloons (761)
- *25158 Little Teton Rd*
- *(605) 673-2520*
- *blackhillsballoons.com*

Witness untouched wilderness, a breathtaking 360-degree sunrise and local wildlife from a hot air balloon! Flights take place daily at sunrise – weather permitting – from May 1st through Oct 31st. Guests can expect an hour flight over the historic and beautiful Black Hills, with a champagne toast and a souvenir flight certificate included. For most of us, flying in a hot air balloon is a once-in-a-lifetime, bucket-list adventure. Here in the southern Hills, the experience is even more spectacular as the craft flies over some spectacularly rugged terrain in Custer Valley and Custer State Park. There are mountains, valleys, lakes and prairies to view as you drift along on the morning breeze. Guests quite often see some unique wildlife including elk, antelope, buffalo and mule deer. If you're really lucky, you might even spot a mountain lion from the secure gondola! There's nowhere else in the world quite like it. Reservations are required. Adults are $295 each, and children 4-12 are $245 (2016 prices).

Blue Bell Stables (762)
- *25453 Highway 87*
- *(605) 255-4531*
- *custerresorts.com/lodges-and-cabins/blue-bell-lodge*

Blue Bell Lodge in Custer State Park operates stables where you can go on horseback rides or take in a chuck wagon cookout. A hayride travels back roads to a quiet meadow where you'll be treated to a feast and entertainment. Or explore the 71,000-acre wildlife preserve on a peaceful, guided horseback ride. Beginners and experts are welcome, and there are one-hour to full-day rides available (5+ kids can ride the trail and there are pony rides for children under 5.

Custer Farmers' Market (763)
- *400 Mt. Rushmore Rd*
- *(605) 673-5230*
- *gdcleveland@goldenwest.net*

The market takes place at Way Park on Mt. Rushmore Road and 4th Street every Saturday morning beginning at 8, from June to October.

Four Mile Old West Town (764)
- *11921 West Highway 16*
- *(605) 673-3905*
- *fourmileoldwesttown.com*

From mid-May until early October you can visit the ghost town of Moss City, about four miles west of Custer on Hwy 16. There are about fifty buildings including a school, saloon, jail, sheriff's office and a log cabin. Actors portray Western characters: call for schedule. Admission is $5 per person (kids 6 & under are free). Pet friendly.

Frontier Photo (765)
- *512 Mt. Rushmore Rd*
- *(605) 673-2269*
- *frontierphotos.com*

This studio has all the props you need to have your photograph taken in the Old West., or on a motorcycle. Drive your bike right in! There's also a wide range of wildlife prints, and bike rentals for the Mickelson Trail.

Grizzly Gulch Adventure Golf (766)
- *231 West Mt Rushmore Rd*
- *(605) 673-1708*
- *18 hole mini-golf, 9:00 AM to 10:00 PM.*

Rocky Knolls Golf Course - 9 Hole (767)
- *12181 West Hwy 16*
- *(605) 673-4481 or (605) 517-1107*
- *rockyknollsgolfcourse.com*

This is one of the prettiest 'interrupted walks' in the Hills, and the course is a teaser with narrow, tree-lined fairways, sloping greens, a few quite long holes, ponds, wildlife and sand traps. Great fun. Just west of town on Hwy 16.

Operation Black Hills Cabin (768)
- *605-517-1830*
- *operationblackhillscabin.org*

This all volunteer program offers a vacation in the Hills at little or no expense to qualified wounded Veterans from the Iraq and Afghanistan campaigns.

Beaver Lake Water Slide (769)
- *12005 West Hwy 16*
- *(605) 673-2464*

Max and Cindy Hammer operate the Beaver Lake Campground, and right out by the highway they have a nice water slide that's open to the public for $10 a day per person, with a discount for campers.

Dakota Frontier Tours (770)
- *(866) 978-3553*
- *dakotafrontiertours.com*

Personalized, narrated, guided tours of the southern and northern Hills, and Badlands.

L&J Golden Circle Tours (771)
- *12021 US Hwy 16*
- *(605) 673-4349*
- *goldencircletours.com*

Guided tours of the Black Hills and the surrounding area.

Grand Magic (772)
- *370 West Main St*
- *(406) 291-2004*
- *grandmagicshow.com*

Magic show with illusionist Duane Laflin, 7:30 PM nightly in the summer.

Rockin R Trail Rides (773)
- *24853 Village Ave*
- *(605) 673-2999*
- *rockingrtrailrides.com*

Trail rides and over-night trips with owners Randy and Peggy to capture the spirit of the Old West. There's a variety of rides, including 1 hour, 1½ hour, 2 hour and half day. Riders of all ages and experience welcome.

Jewel Cave National Monument (774)
- *11149 US Hwy 16*
- *(605) 673-8300*
- *nps.gov/jeca/index.htm*

"Immerse yourself within the third longest cave in the world. With over 180 miles of mapped and surveyed passages, this underground wilderness appeals to human curiosity. Its splendor is revealed through fragile formations and glimpses of brilliant color. Its maze of passages lure explorers, and its scientific wealth remains a mystery. This resource is truly a jewel in the National Park Service." They're not wrong. This is a family adventure that's hard to top. It's surprisingly accessible, especially the Discovery Talk program: "This 20-minute ranger talk is a brief introduction to Jewel Cave's natural and cultural histories. Participants view one large room of the cave. This easy cave visit enters and exits the cave by elevator in the Visitor Center, and involves walking up and down 15 stair steps. The Discovery Talk is wheelchair accessible for people who have trouble negotiating stairs, and the tour is limited to 20 participants." For people with no physical challenges, there's the popular scenic tour (a 1 hour 20 minute moderately tiring hike); the relatively strenuous but very engaging historic lantern tour that feels like a 1930s adventure; or the scrambling, belly-crawling, very strenuous 3 to 4 hour Wild Caving tour. Visit the website before deciding!

Where To Eat – Custer

Blue Bell Lodge (785)
- *25453 Hwy 87*
- *(605) 255-4531*

   Comfortable Old West saloon-style setting. Specialty burgers and sandwiches, salads, buffalo and steak. Peaceful patio overlooking French Creek.

Legion Lake Lodge (786)
- *12967 Hwy 16A*
- *(605) 255-4521*

   Relaxed and inviting atmosphere for families on the go. Breakfast, lunch and dinner on the lakeside deck. Hard ice cream, fresh baked pies and Starbucks®.

State Game Lodge (787)
- *13389 Hwy 16A*
- *(605) 255-4541*

   Eloquently historical. Dinner is a culinary treat. Entree selections highlight local game such as trout, pheasant, buffalo and elk. Reservations recommended.

Sylvan Lake Lodge (788)
- *24572 Hwy 87*
- *(605) 574-2561*

   Fantastic forest views! Newly remodeled. Features buffalo, fresh fish and wapiti (elk) tenderloin. Reservations recommended.

1881 Bank Coffee House (789)
- *548 Mt. Rushmore Rd*
- *(605) 673-2497*
- *bankcoffeehouse.com*

Annie's Emporium (790)
- *325 Mt. Rushmore Rd*
- *(605) 673-5600*
- *facebook.com/anniesemporiumrc*

Baker's Bakery & Café (791)
- *541 Mt. Rushmore Rd*
- *(605) 673-2253*
- *bakersbakerycafe.com*

Begging Burro Mexican Bistro (792)
- *529 Mt Rushmore Rd*
- *(605) 673-3300*
- *facebook.com/beggingburro*

Bitter Esters Brewhouse (793)
- *607 Mt. Rushmore Rd*
- *(605) 673-3433*
- *facebook.com/bitterestersbrewhouse*

Black Hills Burger and Bun Co. (794)
- *441 Mt. Rushmore Rd*
- *(605) 673-3411*
- *blackhillsburgerandbun.com*

Oliver's Twist (795)
- *29 N. 5th St*
- *(605) 673-3039*

Bobkat's Purple Pie Place (796)
- *19 Mt. Rushmore Rd*
- *(605) 673-4070*
- *purplepieplace.com*

Buglin' Bull Restaurant and Sports Bar (797)
- *511 Mt. Rushmore Rd*
- *(605) 673-4477*
- *buglinbull.com*

Captain's Table (798)
- *220 West Mt Rushmore Rd*
- *(605) 673-3195*
- *blackhills.net/captainstable*

Custer County Candy Company   (799)
- *506 Mt. Rushmore Rd #1*
- *(605) 673-3911*
- *custercountycandycompany.com*

Dairy Queen (800)
- *335 Mt. Rushmore Rd*
- *(605) 673-5556*
- *dairyqueen.com*

Dakota Cowboy Inn Restaurant   (801)
- *216 West Mt. Rushmore Rd*
- *(605) 673-4613*
- *dakotacowboyinncuster.com*

Espresso and More (802)
- *86 Centennial Dr.*
- *(605) 673-3999*

Frontier Grill (803)
- *680 Mt Rushmore Rd*
- *(605) 673-8870*
- *facebook.com/TheFrontierBarAndGrill*

Gold Pan Saloon (804)
- *508 Mt. Rushmore Rd*
- *(605) 673-8850*
- *facebook*

Laughing Water Restaurant (805)
- *12151 Avenue of the Chiefs*
- *(605) 673-4681*
- *crazyhorsememorial.org/our-campus.html*

Maria's Mexican Food Truck (806)
- *731 Mt Rushmore Rd*
- *(605) 440-2269*
- *facebook*

Naked Winery (807)
- *430 Mt. Rushmore Rd*
- *(605) 673-2733*
- *nakedwinerysd.com*

On The Rocks Chophouse – Bavarian Inn (808)
- *907 North 5th St*
- *(605) 673 5540*
- *ontherockschophouse.com*

Our Place (809)
- *738 Mt. Rushmore Rd*
- *(605) 673-5255*

Pizza Hut (811)
- *12193 US Highway 16*
- *(605) 673-3330*
- *order.pizzahut.com*

Pizza Mill (812)
- *904 Mt. Rushmore Rd*
- *(605) 673-3306*
- *facebook.com/PizzaMill*

Pizza Works (813)
- *429 Mt. Rushmore Rd*
- *(605) 673-2020*
- *custerpizzaworks.com*

Rosestrudel (814)
- *437 Mt Rushmore Rd*
- *(605) 673-5344*
- *facebook*

Sage Creek Grille (815)
- *611 Mt. Rushmore Rd*
- *(605) 673-2424*
- *sagecreekgrille.com*

Subway (816)
- *926 Mt. Rushmore Rd*
- *(605) 673-2722*
- *subway.com*

Wrangler Café (817)
- *302 Mt. Rushmore Rd*
- *(605) 673-4271*
- *facebook.com/WranglerCafe*

VFW Post 3442 (818)
- *721 Mt. Rushmore Rd*
- *(605) 673-4262*
- *vfw.org/oms/findpost.aspx*

Where To Stay – Custer

('Camp' below is an abbreviation for Campground, and CH* denotes Crazy Horse town)

Bavarian Inn (835)	855 N. 5th St	(605) 673-2802
Beaver Lake Camp & Cabins (837)	12005 W. Hwy 16	(605) 673-2464
Best Western Buffalo Ridge Inn (838)	310 W Mt. Rushmore Rd	(605) 673-2275
Big Pine Camp & Cabins (839)	12084 Big Pine Rd	(605) 673-4054
Black Hills Mile Hi Motel (840)	244 Mt. Rushmore Rd	(605) 673-4048
Black Hills Bungalows (841)	24941 America Center Rd	(605) 673-5253
Black Hills Ponderosa Place (842)	915 Gordon St	(605) 366-7461
Blue Bell Lodge Cabins (843)	25453 Hwy 87	(605) 255-4531
Broken Arrow - Horse & RV (844)	25548 Flynn Creek Rd	(605) 517-1964
Buffalo Ridge Camp Resort (845)	422 Mount Rushmore Rd	(605) 673-4664
Calamity Peak Lodge (846)	12557 Hwy 16A	(605) 673-2357
Chief Motel (847)	120 Mt Rushmore Rd	(605) 673-2318
Comfort Inn & Suites (848)	339 W Mt. Rushmore Rd	(605) 673-3221
Creekside Lodge (849)	13389 Hwy 16A	(605) 255-4541
Crazy Horse Camp & Cabins (850)	1116 North 5th St	(605) 673-2565
Custer-Mt. Rushmore KOA (851)	12021 US Hwy 16	(605) 673-4304
Custer's Gulch RV & Camp (852)	25112 Golden Valley Rd	(605) 673-4647
Dakota Cowboy Inn (853)	208 W Mt. Rushmore Rd	(605) 673-4659
Dakota Dream B&B & Horse (854)	12350 Moss Rock Lane	(605) 517-2292
Days Inn of Custer (855)	519 Crook St	(605) 673-4500
Double Diamond Ranch B&B (856)	23818 Hwy 385	(605) 574-4560
Econo Lodge (857)	342 Mt. Rushmore Rd	(605) 673-4400
Fort Welikit Family Camp (858)	24992 Sylvan Lake Rd	(605) 673-3600
French Creek RV Park (859)	144 S 4th St	(605) 673-3727
Gold Camp Cabins (860)	11965 Pleasant Valley Rd	(605) 673-2720
Heritage Village Campground (861)	24827 Village Ave, CH*	(605) 673-5005
Holiday Inn Express (862)	433 W Mt. Rushmore Rd	(605) 673-2500
Legion Lake Lodge Cabins (863)	12967 Hwy 16A	(605) 255-4521
Mystic Valley Inn (864)	25085 Spring Pl	(605) 673-4819
Outlaw Ranch - Lutheran (865)	12703 Outlaw Ranch Rd	(605) 673-4040
Rock Crest Lodge & Cabins (866)	15 Mt. Rushmore Rd	(605) 673-4323
Rocket Motel (867)	211 Mt. Rushmore Rd	(605) 673-4401
Roost Resort Camp & Cabins (868)	12462 Hwy 16A	(605) 673-2326
Shady Rest Motel (869)	238 Gordon St	(605) 673-4478
State Game Lodge (870)	13389 Hwy 16A	(605) 255-4541
Super 8 (871)	535 W Mt. Rushmore Rd	(605) 673-2200
Sylvan Lake Lodge (872)	24572 Hwy 87	(605) 574-2561
Way Back Inn (873)	26699 Remington Rd	(605) 673-2679

Where To Shop – Custer

Custer State Park (890):
- *13329 Hwy 16A*
- *(605) 255-4515*

A gift shop is located at the State Game Lodge, and general stores can be found at Legion Lake, Blue Bell and by Sylvan Lake. The Coolidge General Store is a short distance from the State Game Lodge. All are stocked with souvenirs and supplies, including apparel, bison and wildlife items, personal care products, groceries and beverages (beer and liquor at some locations), grab-and-go food, camping supplies, fishing supplies and licenses. There's gasoline at the Blue Bell and Coolidge general stores, and watercraft rentals at the Legion Lake and Sylvan stores.

Annie's Emporium (780)
- *325 Mt. Rushmore Road*
- *(605) 673-5600*

Located in a 120-year old house, you'll find locally crafted jewelry, fibers, art, leather, spices, honey, chocolate, the French Creek Tea Company, and homemade pretzels.

Art Expressions Gallery of Custer (891)
- *36 S. 6th St, Custer*
- *(605) 673-3467*

Cooperative-style gallery featuring the artwork of more than 30 local, regional and nationally-known artists who work in the following mediums: wood furniture; bronze sculpture; stained glass; watercolor; acrylic; oils; pastels; photography; stone; fiber; jewelry; books and more.

Mini-Needles Art Studio (892)
- *24948 American Center Rd*
- *(605) 673-3086 or (308) 760-8145*

The Mini-Needles Art Studio "will be displaying artist's original work in oils, acrylics, watercolors and various mixed mediums. All work on display will be for purchase. The Studio will feature special conversation art pieces for the buyer's selection."

Paul Horsted, Dakota Photographic LLC (893)
- *24905 Mica Ridge Road*
- *605) 673-3685*
- *paulhorsted.com*

A widely celebrated regional photographer whose work is featured in the books *The Black Hills Yesterday & Today, Exploring With Custer* and *Custer State Park: From the Mountains to the Plains*. To learn more, visit facebook.com/AuthorPaulHorsted

Richard Tucker, Bronze Sculptor (894)
- *24946 America Center Road*
- *(605) 673-2463 or (605) 440-2280*
- *richardtucker.net*

Richard Tucker creates sculptures of various subjects including wildlife, the American West, and the human figure.

Carson Drug (896)
- *521 Mt Rushmore Rd*
- *(605) 673-2225*

Full-service pharmacy, Russell Stover candies, greeting and postcards, Yankee Candles, film, souvenirs. Ship via UPS

A Step Back In Time (897)
- *522 Mt Rushmore Rd*
- *(605) 673-2217*

Gifts and antique store in a Victorian building setting.

A Walk in the Woods (898)
- *506 Mount Rushmore Rd*
- *(605) 673-6400*

Very nice store with gifts, home décor, clothing, furniture, kitchen/dining and more.

Dakota's Best Wine & Gifts (899)
- *529 Mt. Rushmore Rd*
- *(605) 673-3585*

The largest selection of Dakota made products, including gourmet foods such as jams, salsa, sauces, pasta, oils, meats, cheeses and the greatest selection of SD made wine. Wine tastings daily

Flora's Jewelry & Western Wear (900)
- 601 Mt. Rushmore Rd
- (605) 673-4754

In business for 48 years (same location), this store offers Western wear, Black Hills gold jewelry and custom gold jewelry. There's a goldsmith on site, jewelry repair, American made gifts, boots, belts, hats, buckles, horse riding gear, pack supplies, hiking gear, camping supplies, T-shirts, sweatshirts, gloves, native gifts, Western art, leathers, pictures and cookbooks.

Jenny's Floral (901)
- *1528 Mt. Rushmore Rd*
- *(605) 673-3549*

Fresh flowers, plants and home decor

Claw, Antler and Hide Co. (902)
- *735 Mount Rushmore Rd*
- *(60)673-4345*
- *clawantlerhide.com*

Exactly what it sounds like.

Ken's Minerals & Trading Post (903)

- *12372 Hwy 16A*
- *(605) 673-4935*

kensminerals.net

Back in 1936, Ken Spring opened this rock hound's paradise and it has been an iconic stop for eight decades now. The store, inside and out, is brimming with rare fossils, beautiful gemstones, hand-crafted jewelry, diverse agates, rare Fairburn agates and more. There's a private collection of rocks, minerals and fossils that will blow your socks off.

Main Street Market Place – Ice Cream (904)

- *529 Mt. Rushmore Rd*
- *(605) 673-3300*

Three stores with a variety of sweatshirts, t-shirts, ball caps, kids toys and an ice cream and coffee shop.

Shanklin's of South Dakota, Inc. (905)

- *12702 Miller Court*
- *(605) 673-2099*

A flooring store that also carries souvenirs, tie-dyed apparel, tank tops, hoodies, sweatshirts, jewelry, gifts and locally made items.

SoDak Honest (906)

- *25528 Flynn Creek Rd*
- *(605) 450-9957 or (605) 450-9956*
- *sodakhonest.com*

Custom, functional goods from fallen trees, barn wood, antler sheds, scrap metal and more, including furniture, fireplace mantels, signs, jewelry and kitchen utensils.

Hill City
ZIP: 57745

Things to See and Do – Hill City

Known as a center of the arts, Hill City's downtown is home to five nationally known galleries. But the biggest attraction in town is the 1880 Train, where steam and diesel locomotives still pull passengers through some of the prettiest country in the West. They make up to five round trips every day in the summer to neighboring Keystone, at the base of Mount Rushmore.

1880 Train and SD Railroad Museum (929)
- *222 Railroad Avenue*
- *(605) 574-2222*
- *1880train.com*

An absolute must on anyone's Black Hills to-do list, this is a two-hour, narrated 20-mile round trip between Hill City and Keystone. Passengers view vistas of Harney Peak and mining encampments and get a very real sense of what travel was like in the Hills a hundred and more years ago. The Black Hills Central Railroad is the oldest continuously operating tour railroad in the nation. It operates three steam and two diesel engines throughout the season (May through December). One of the steam engines is close to 100 years old. You can download the brochure from the website. Ticket prices (early 2016) are $28 round trip for adults, or $23.00 one way. Children between 3 and 12 are $12 RT and $10 OW. Children 2 and under are free.

The Highliner Snack Shoppe in Hill City is a restored railcar offers that serves meal deals and has outdoor seating. Its concessions are sold onboard the train from Memorial Day through Labor Day weekend. There are gifts shops in the depots at both Hill City and Keystone where you'll find t-shirts, hats, books, train memorabilia and even local wines. And the **South Dakota State Railroad Museum**, next to the depot in Hill City, is only $6 for adults and free to kids under 11. More info at sdsrm.org and the Museum's phone number is (605) 574-9000.

High Country Guest Ranch (930)
- *12138 Ray Smith Drive*
- *(605) 574-9003*
- *highcountryranch.com*

You don't have to be a guest to enjoy music and entertainment by the award-winning Native American group Brule, or the Circle B Chuckwagon Show. But if you're planning on staying in the southern Hills, High Country has log vacation homes, cabins and RV sites in a serene mountain meadow. Visitors can also take a trail ride with experienced wranglers in the Black Hills National Forest., rent ATVs and explore more than 3,000 miles of marked trails in the Hills, or rent bicycles and travel the Mickelson Trail. The ranch is located 4 miles west of Hill City, on Deerfield Road.

Rabbit Bicycle Shuttle (931)

- *175 Walnut Ave.*
- *(605) 574-4302*
- *rabbitbike.com*

This is 'the only full service bicycle shop right on the Michelson Trail' and it offers bicycle rentals for children and adults. But the staff also offer a shuttle service to provide longer rides by dropping you at designated trail heads. The store has everything you may need or want for a day of biking, including a certified mechanic, apparel and food. The trail (gfp.sd.gov/state-parks/directory/mickelson-trail) is 109 miles long and contains more than 100 converted railroad bridges and 4 rock tunnels. The trail surface is primarily crushed limestone and gravel. There are 15 trailheads, all of which offer parking, self-sale trail pass stations, vault toilets, and tables. It's one of South Dakota's greatest treasures.

Everything Prehistoric & The Geological Museum (932)

- *117 Main Street*
- *(605) 574-3919*
- *bhigr.com/museum*

South Dakota once had seaside property. During the Cretaceous era, when T Rex roamed the land, a seaway spanned central South Dakota and hosted an abundance of sea creatures. The Museum at the Black Hills Institute curates a collection that includes many of these strange and amazing animals, plus dinosaurs, fossils, minerals and collectibles from all over the world. Adults 16 and over are $7.50; seniors, Vets and active military are $6; kids 6-15 are $4 and children 5 and under are free (2016).

Everything Prehistoric is the impressive gift shop at the Black Hills Institute, located in the lobby. It offers a broad variety of fossils, minerals, agates and meteorites. There is an extensive book section, educational toys, stone housewares, carvings and a natural gemstone jewelry. Smaller museum, highly recommended. *(Image courtesy of BHIGR)*

Dakota Stone's Rock Shop (933)

- *23850 Hwy 385*
- *(605) 574-2760*
- *dakotastone.net*

Billed as 'a fun and enjoyable experience for the whole family', this is a great hands-on thing for kids to do. They can pan for gemstones and fossils, hunt for hidden treasure in an underground mine, look for gold and crack open a geode.

Jon Crane Gallery (934)

- *256 Main*
- *(605) 574-4440*
- *joncranewatercolors.com*

Crane is renowned for his ability to capture great detail in his landscape watercolors, and for preserving the memory of historic places. Impressive gallery and frame shop.

Warrior's Work & Ben West Gallery (935)

• *277 Main Street*
• *(605) 574-4954*
• *warriorswork-benwestgallery.com*

This is 'a Native American and Contemporary Fine Art Gallery', showcasing the work of 30 artists from the Black Hills, South Dakota, Colorado and the Southwest. Media include bronze, wood, stone, watercolor, oil, acrylic and mixed media. Exquisite work – a treat for your senses. Check out Randy Berger's incredible leather frames.

Sandy Swallow Art Gallery (936)

• *280 Main Street*
• *(605) 642-7847 or (605) 641-2950*
• *sandyswallowgallery.com*

This gallery is Native American owned and operated by Sandy Swallow, and it features Oglala Lakota artists. The work includes fine art, handcrafted jewelry, designer casual apparel and many unique Native American crafted items.

ArtForms Gallery (937)

• *280 Main Street*
• *(605) 574-4894*
• *artformsgallery.org*

Nestled in the back of the Old World Plaza on Main St, this gallery is owned and operated by 20 local artists. You'll find affordable art in every medium imaginable: woodcraft, jewelry, painting, sculpture, pottery, weaving, glass, photography, basketry and more. Stop in and say hello to the artist of the day.

Dakota Nature & Art Gallery (938)

• *216 Main St*
• *(605)-574-2868*
• *dakotanature.com*

This is a family owned gallery featuring art, jewelry home décor, rugs, glasswork, pottery and woodturning by local artists. Their slogan is 'Decorate your home with the feel of the Hills', which is appropriate to their inventory. There are original and Giclée prints, turned vessels by Jerry Green, photography, cedar furniture, petrified wood tables and bookends, minerals from around the world and more. Eclectic, affordable.

Twisted Pine Winery (939)

• *124 Main Street*
• *(605) 574-2023*
• *facebook.com/twistedpinetastingroom*

"Largest selection of Dakota made wines, foods and gifts. We also carry wines from around the world, and offer daily wine tastings. In addition we carry olive oils and balsamic vinegars, sauces, dips, meats and cheese."

Prairie Berry Winery (940)

- *23837 Highway 385*
- *(877) 226-9453*
- *prairieberry.com*

Located three miles northwest of town on Hwy 385, fifth generation winemaker Sandi Vojta handcrafts each wine, often using old family recipes. From the popular Red Ass Rhubarb to seasonal releases, Prairie Berry wines have earned more than 850 awards since 2001. Enjoy a free tasting of up to five wines, including Anna Pesä handcrafted traditional European wines, or crisp, dry wines and robust, oak-aged reds to sweet, fruity varieties. Online shopping available.

Miner Brewing (941)

- *23845 Hwy 385*
- *(605) 574.2886*
- *minerbrewing.com*

Opened in the Fall of 2013, the brewery is located next door to Prairie Berry Winery on Highway 16, just past the junction with Highway 385. It includes a taproom and outdoor beer garden, and features a rotating tap of year-round, seasonal and specialty beers. *The Daily Share* has included Miner Brewing Company among their ranking of the best craft breweries in the United States.

Stone Faces Winery (942)

- *12670 Robins Roost Rd*
- *(605) 574-3600*
- *stonefaceswinery.com*

Named for the presidents on the National Memorial, this is 'one of South Dakota's finest wineries specializes in South Dakota native wild grape Vitis riparia and cold climate hybrid wines, as well as traditional grapes with a uniquely South Dakota feel. Dry, sweet, grape or other fruit wine, Stone Faces Winery has your palate covered.' About 2-1/2 miles north of town.

Naked Winery and Sick-N-Twisted Brewing Company (943)

- *23851 Hwy 385*
- *(605) 673-2733*
- *nakedwinerysd.com*

This is a winery that "takes the pecksniffery out of wine tasting. We'll set the mood and tease your senses with our romantically playful, traditional grape wines. Naked Winery® offers a wide variety of grape wines, including red, white and blush varieties. We also offer a few select fruit wines. All of our wines are presented in a fun way that will spark your passion. At Naked Winery, we want you to drink what you like and have fun doing it! Let the romantic atmosphere put you at ease as you enjoy a glass of wine by the fire with friends and family. Naked Winery has tasting rooms in Hill City and Custer. The Hill City location now offers over 100 revolving microbrews, with 34 on tap."

Sheridan Lake (944)

- *1019 N. 5th Street, Custer, SD 57730 (Black Hills National Forest)*
- *(605) 673-9200*

This is a small reservoir just north of Hill City that is fed and drained by Spring Creek. It was created in 1939 with the construction of a dam that flooded the valley and the original town of Sheridan, which was the first Pennington County seat. The lake is administered by the US Forest Service and there is a commercial marina (see next entry), a swimming beach, some campgrounds, plus several picnic and overlook areas. Fish species include brown trout, largemouth bass, Northern pike, rainbow trout, white crappie and yellow perch. There is no public boat ramp.

Sheridan Lake Marina (945)

- *16451 Sheridan Lake Road (Rapid City address)*
- *(605) 574-2169*
- *sheridanlakemarina.com*

This is a commercial marina located about six miles northeast of Hill City on Hwy 385 on the shore of 383-acre Sheridan Lake. Surrounded by forested hills, this is a very beautiful spot. The Marina offers boat rentals (speedboat/ski, pontoon, 16 ft aluminum fishing boats, canoes and kayaks), bait and fishing tackle, convenience foods, Wave Runner jet skis, and even a waterfront apartment with a deck overlooking the lake.

Wade's Gold Mill (946)

- *12401 Deerfield Road*
- *(605) 574-2680*
- *wadesgoldmill.com*

Built around a collection of antique mining equipment, this is a place where visitors can learn about gold mining in the Black Hills, plus some geology, and even cool their heels in the creek while panning. Take a hands-on tour of the equipment, and meet a modern placer gold mill. Fun and educational. The 75-minute tour is $9 for adults, $5 for 16 and under, kids under 5 are free. The gold panning lesson is $18 for adults, $14 6 to 14-year-olds, and includes a sample of gold ore that is guaranteed to contain gold.

Sylvan Rocks Climbing School (947)

- *208 Main St*
- *(605) 484-7585*
- *sylvanrocks.com*

Daryl and Cheryl Stisser and their crew have been teaching people how to climb in the hills since 1989. Their goal is to teach beginning climbers right, and take experienced guests to the best summits the area has to offer. This is the only *American Mountain Guides Association* accredited climbing guide service operating in the Black Hills, and at Devils Tower National Monument. It's a full service guide school that can host groups from 1 to 80+ people. This team was chosen to work on the film *National Treasure 2*, and has also worked on location in the Black Hills with Bear Grylls, a British adventurer who hosts a television series called *Man vs. Wild*.

Civilian Conservation Corps Museum of South Dakota (948)
- *23935 Hwy 385*
- *(605) 389-3410*
- *southdakotaccc.com*

In March of 1933, President Franklin Delano Roosevelt (FDR) established the Civilian Conservation Corps (CCC), a public work relief program that operated from 1933 to 1942. It found work for unemployed, unmarried men as part of the New Deal. The museum honors those men who thinned trees, fought forest fires, built rock bridges and structures, planted trees, constructed fire trails, worked on soil conservation projects, built dams and generally helped frame the beauty of South Dakota – all for a dollar a day. Families needed food and these men were willing workers who received housing, medical care, food and on the job training. The museum features a video of the history, artifacts, photos and a searchable database of the men who worked in the CCCs in SD, including many from North Dakota, Nebraska and other states. The museum is located upstairs at the Visitor Center (the number for the center is 605-574-2368). It's wheelchair accessible.

The Stables at Palmer Gulch (949)
- *12620 Hwy 244 (located at the Mount Rushmore KOA)*
- *(605) 574-3412*
- *ridesouthdakota.com*

For more than fifty years, this business has been putting Black Hills visitors in the saddle. They offer horseback riding, a chuck wagon dinner show and horse-drawn wagon rides. These are fun trail rides into the most beautiful places in the National Forest, such as the Norbeck Wildlife Preserve and the Black Elk Wilderness Area. provide spectacular scenery that no other trail ride barn can match. The chuck wagon dinner shows are offered several nights a week with real cowboy cooking (don't worry, it's actually a whole lot better than the original cowboys used to eat!), hear old cowboy stories, and listen to real cowboys sing.

Black Hills Open-Top Tours (950)
- *1 White Horse Rd*
- *(605) 644-6736*
- *blackhillsopentoptours.com*

Operating out of Hill City (and also Rapid City, Keystone, Custer, Deadwood, Lead and Sturgis), they provide Black Hills sightseeing tours using comfortable, distinctive, convertible top tour vehicles. Their tours never rush you and make frequent stops for photo ops and breaks. The vehicles are never crowded, seating 2 to 12 guests, all with excellent viewing. Options include convertible-top 'Safari' wildlife tours, Jeeps in the Badlands, handicap accessible vehicles and multilingual narrated tours. Their new Buffalo Safari Van has a distinctive see-through Lexan™ top, and is a comfortable 10 passenger all-weather vehicle with removable side windows for excellent viewing, and standing photo ops.

Hill City Visitor Information Center (951)
- *23935 Highway 385*
- *(605) 574-2368*
- *hillcitysd.com*

One of the best visitor resources in the region, the professional and friendly staff at the VIC will tell you all there is to know about lodging, dining, sight-seeing, and planning activities in the area. They can even plan day trips for you, according to your needs. This is where to go for trail maps, ATV passes, attraction brochures, restaurant menus, local coupons, and they'll also tell you where to find emergency items on the road such as a spare widget for the RV or a new collar for the dog.

Unfortunately, they're closed on weekends.

Where To Eat – Hill City

Alpine Inn (970)   133 Main St   (605) 574-2749
Ethnic European and contemporary lunches, filet mignon for dinner.

Annie Lode Coffee Cabin (971)   23828 Highway 385   (605) 574-4722
Drive-through coffee cabin with exterior seating and treats.

Bumpin Buffalo (972)   245 Main St   (605) 574-4100
Burgers and steaks.

Chute Roosters (973)   850 Chute Rooster Dr.   (605) 574-2122
Family dining, dancehall, bar, and BBQ grill.

Dairy Queen (976)   281 Main St   (605) 574-4735
Chain, ice cream and food, closed in winter.

Dairy Twist (977)   12647 S Hwy 16   (605) 574-2380
Mid-April through mid-September, burgers and dogs, malts, shakes, Indian tacos, etc.

Desperados Cowboy Cuisine (978)   301 Main St   (605) 574-2959
American cuisine including buffalo burgers.

Golden Spike -Best Western (980)   601 E Main St   (605) 574-2577
Hotel restaurant with great breakfast reviews.

Hill City Café (981)   209 Main St   (605) 574-4582
Traditional breakfast lunch and dinner diner menu.

Horse Creek Inn at Sheridan Lake (982)   23570 Highway 385, RC   (605) 574-2120
Steakhouse, prime rib.

Hub Cap Diner (983)   317 Main St   (605) 574-3800
50s/60s style diner.

Mac's Grub (984)   355 E Main St   (605) 574-2575
BBQ and more. Good reviews.

Mangy Moose Saloon (985)   240 Main St   (605) 574-9502
Bar food.

Miner Brewing Co (986)   23845 Hwy 385   (605) 574-2886
Lots of tap beers, some food.

Mountain Treats (987)   269 Main St   (605) 574-2514
Ice cream, fudge, pie.

Naked Winery Kitchen (988)   23851 Hwy 385   (866) 355-7889
Pizza, pretzels, meat and cheese platters.

Ponderosa Restaurant (989)   12620 Highway 244   (605) 574-9559
Sandwiches, burgers etc.

Prairie Berry Winery (990)   23837 Hwy 385   (877) 226-9453
Gourmet sandwiches, soups, desserts.

Rico's (991)   148 Main St   (605) 574-2932
Homemade Mexican.

Silver Dollar Saloon (993)   24090 Highway 385   (605) 574-4417
Known for pizza.

Slate Creek Grille (994)   158 Museum Dr.   (605) 574-9422
Walleye, game and steakhouse fare.

Subway (995)   451 E Main St   (605) 574-4174
  Chain.
Turtle Town (996)   205 Main St   (605) 574-4124
  Fudge, candy, ice cream.

Where To Stay – Hill City

Alpine Inn (1020)
- *133 Main St*
- *(605) 574-2749*
- *alpineinnhillcity.com*

4 lodging rooms available on the second floor of a historic hotel built in 1884.

BackRoads Inn and Cabins (1021)
- *901 Echo Valley Rd*
- *(605) 209-3971*
- *cabinsoftheblackhills.com*

Best Western Golden Spike Inn & Suites (1022)
- *601 E. Main St*
- *(605) 574-2577*
- *bestwesterngoldenspike.com*

Black Hills Trailside Park Resort (1023)
- *24024 Hwy 16*
- *(605) 574-9079*
- *trailsideparkresort.com*

Creekside Country Resort (1024)
- *12647 S Hwy 16*
- *(605) 574-2380*
- *creeksidecountryresort.com*

Mini golf, restaurant.

Crooked Creek Resort and RV Park (1025)
- *24184 Hwy 385*
- *(605) 574-2418*
- *crookedcreeksd.com*

Derby Elk Resort (1026)
- *12446 Log Cabin Rd*
- *(605) 877-5544*
- *derbyelkresort.net*

Horses welcome

Double Diamond Ranch (1027)
- *23818 Hwy 385*
- *(605) 574-4560*
- *doublediamondcabins.com*

Happy Trails Cabins (1028)
- *9309 Main St*
- *(605) 574-2177*
- *happytrailscabins.com*

Harney Peak Inn (1029)
- *125 Main St*
- *(605) 574-2544*
- *harneypeakinn.com*

Heart of the Hills Vacation Homes (1030)
- *349 Main St*
- *(605) 574-2250*
- *hillcityvacation.com*

High Country Guest Ranch Cabins & Camping (1031)
- *12138 Ray Smith Dr.*
- *(605) 574-9003*
- *highcountryranch.com*

Hillside Country Cabins (1032)
- *13315 South Hwy 16*
- *(605) 342-4121*
- *hillsidecountrycabins.com*
Year round.

Holiday Inn & Suites (1033)
- *12444 Old Hill City Rd*
- *(605) 574-4040*
- *ihg.com*

Holly House B&B (1034)
- *23852 Hwy 385*
- *(605) 574-4246*
- *bbonline.com/united-states/south-dakota/hill-city/hollyhouse.html*

Janssen's Lode Stone Motel & Cabins (1035)
- *23884 Hwy 385*
- *(605) 574-2347*
- *lodestonemotel.qwestoffice.net*

Lantern Inn (1036)
- *580 East Main St*
- *(605) 574-2582*
- *lanterninn.com*

Lodge at Palmer Gulch & KOA (1037)
- *12620 Hwy 244*
- *(605) 574-2525*
- *palmergulch.com*

Mountain View Lodge & Cabins (1038)
- *12654 South Hwy 16*
- *(800) 789-7411*
- *mountainviewlodge.net*

Mountains to Prairies B&B (1039)
- *200 East Main St*
- *(605) 574-2424*
- *mountainstoprairiesbb.com*

Mt. Meadow Cabins & Campground (1040)
- *11321 Gillette Prairie Rd*
- *(605) 574-2636*
- *mtmeadow.com*
Snowmobile and ATV/UTV rentals

Newton Fork Ranch Cabins (1041)
- *12407 Deerfield Rd*
- *(605) 574-2220*
- *newtonforkranch.com*
Horses welcome

Pine Rest Cabins (1042)
- *24063 South Hwy 385*
- *(605) 574-2416*
- *pinerestcabins.com*

Quail's Crossing, Motel and Cabins (1043)
- *24060 Hwy 385*
- *(605) 391-3217*
- *quailscrossing.net*

Quality Inn (1044)
- *616 Main St*
- *(605) 574-2100*
- *choicehotels.com*

Rafter J Bar Ranch Camping (1045)
- *12325 Rafter J Rd*
- *(605) 574-2527*
- *rafterj.com*

Restmore Inn & Cabins (1046)
- *24191 Hwy 385*
- *(605) 574-2593*
- *restmoreinn.com*

Robin's Roost Cabins (1047)
- *12630 Robins Roost Rd*
- *(605) 574-2252*
- *robinsroostcabins.com*

Spring Creek Inn (1048)
- *23900 Hwy 385*
- *(605) 574-2591*
- *springcreekinn.com*

Super 8 (1049)
- *109 Main St*
- *(605) 574-4141*
- *super8.com*

Guinness World Record "Largest Teddy Bear Collection", with over 9000 bears.

Three Forks Campground (1050)
- *23821 Hwy 385*
- *(605) 574-4546*
- *blackhills.net/threeforkscampground*

Trails End Cabins & Motel (1051)
- *320 Park St*
- *(605) 574-4900*
- *hillcitycabin.com*

Whispering Winds Cottages/Camping (1052)
- *12720 S Hwy 16*
- *(605) 574-9533*
- *whisperingwindsblackhills.com*

Where To Shop – Hill City

Broken Arrow Trading Co. (1053)
- *249 Main St*
- *(605) 574-4275*

Buffalo Bobs (1054)
- *381 Main St*
- *(605) 574-4791*

Country Store At The Forks (1056)
- *23820 Hwy 385*
- *(605) 574-4377*

Dakota Stone Rock Shop (1057)
- *23850 Hwy 385*
- *(605) 574-2760*

Dakota's Best Gifts (1058)
- *124 Main St*
- *(605) 574-2023*

Everything Prehistoric (1059)
- *117 Main St*
- *(605) 574-3919*

Gold Diggers (1060)
- *241 Main*
- *(605) 574-3332*

Granite Sports (1061)
- *201 Main Street*
- *(605) 574-2121*
- *granitesports.biz*

Heart of the Hills Antiques (1062)
- *280 Main St*
- *(605) 574-2821*

Hill City Harley-Davidson (1063)
- *261 Main*
- *(605) 574-3636, (605) 342-9362*

Hill City Mercantile & Quilt Co. (1064)
- *227 Main St*
- *(605) 574-2001*
- *hillcitymercantile.com*

Jenny's Floral (1065)
- *243 Elm St*
- *(605) 574-3549*

Jewels of the West (1066)
- *208 Main St*
- *(605) 574-2464*

Just Dandy (1067)
- *273 Main St*
- *(605) 574-2085*
- *facebook*

Mount Rushmore Memories (1069)
- *263 Main St*
- *(605) 385-0251*
- *mountrushmoresociety.com*

Rafter J Bar Ranch Store (1070)
- *12325 Rafter J-Bar Rd*
- *(605) 574-2527*

Stage Stop Leather & Gifts (1072)
- *224 Main St*
- *(605) 574-2646*

Teddy Bear Town (1074)
- *108 Main St*
- *(605) 574-2266*

The Farmer's Daughter (1075)
- *164 Main St*
- *(605) 574-9095*
- *thefarmersdaughtersd.com*

The Handbag Store (1076)
- *253 Main St*
- *(605) 574-9585*

Things That Rock (1077)
- *156 Main St*
- *(605) 574-9096*

Warrior's Work & Ben West Gallery (1078)

- *277 Main St*
- *(605) 574-4954*

Depot Gift Shop -1880 Train (1079)

- *222 Railroad Ave*
- *605-574-2222*
- *1880train.com*

Jon Crane Gallery & Frame Shop (1080)

- *333 Main St*
- *605-574-4441*
- *store.joncranewatercolors.com*

Hot Springs
ZIP: 57747

Things to See and Do – Hot Springs

For more than a hundred and fifty years, people have been bathing in the warm mineral waters of Hot Springs. Today, the town has a well-preserved historical district that includes many of its original red sandstone structures. In 1891, Evan's Plunge baths were developed, and they're still operational today. The town is also home to a Veterans' residence and hospital, and an airport that can handle small jets. There's a great 4th of July parade, and the Christmas In The Hills festival of lights also includes a parade after dusk at the beginning of December.

Angostura Recreation Area (1100)
About ten miles southeast of Hot Springs on Hwy 385/18, Angostura Reservoir is a water-lover's dream with lots of sandy beaches and shoreline, plus 4 campgrounds (169 campsites and 12 cabins). There are walleye, smallmouth bass, crappie, northern pike, largemouth bass, perch and bluegill in the lake. There's a privately-operated resort with marinas and rental lodges (800-364-8831), a convenience store and lots of boat ramps. Visitors can also rent kayaks/canoes, fishing rods and paddleboards. The daily fee for a vehicle is only $6 (2016), and campsites run less than $20. Or stay in town and drive to the lake (15 minutes) to spend the day. And check out Shep's Canyon Recreation Area.
gfp.sd.gov/state-parks/directory/angostura   *13157 N Angostura Rd   (605) 745-6996*

Black Hills Parks & Forest Association (1101)
This is a nonprofit organization designed to "promote public understanding, appreciation, and stewardship of the Black Hills natural and cultural heritage". If you're looking for reading materials for your trip, visit the BHPFA website or stop by one of their fourteen physical bookstores that are located in Black Hills facilities run by the National Park Service, National Forest Service, National Grasslands, and South Dakota State Parks. When you shop BHPFA, the profits are used to print interpretive publications, fund internship positions, purchase educational supplies and equipment, serve as matching funds for grant requests, and provide assistance in research projects.
blackhillsparks.org   *26611 Us Highway 385   (605) 745-7020*

Black Hills Wild Horse Sanctuary (1102)
Hundreds of unadopted BLM wild horses run free at this non-profit which receives no state or federal funding. Two-hour guided bus tours are offered (see rates online).
wildmustangs.com   *12165 Highland Rd   (605) 745-5955*

Cascade Falls (1103)

Cascade Spring is the largest single spring in the Black Hills, and the source of Cascade Creek. This breathtakingly beautiful spot is located about seven miles south of Hot Springs, on Hwy 71. The Black Hills National Forest manages two picnic areas: the J.H. Keith Park and Cascade Falls Picnic Ground. There are several rare South Dakota plant species found only here, including tulip gentian, beaked spike-rush, southern maidenhair fern and stream orchid. The Forest Service wants you to know that: "Cascade Falls and Springs both have gravel or concrete pathways and are just a few minutes walk from the parking areas. There is a stairway down a steep bank to Cascade Falls, where swimming is allowed. Swimming is not permitted in Cascade Springs. Be aware that poison ivy is abundant in some areas adjacent to Cascade Creek, and there is always the possibility of a prairie rattlesnake. Please stay on established trails." *fs.fed.us/wildflowers/regions/Rocky_Mountain/CascadeSprings/index.shtml* *(307) 746-2782*

Cold Brook Lake (1104)

This is one of those quiet little treasures that locals enjoy and tourists tend to miss. The Army Corps of Engineers administers this small reservoir about a mile north of Hot Springs. The dam was constructed for flood control, and the lake "offers an excellent variety of recreational activities year-round including canoeing, fishing, swimming, wildlife viewing, and camping. Winter activities include ice fishing, skating, and cross-country skiing." Go north on Hwy 385, take a left on Badger Clark Road, right on Evans Street, left on Larive Lake Road and the first right (about 100 feet), which will take you around the lake to the beach. The Corps' number is (605) 745-5476.

Cottonwood Springs Lake (1105)

Another hidden gem, this one is located about five minutes west of Hot Springs on Hwy 18. It offers primitive camping only (no hookups), hiking, fishing (only electric motors), and picnicking. This is where you go to enjoy nature and leave the world behind. Follow Hwy 18 to County Rd 17 on your right. At the Y in the road take 17 to the left (not 17C to the right), and in about a quarter of a mile take another right. After a minute, check out the picnic area on your right, and then go back to the road and follow it to the beach.

The Freedom Trail & City Parks (1106)

This walk/run trail is approximately 2.3 miles long and begins behind the Mueller Center, which is at 801 South 6th St. It then follows the Fall River up to Kidney Springs Park, which has a natural spring emerging from the side of the hill, under a gazebo. There are benches along the Trail, and lots of little parks to wander through. Chatauqua Park has fallen rocks, picnic spots and a stone bridge over the river. Both South River Park and Brookside Park have playgrounds, picnic tables and swimming spots along the river. You can also cross the footbridges and do some downtown shopping or dining. There's an old train depot by Kidney Springs. (605) 745-3135

Evan's Plunge (1107)

This is a renowned waterpark built around natural warm springs. The main pool completely recycles itself every hour and a half, and stays a consistent 87° F year round. The water is very gentle: it doesn't contain the harsh minerals often found in other springs. In addition to several water slides there's a health club, two hot tubs, a sauna, steam room, lap swim, water exercise classes, spinning class, weight room, cardio room, boutique fitness classes, two kid's pools, volleyball, basketball, Tarzan rings, inflatable tubes and more. Daily rates (2016) are 2 and under, free; 3-15 years old $10.00; and 16 and older $14.00. There are Military, Senior and AAA discounts. The facility has been in business since 1890 and is the oldest tourism attraction in the Black Hills. There's food on site, as well as a gift shop.

evansplunge.com *1145 North River St* *(605) 745-5165*

The Mammoth Site (1108)

South Dakota's greatest fossil treasure, this was a spring-fed pond some 26,000 years ago that trapped a large number of Columbian and woolly mammoths (61 have been unearthed so far, along with a number of other animal species). The sinkhole was discovered in 1974, and is now enclosed in a large, climate-controlled building. The site, run by a nonprofit, is on the southwest side of town, north of Hwy 18 and beside the Super 8. The 2016, admission is 12 and over $11, age 4 to 12 $8, and under 3 free. There's a senior discount. Open in summer from 8 to 8: call for fall through spring curtailed hours. This is about a two-hour adventure, centered on a 30-minute guided tour. You can stroll through "the dig area at your own pace. Then, explore the many exhibits in the Ice Age Exhibit Hall and peek in the windows of a working paleontology laboratory. Plus…view numerous short educational films on geology, Mammoth Site history, Hunting Mammoths with Dr. Larry Agenbroad, early North America and the people and animals that lived here during the Ice Ages, and museum laboratory procedures".

(The Columbian mammoth shown here was not provided by the site: it's from a painting by Charles R. Knight, c.1909.)

mammothsite.com *1800 Us-18-Truck* *(605) 745-6017*

Pioneer Museum (1109)

Housed in a magnificent 19th century sandstone school, the museum has some 25 exhibit areas and also features work by local artists and sculptors. "Handcrafted Tools, old washing machines, wood cook stoves, and kerosene lamps the pioneer farmers and ranchers used in their daily lives are displayed here. When you view the doctor's office you'll almost smell the liniment! You'll stand in an authentic 19th century classroom and visit a country store complete with supplies!" From May 15 to October 1, the museum is open Monday-Saturday from 9 to 5. Admission for adults is $6 (seniors $5), and under 12s are free. There's even a $15 family package.

pioneer-museum.com *300 N. Chicago Street* *(605) 745-5147*

Ramblin' Rangers (1110)

The husband and wife team of Bonnie Jo and Brad Exton present musical interpretive programs throughout the southern Hills during the summer. They describe their sound as cowboy, country and collectible tunes. Beautiful voices, very relaxing. You can download samples, and their schedule.

ramblinrangers.com/calendar.html   *12601 Darlene Lane*   *605-745-5015 or 440-1957*

Rock & Pine Adventures, Edgemont (1111)

About twenty-five minutes west of Hot Springs is an adventure that soaks in the spirit of the Hills. In Edgemont, John and Janet Koller lead three-hour guided tours of ancient Native American petroglyphs and pictographs, cavalry campsites and incredible natural wonders. "Prehistoric and historic archaeology, native culture and ancient rock art of the earliest area inhabitants are featured at the Buffalo Cave archaeology site. Listed on the National Register of Historic Places, the petroglyphs carved here on rocky cliffs possibly date back as much as 8,000 years ago, and stone teepee rings mark the site of Native campsites." Prices are $25 for adults and half that for 12 and under. Tours begin in downtown Edgemont at the City Park on the main street (Second Avenue) at 9 a.m. and 1 p.m., Monday through Saturday. Visit the website first for guidelines on what to wear and pack. Not recommended for anyone with a physical disability, or health conditions that prevent them from negotiating vertical stairs. An absolute must-do if you want to get the 'feel' of these ancient Hills. Kids will be completely absorbed.

rockandpine.blogspot.com   *City park, Edgemont*   *(605) 662-7332*

Southern Hills Community Theatre (1112)

This is a volunteer, non-profit, very good, community actors' group that is 'dedicated to presenting quality live, family-friendly theatre'. Performances are at the Mueller Civic Center on summer evenings, with some dinner theater performances at Woolly's Restaurant. Ticket prices vary, but are very reasonable.

shct.org   *Mueller Civic Center, 801 S 6th St*   *(605) 745-4837*

Southern Hills Golf Course (1113)

This is an 18-hole par 70, beautiful undulating course that nips in and out of the trees and has gorgeous mountain views. 2016 rates are $26 and $42 for nine and eighteen respectively. Cart rental is $10 and $16.

hotspringssdgolf.com   *1130 Clubhouse Drive*   *(605) 745-6400*

Trout Haven Ranch (1114)

The trout are always biting here! Everything is furnished and no license is needed. You pay only for what you catch. The hatchery raises more than a million trout each year for stocking in ponds and streams in Canada and the USA. It's located nine miles north of Hot Springs, just off Hwy 385 and 79.

ohwy.com/sd/t/trharahs.htm   *Highway 101 in Buffalo Gap*   *(605) 833-2571*

Windcross Spanish Mustang Conservancy (1115)

This is an organization dedicated to preserving the first horse breed that roamed the great plains. There are daily guided walking tours among the herd – it's a very hands on experience. The animals are quite beautiful, and riders of all ages will enjoy the visit. Adults $20, seniors $15, and children under 12 are $5. The Conservancy also offers a 2-hour session for children in basic horsemanship ($50). They will learn grooming, saddling and the basics of training/riding. Class size is extremely limited and by reservation only. The Conservancy is a non-profit.

windcrossconservancy.org   *404 Main St, Buffalo Gap*   *(605) 833-2336*

GeoFunTrek Tours (1116)

This company specializes in day-long adventures in the Black Hills, the Badlands region and the surrounding states. They follow traditional itineraries such as Mount Rushmore, Crazy Horse and Custer State Park, or offer unique and novel experiences such as sunset and stargazing tours of the Badlands, or dinosaur and fossil tours, mining history, wineries and art galleries, walking tours and other specialty tours.

geofuntrek.com   *24430 Nellie Lane*   *(605) 923-8386*

Sage Meadow Ranch (1117)

Situated on acres of prairie, pines and rolling hills, the ranch is located near the scenic and historic Red Canyon, where the Deadwood stage and General Custer and his troops once passed through. Beginner, intermediate and advanced options.

sagemeadowranchllc.com   *26840 Iron Shoe Trail*   *(605) 745-4866*

Bison Express Tours (1118)

This company offers day tours with ample wildlife viewing. The day tour begins in Hot Springs and takes visitors into Wind Cave National Park and Custer State Park to view bison, antelope, deer, prairie dogs and other wild animals. Additional stops on this tour include Mt. Rushmore and Crazy Horse. Admission charges for all locations are included in the tour fee, but lunch is not included. A two-hour evening tour leaves Hot Springs at 7PM and takes in Wind Cave National Park and it's wildlife. Evening is the perfect time to see some of the park's more elusive creatures, and on this tour adults are $20, 6-12 are $10 and children under 5 are free (limit 2).

bisonexpresstours.com   *309 Canton Ave*   *(605) 891-8345*

Battle Mountain Lookout (1119)

A mile northeast of downtown, this is a moderately strenuous 1.4 mile hike (or a short drive in a 4WD vehicle). The hill was the site of a 19th century battle between the Cheyenne and the Sioux for access to the warm springs below. From Highway 385 go two blocks east on Battle Mountain Avenue (beside Evans Plunge), and after the bend take a right on Thompson Avenue/Skyline, which goes to the summit. There are lots of antennae on top.

summitpost.org/battle-mountain/708028   *740 Battle Mountain Ave*   *(605) 745-5445*

Hot Brook Canyon (1120)

The Fall River rises in this canyon, just outside town. It's a nice hike to pick up the stream in one of the parks (Upper Chautauqua is the closest) and follow the winding water up the canyon to the source, which is about a mile and a half away.

Wind Cave National Park (1121)

"Bison, elk, and other wildlife roam the rolling prairie grasslands and forested hillsides of one of America's oldest national parks. Below the remnant island of intact prairie sits Wind Cave, one of the longest and most complex caves in the world. Named for barometric winds at its entrance, this maze of passages is home to box-work, a unique formation rarely found elsewhere." Teddy Roosevelt signed the bill creating this, the eighth National Park, in 1903, and today it encompasses an impressive 33,851 acres. There are no fees to drive through or hike in the park. The Garden of Eden cave tour is $10 for adults (2016), half price for children 6-16 and under 6 are free. Three other tours – Natural Entrance, Fairgrounds and Candlelight are a couple of dollars more, and the Wild Cave tour, which is four hours, runs $30.00 (minimum age is 17 and reservations are required). To get some idea of the treat waiting for visitors, go to the website, click on 'Learn About The Park', and then scroll down to 'Photos and Multimedia', and then 'Photos'. Wind Cave is a must-do on a Black Hills vacation.
nps.gov/wica/index.htm   *26611 US Highway 385*   *(605) 745-4600*

Where To Eat – Hot Springs

American Legion Club Post 71 (1141)   1045 Jennings Ave   (605) 745-3213
Check out the Friday night fish fry!

China Buffet (1143)   333 N. River St   (605) 745-4126
The lunch buffet gets good reviews.

Chops & Hops (1144)   27631 Why 79   (605) 745-4677
Steakhouse classics and some surprises like fried deviled eggs…

Daily Bread Bakery & Café (1145)   431 N. River St   (605) 745-7687
Breakfast and lunch with bakery items.

Dairy Queen (1146)   901 Jensen Hwy   (605) 745-5777
Chain. Brazier.

Dale's Family Restaurant (1147)   745 Battle Mountain Ave   (605) 745-3028
Family fare.

Dew Drop Inn (1148)   1204 Sherman St   (605) 745-7500
Good burgers and shakes.

Gus' Best Ice Cream (1149)   345 N River St   (605) 745-6506
Strong reviews. Malts, shaved ice etc.

Hot Springs Coffee Kiosk (1150)   648 Jennings Ave   (605) 745-3912
5 out of 5 on Yelp. The coffee must be good.

Hot Springs Vault (1151)   329 N River St   (605) 745-3342
Coffee house, bar and grill. Breakfast, lunch and dinner.

JP's Family Dining (1152)   627 N River St   (605) 745-7877
Used to be Bumpers Grub & Pub.

Mornin' Sunshine Coffee Shop (1153)   509 North River Street   (605) 745-5550
Pretty store, good coffee. Try the homemade pastries and monkey bread.

Pizza Hut (1154)   723 Jensen Hwy   (605) 745-5443
Chain.

Smokin' T/D BBQ (1155)   239 North River Street   (605) 745-5070
Outdoor seating. Reasonable prices for families.

Subway (1156)   733 Jensen Hwy   (605) 745-6611
Chain.

Taco John's (1157)   1145 Jensen Hwy   (605) 745-6880
Chain.

Winner's Circle Lanes & Games (1158) 733 Jensen Hwy   (605) 745-5414
Food and bowling.

Woolly's Grill & Cellar (1159)   1648 Hwy 18 Bypass   (605) 745-6414
A wide gamut from chicken tortilla soup to walleye and jalapeño burgers. Brewery.

Where To Stay – Hot Springs

Hotels/Motels

Americas Best Value Inn (1180)	602 N West River St	(605) 745-4292
Angostura Lodge (1181)	13297 North Angostura Rd	(605) 343-0234
Baymont Inn & Suites (1182)	737 S 6th St	(605) 745-7378
Braun Historic Hotel (1184)	902 N River St	(605) 745-3187
Dollar Inn (1185)	402 Battle Mountain Ave	(605) 745-3182
FlatIron Historic Inn (1186)	745 N River St	(605) 745-5301
Hide-A-Way Cabins (1187)	422 S Chicago St	(605) 745-5683
Hills Inn (1188)	640 S 6th St	(605) 745-3130
Historic Log Cabin Motel (1189)	1246 Sherman St	(605) 745-5166
Motel 6 (1190)	541 Indianapolis Ave	(605) 745-6666
Red Rock River Resort & Spa (1191)	603 North River St	(605) 745-4400
Riverside Suites (1192)	646 S 5th St	(605) 745-4295
Skyline Motel (1193)	1145 Sherman St	(605) 745-6980
Smith Fargo Suites (1194)	321 N River St	(605) 890-0585
Stay USA Hotel & Suites (1195)	1401 Highway 18 Bypass	(605) 745-4411
Super 8 (1196)	800 Mammoth St	(605) 745-3888

Bed & Breakfast

Double D Bed & Breakfast (1205)	26575 Jackpine Rd	(605) 673-4214

Campgrounds

Allen Ranch (1215)	13065 Fall River Rd	(605) 745-1890
KOA (1216)	27585 SD Hwy 79	(605) 745-6449
Angostura State Park		
Four Campgrounds (1218)	13157 N Angostura Rd	(605) 745-6996
Cold Brook Lake Campground (1219)	27279 Larive Lake Rd	(605) 745-5476
Kemo Sabay Campground (1220)	27288 Wind Cave Rd	(605) 745-4397
Larive Lake Resort (1221)	1802 Evans Street	(605) 745-3993
Elk Mountain/Wind Cave (1222)	26611 US Hwy 385	(605) 745-4600
Cottonwood Springs (1223)	County Rd 17	(605) 745-5476

Where To Shop – Hot Springs

Black Hills Books & Treasures (1230)
- *112 S. Chicago*
- *(605) 745-5545*
- *blackhills-books.com*

Wanda's Finds (1231)
12,000 square feet of Montana Silversmith, Depression glass (mostly pink), collectibles and antiques (closed Sunday and Monday).
- *27237 Wind Cave Rd*
- *(605) 745-4040*
- *wandasfinds.com*

Heartsong Quilts (1232)
- *345 N River St*
- *(605) 745-5330*
- *h eartsongquilts.com*

Earth Goods Natural Foods (1233)
- *738 Jennings Ave*
- *(605) 745-7715*
- *earthgoodsnaturalfoods.com*

Fall River Fibers (1234)
- *207 S. Chicago St*
- *(605) 745-5173*
- *fallriverfibers.com*

Lucy and the Green Wolf Earth Friendly Goods (1235)
- *740 Jennings Ave*
- *(605) 745-3415*
- *facebook.com/lucyandthegreenwolf/info/?tab=overview*

Rustic Country & Candy Store (1236)
- *309 S. Chicago St*
- *(605) 517-0869*
- *rusticcountrycandystore.net*

Designs by Delise (1237)
- *401 N River St*
- *(605) 890-1898*
- *facebook.com/designsbydelise*

Keystone
ZIP: 57751

Things to See and Do – Keystone

Nope, the Keystone Cops didn't originate here. But the town does have a lot of history: it was named after the Keystone mine, which was opened in 1891. Built on the ghosts of an older settlement named Harney, Keystone swelled and shrank in response to gold finds for half a century. It settled into relative stability with the arrival of Gutzon Borglum, the man who sculpted the Presidents. In the summer of 1927, when President Coolidge set up his summer White House at Custer State Park, Borglum prevailed upon him to dedicate the work at Mount Rushmore. That led to publicity and fundraising, and modern Keystone found its feet. Unlike some tourist destinations, Keystone has kept its small town identity: the population is still only about 325 and the reception for visitors is warm and welcoming. Among the town's attractions are the Black Hills Central Railroad (the 1880 Train), the Big Thunder Gold Mine, the Rushmore Borglum Story (museum), and a wax museum featuring the Presidents of the United States. Laura Ingalls Wilder's sister Carrie arrived here in 1911 to run the local newspaper, and stayed here until her passing in 1946: check out her story at the free Keystone Historical Museum...

Mount Rushmore National Memorial (1250)
Doane Robinson was born in Sparta, Wisconsin in 1856, and eventually became the South Dakota state historian. He was very interested in attracting tourists to the Black Hills, and his initial plan was to carve famous figures on the Needles – a concept that was strongly opposed by Lakota interests and local conservationists. His choice for a sculptor was Gutzon Borglum, and when the initial project fell through, Borglum suggested carving Presidents on Mount Rushmore.

The purpose, he said, was to "communicate the founding, expansion, preservation, and unification of the United States with colossal statues of Washington, Jefferson, Lincoln, and Theodore Roosevelt." Almost three million people visit the site each year, and it has become a national symbol over the decades. If you're within a day's drive, it is absolutely worth taking the time. There is no entrance fee, but there is a charge to park a car ($11), and that ticket is good for as many visits as you like in one calendar year. Pets on a leash (no longer than six feet – the leash, not the pet!) are permitted only in the parking garages, and in the pet exercise areas adjacent to them. Service dogs are permitted to accompany visitors with disabilities in all areas. There are ample food choices and gift shops on site. Wander down past the front of the auditorium or take the trail along the base of the mountain and you may see some beautiful, snow white mountain goats wandering around in the trees. There are chipmunks, yellow bellied marmots, tree frogs, red squirrels and mule deer along the trails, too. If you have kids in your party, visit the website and download the Student Guide before you visit (nps.gov/moru/learn/kidsyouth/upload/MORU-Student-Guide-2014.pdf). It's a comprehensive and fun guide with a historic timeline, pictures of animals and so on, that can be viewed on a tablet or even a phone in the car on the drive there. Be aware that, around the 4th of July and during the Sturgis motorcycle rally, there will be some delays. Hours are 8 to 5 from October through May, 8 to 10 from June through mid-August, and 8 to 9 from mid-August through September.

nps.gov/moru   *13000 Highway 244*   *(605) 574-2523*

Big Thunder Gold Mine (1251)

The mine was opened in 1892 and skillfully dynamited so that, more than a century later, it is still one of the safest shafts in the hills – so safe, in fact, that it was designated as the town's fallout shelter. The mine extends 680 feet into the mountain, and 240 feet underground. There's a restaurant (on the menu are elk, buffalo, duck, pheasant and... rattlesnake!), a gift shop, wine tasting, gold panning, tours (adults $9.95 and kids 5-12 $6.95 in 2016), and a mining museum with a real stamp mill on display.

bigthundermine.com   *604 Blair Street*   *(605) 666-4847*

Black Hills Central Railroad – Keystone (1252)

The other end of the hill City 1880 Train ride, this is a two-hour, twenty-mile round trip through the Black hills National Forest. One-way and return tickets are available: booking is available on site or online, and there's a Depot Gift Shop.

1880train.com   *103 Winter Street*   *(605) 574-2222*

Rushmore Borglum Story (1253)

"Explore the life and times of Gutzon Borglum, creator of Mount Rushmore! An exciting, entertaining and educational experience for the entire family. Watch the blasting and carving in our exclusive film. Family rates. Must see to enhance your Mount Rushmore visit. Summer months only. Great gift/book shop.

rushmoreborglum.com   *342 Winter Street*   *(605) 666-4448*

Keystone Fun Zone (1254)

The Mirror Maze is an old-fashioned fun hall of mirrors; the 3D Dragon Blaster is a black light, high energy air cannon game with foam balls for 2-12 players at a time; and the Free Fall is a rush of adrenaline when you step off the platform and land safely, 40 feet below!

keystonefunzone.com   *221 Swanzey St*   *(605) 666-4200*

Harney Peak (1255)

This 7,242 foot summit is the highest point between the Rockies and the Alps. There's a fire tower on top that provides exquisite views of the southern Hills. Access is on a strenuous, three-and-a-half mile hike from Custer State Park. This is the Black Elk Wilderness area and there are restrictions on use. There's no road to the summit. Black Elk (1863-1950) was a Lakota medicine man and a cousin of Crazy horse. His story is told in *Black Elk Speaks* by John G. Neihardt (William Morrow & Co., 1932, later republished by the Nebraska University Press). He fought at Little Big Horn as a young teenager, and survived the Wounded Knee Massacre.

The peak is named for Bvt. Major General William S. Harney (1800-1889), a U.S. Cavalry officer. In June 1834 while still a major, Harney was charged with the murder of a female slave by whipping her to death over some keys, and he had to flee a mob. He was eventually acquitted in a state where no white man would have been found guilty. In the mid-1850s he led attacks against the Sioux, the last of which was the Battle of Ash Hollow where his 600 troops attacked 250 men, women and children and killed 86 of them, many of whom had taken refuge in caves along the Platte River under a flag of truce. Harney later professed remorse for this. He served in the Union Army during the Civil War but proved to be an incompetent administrator, mishandling riots in St. Louis. He then spent a couple of years as an administrator in Washington, before retiring in 1863. In 2015, *USA Today* ran a piece on the naming controversy surrounding Harney Peak, which the paper said was "named for a particularly brutal Army general". Despite the history, and heartfelt appeals by Lakota tribal members, the South Dakota Board on Geographic Names voted 4-1 to retain the name.

Holy Smoke Trail Rides (1256)

The Holy Smoke Resort is open mid-May through September, and the one-hour trail rides are mostly on US Forest Service trails.

Holysmokeresort.com   *24105 Hwy 16A*   *(605) 666-4444*

Holy Terror Mini Golf (1257)

Nestled on the side of a pine-covered slope, the course was named after the last active gold mine in Keystone. The 18 holes run up and down the hillside, unified by a gold mining motif and rushing water that flows through sluices, over a waterwheel and into a millpond. There are three kinds of artificial turf that simulate fairways, sand traps and rough. The course is fully lighted and open from 8AM to 9PM from May 15th through October 31st (weather permitting). Adults $9, 6-12 $7, under 6 free (2016).

holyterrorminigolf.com   *609 Hwy 16A*   *(605) 666-5170*

Keystone Historical Museum & Walking Tour (1258)

Located in a beautiful old 1900 schoolhouse, the museum has a small playground and gazebo outside – an ideal spot for a picnic lunch. Inside, one learns about the discovery of gold in Battle Creek, the Black Hills tin boom, Gutzon Borglum and Mount Rushmore, Peter Norbeck and the Iron Mountain Road, C.C. Gideon and the Pigtail Bridges, Carrie Ingalls and The Little House on the Prairie, Wild Horse Harry Hardin, Sugar Babe and a lot of other local history. For a town with fewer than 300 inhabitants, this is an impressive resource and well worth a visit. Original log schoolhouse on site. The Old Town Walking Tour is self-guided. Follow the numbered signs and read about the history of one of the fastest growing boom towns in the Hills. There are 19 stations on the walking tour, each with a sign describing the location. It's a fun family activity.

keystonehistory.com/index.php/walking-tour   *410 3rd Street*   *(605) 666-4494*

National Presidential Wax Museum (1259)

This unique museum features realistic, life-sized wax figures of every President of the United States. Experience the feeling of being with President Roosevelt at Yalta, Dolly Madison at a White House reception, or Richard Nixon aboard the U.S.S. Hornet as he welcomes returning astronauts from their moon flight. There are lifelike, life-size figures of all the Presidents in authentic period costumes, and accurately detailed surroundings. There's a state-of-the-art narration system, and the historical artifacts include everything from Bill Clinton's red, white and blue saxophone to the Florida 2000 presidential election's controversial ballot boxes. The gift shop has a special selection of Black Hills Gold, plus fine porcelains and pewter, sculptures, presidential china and other exhibits.

presidentialwaxmuseum.com   *609 Hwy 16A*   *(605) 666-4455*

Rushmore Tramway Adventures (1260)

The original attraction here – still just as good in an updated version fifty years later – is a chairlift (like those in ski resorts) that takes you up a mountain just west of the Rushmore carvings. The views are absolutely spectacular, and at the top of the hill there is a whole array of pretty cool things to do, such as swooshing down an Alpine slide (you control the speed – it's like a bobsled ride without the snow), or flying along a zip-line. There's an Aerial Park that offers rope courses for climbers of all skill-levels, and plenty of hiking trails and gardens for those who prefer to keep their feet firmly planted on the ground. You can have lunch at the Mountain-Top Grille too, amid viewing decks, waterfalls and beautiful flower gardens. The chairlift up/Alpine slide down combo is $12. A round-trip on the chairlift up and down runs $9. The Aerial adventure (climb through the huge Ponderosa pines in harness, on ropes, and travel between more than 80 treetop platforms) is $39. The zip-line is $15 and so is the new free-fall jump tower that invites you to take a 60-foot high bungee-jump step into space. Prices quoted for 2016. This is one of the best places to take a carload of bickering kids, and let them gorge on adrenaline while you feast on the outdoor deck at the Grille, sip a cool beer, or just enjoy an ice-cream and a unique view of Mount Rushmore.

rushmoretramwayadventures.com   *203 Cemetery Rd*   *(605) 666-4478*

Rush Mountain Adventure Park & Rushmore Cave (1261)

There are four attractions in one location here. There's the Rushmore Mountain Coaster, a three-and-a-half-thousand foot long eight minute roller coaster track with little individual cars that zoom through the forest (you can control the speed). The Soaring Eagle Zip-line feels like flying as you accelerate down 630 feet of altitude on a formed seat (with seatbelts!) suspended beneath a taut cable. Check out the video on the website. You can shoot bandits at the Gunslinger 7-D Interactive Ride, a multi-sensory experience where you'll feel the seat move and the wind in your hair as you shoot a laser gun at targets. Or experience the stalactite-filled caverns on a tour of the cave.

rushmorecave.com *13622 Hwy 40* *(605) 255-4384*

Rushmore Helicopters, Inc. (1262)

This company has six standard tour packages ($49 to $229 per person, 2016).

coptertours.com *103 Hwy 16A* *(605) 666-5580*

Horse Thief Lake (1263)

Horse Thief Lake Campground has 36 primitive tent and RV camping sites on a recreational lake just 2 miles from Mount Rushmore. It sees heavy usage, and to make reservations, call (877) 444-6777. To find the lake, go northwest on Hwy 244 from the Rushmore monument and look for Horse Thief Lake Road on your left. The GPS coordinates are 43.895104 -103.484232

fs.usda.gov *Horse Thief Lake Rd* *(605) 673-4853*

Wrinkled Rock (1264)

A 'climbing area' in the Black Hills National Forest, its trailhead is on Hwy 244 and it borders the National Memorial. This facility was designed to provide parking, bivy sites and bathroom facilities for rock climbers. Note than climbing the Mount Rushmore sculpture is prohibited, but there are many other climbing opportunities in the vicinity. There's no potable water. Large vehicles can't access the area. There's no fee. A climbing brochure is available from the Lincoln Borglum Museum, or at the Information Center in the Memorial: call (605) 574-2523. The number below is the Forest Service, who can tell you more about this specific climbing area.

fs.usda.gov *Hwy 244* *(605) 673-9200*

Where To Eat – Keystone

Barlee's (1286)
American, Mexican
253 Swanzey St   *(866) 883-6730*

BrGr 61 (1287)
American, family, burgers
221 Swanzey St   *(605) 666-5500*

Big Thunder Gold Mine (1288)
bigthundermine.com
South Dakota traditional
604 Blair St   *(605) 666-4847*

Big Time Pizza (1289)
rosyinn.com
Pizza, subs, beer & wine
206 Cemetery Rd   *(605) 666-4443*

Carver's Café (1265)
mtrushmorenationalmemorial.com
The restaurant at the Memorial
13000 Hwy 244   *(605) 574-2515*

Cruizzers (1266)
facebook.com/cruizzers
Pizza, calzones, subs, pasta
110B Winter St   *(605) 666-4313*

Dairy Queen (1267)
dairyqueen.com
Brazier
804 Hwy 16A   *(605) 666-4441*

Eno's Pizza (1268)
enospizza.com
Large Italian menu, with bar
804 Hwy 16A   *(605) 666-4771*

Grapes & Grinds (1269)
Grapesgrinds.com
Seasonal. Wine, coffee, dessert, snacks
609 Hwy 16A   *(605) 666-5142*

Grizzly Creek (1270)
grizzlycreekrestaurant.com
American, bar.
624 Hwy 16A   *(605) 666-4633*

Holy Terror Coffee Co. (1272)
Espresso, chocolate, desserts
804 Hwy 16 A   *(605) 999-2055*

Jane's Boardwalk Pizza (1273)
facebook
Pizza, ice cream, sandwiches, salads
160 Winter St   *(605) 666-4713*

Keystone House/Mijo's (1274)
Check reviews on Yelp and Tripadvisor
217 Winter St   *(605) 666-4775*

Mount Rushmore All American (1275)
AKA 'Pie For The People'
Pizzeria (branches in CA, WA and SD)
212 Winter St   *(605) 666-5218*

Peggy's Place (1277)

Home cooking café
434 Hwy 16A   *(605) 666-4445*

Powder House Lodge (1278)
powderhouselodge.com/restaurant

Steak, buffalo, wine & bar
24125 Hwy 16A   *(605) 666-5214/4646*

Railhead Family Restaurant (1279)

Family style
102 Winter St   *(605) 666-5210*

Red Garter Saloon (1280)
redgartersaloon.com

Bar, music, theater
124 Winter St   *(605) 666-4274*

Ruby House (1281)
Rubyhousekeystone.com

Steaks, seafood, ribs, elegant.
124 Winter St   *(605) 666-4404*

Subway (1282)
subway.com

Sandwiches. Closed in winter.
804 Hwy 16A   *(605) 666-5201*

Teddy's Deli (1283)
teddysdeli.com

Sandwiches, soup and salads
236 Winter St   *(605) 666-4500*

Turtle Town (1284)
turtletown.com

Chocolate and fudge
117 Winter St   *(605) 666-4675*

Where To Stay – Keystone

American Pines Cabins (1300)
americanpines.com   1315 Old Hill City Rd   (605) 666-5475

Backroads Inn & Cabins (1301)
cabinsoftheblackhills.com   901 Echo Valley Rd   (605) 342-2246

Battle Creek Lodge (1302)
battlecreeklodge.us   404 Reed St   (605) 666-4800

Buffalo Rock Lodge (1303)
buffalorock.net   24524 Playhouse Road   (605) 666-4562

Brookside Motel (1304)
brooksidekeystonesd.com   603 Reed St   (605) 666-4496

Dee'zz Inn (1305)
cabinsatrushmore.com   436 Old Hill City Rd   (605) 666-4854

Econo Lodge Near Mt. Rushmore Memorial (1306)
choicehotels.com   908 Madill St   (605) 666-4417

Elk Ridge Bed & Breakfast (1307)
erbnb.com   12741 Matthew Ct   (605) 574-2320

Holiday Inn Express & Suites (1308)
ihg.com   321 Swanzey St   (605) 666-4925

Holy Smoke Resort (1309)
holysmokeresort.com   24105 Hwy 16A   (605) 666-4616

K Bar S Lodge Hotel (1310)
kbarslodge.com   434 Old Hill City Rd   (605) 666-4545

Kemp's Kamp (1311)
kempskamp.com   1022 Old Hill City Rd   (605) 666-4654

Keystone Boardwalk Inn & Suites (1312)
keystoneboardwalk.com   250 Winter St   (605) 666-4990

Presidents View Resort (1313)
rushmorepresidentsviewresort.com   106 Hwy 16A   (605) 666-4212

Mt. Rushmore's White House Resort (1314)
rushmorewhitehouseresort.com   *115 Swanzey St*   *(605) 666-4917*

Powder House Lodge Cabins & Motel (1315)
powderhouselodge.com   *24125 Hwy 16A*   *(605) 666-4646*

Roosevelt Inn Hotel & Restaurant (1316)
rosyinn.com   *206 Cemetery Rd*   *(605) 666-4599*

Rushmore Express Inn & Family Suites (1317)
rushmoreexpress.com   *320 Cemetery Rd*   *(605) 666-4483*

Rushmore View Inn (1318)
No website. Older motel.   *610 Hwy 16A*   *(605) 666-4466*

Rustic Ridge Guest Cabins (1319)
rusticridgeguestcabins.com   *12980 S Hwy 16*   *(605) 666-4848*

Super 8 (1320)
super8.com   *702 Hwy 16A*   *(605) 666-6666*

Spokane Cr. Cabins & Camping (1321)
spokanecreekresort.com   *24631 Iron Mtn Rd*   *(605) 666-4609*

The Lodge at Mount Rushmore   **(1322)**
lodgeatmountrushmore.net   *24075 Hwy 16A*   *(605) 666-4472*

Travelodge Motel (1323)
travelodge.com   *522 Hwy 16A*   *(605) 666-4638*

Triple R Ranch Cabins (1324)
rrrranch.com   *13201 Greyhound Gulch Rd*   *(605) 666-4605*

Washington Inn (1325)
rushmorewashingtoninn.com   *231 Winter St*   *(605) 666-5070*

Where To Shop – Keystone

Big Thunder Gold Mine Co. Store (1340)	308 1st St	(605) 666-4847
Black Hills Gifts & Gold (1341)	166 Winter St	(605) 666-4916
Black Hills Glass Blowers (1342)	909 Old Hill City Rd	(605) 666-4542
Black Hills Souvenirs & Gifts (1343)	207 Winter St	(605) 666-4816
Broken Arrow Trading Company (1344)	220 Winter St	(605) 666-5275
Dahl's Chainsaw Art (1345)	342 Winter St	(605) 834-1149
Earth Treasures Rock Shop (1346)	409 1st St	(605) 666-5222
Emporium (1347)	160 Winter St	(605) 666-4836
Xanterra Gift Shop, Mt Rushmore (1348)	13000 Hwy 244	(605) 574-2515
Grizzly Creek Gifts (1349)	221 Swanzey St	(605) 666-4242
Halley's 1880 Store (1350)	501 1st St	(605) 666-4555
Holy Terror Antique Mall (1351)	221 Swanzey St	(605) 666-5005
Iron Creek Leather & Gifts (1352)	126 Winter St	(605) 666-4732
Iron Mountain Road Gift Shop (1353)	804 Hwy 16A	(605) 666-4609
Key Photo (1354)	232 Winter St	(605) 666-4311
Keystone Mercantile - Souvenirs (1355)	151 Winter St	(605) 666-4946
Mountain Eagle Outpost (1357)	211 Winter St	(605) 666-5965
Rattlesnake Jake's (1358)	804 Highway 16A	(605) 666-4610
Rushmore Mountain Taffy Shop (1359)	203 Winter St	(605) 666-4430
The Indians - Native Art and Crafts (1360)	141 Winter St	(605) 666-4864
The Rock Shed (1361)	515 First St	(605) 666-4813

Zone 3: Wyoming's Black Hills

There are a number of great motorcycle and driving roads here, especially in the hills around Hulett, Sundance and Aladdin. And beyond Devils Tower (above, photo by author), there's a lot to see in towns such as Moorcroft, Newcastle and Sundance – plus lakes to visit, hikes to take and other outdoor and historical gems to explore. Distances between towns can be substantial, but on the Interstate the speed limits are high (75 or 80 MPH), and the back roads are often stunningly beautiful. Summer storms often deliver hailstones, but tornadoes are very rare and we never see those formidable walls of green sky that states east of us such as Minnesota and Wisconsin experience. There's a really nice welcome center on the Interstate at Exit 199, just a few minutes west of the South Dakota-Wyoming line: it offers info, maps, picnic tables and bathrooms, and the staff have a great reputation for being helpful and informative.

Things to See and Do – Wyoming's Black Hills

Devils Tower National Monument (1380)

The tower itself is an igneous monolith that stretches some 1,200 feet (roughly four football fields) above the plains. In 1906, President Theodore Roosevelt made it America's very first national monument. The favored explanation for its creation is that Devils Tower was formed as a 'stock', which is a column of molten magma, and then cooled to become the rock type phonolite porphyry. It began, geologists believe, under layers of sedimentary sandstone beneath an inland sea. As the waters receded, the softer sediment was eroded and eventually revealed the dense, hard column we see today. As the magma cooled, it became crystalline, leaving the long vertical columns that give it such a distinct personality. A sacred site to more than twenty Northern Plains tribes, it is known to the Cheyenne, Lakota and Crow as Bear Lodge (as is the mountain range surrounding it). The Arapaho call it the Bear's Tipi, and the Kiowa know it as Tree Rock. Five great Sioux leaders – Sitting Bull, Crazy Horse, Red Cloud, Gall, and Spotted Tail – once came here together to worship and fast. And the Lakota traditionally held a Sun Dance beneath Matȟó Thípila around the summer solstice each June. It was here on the north face of the tower that they kept their most sacred object, the White Buffalo Calf pipe. And the stream that flows by its base, known today as the Belle Fourche, has long been known in Native culture as the Sun Dance River. There are several Lakota and other cultural legends regarding the formation of Bear Lodge, which visitors can discover during a visit to the information center and gift shop. There are also large souvenir shops just outside the gates, one of which is located in a KOA campground.

The **Devils Tower Natural History Association** operates the nonprofit bookstore inside the park. This is a group of workers that is dedicated to "supporting the historical, educational and interpretive activities of the National Park Service". They have done – and still do – a great deal to augment your experience here. To become part of the effort, or to support their work with a donation, visit DTNHA online at *devilstowernha.org*.

At an elevation of 5,112 feet, the summit of Devils Tower dominates the landscape and defines Wyoming's Black Hills for visitors. The park that houses the Monument encompasses 1,347 acres and hosts about 400,000 people visitors a year. The tower has been widely featured in popular culture, most notably as a location in the 1977 movie *Close Encounters of the Third Kind*.

In 2016, a 7-day non-commercial vehicle pass runs $10, and a motorcycle pass (one rider) is $5. A 7-day individual permit is also $5 (on foot or bicycle), unless you are 15 or younger: then it's free. There is some camping at the Monument (fifty sites at $12 a day). A hike around the base can be a little stressful for people with physical challenges, especially in hot weather, but most visitors have no problem and the experience is memorable.

Getting to the Tower takes about thirty minutes from Sundance. Take Exit 185 from I-90 just west of town, and follow Hwy 14 to Carlisle Junction (look for the Crook County Saloon on your right). Take a right on Hwy 24 to the Tower. And if you start in Belle Fourche, take Hwy 34 at the south end of town by the golf course and go to Aladdin, then keep going straight on Hwy 24 through Hulett to the Tower.

- *192 Highway 110, Devils Tower, WY 82714*
- *(307) 467-5283*
- *nps.gov/deto*

Aladdin General Store (1381)

The state tourism departments says that this is "the best preserved of Wyoming's five remaining 19th-century mercantile stores, and it's been amassing inventory since 1896". For antique buffs, pickers and history enthusiasts, this is a step back in time. There's nothing modern here: it has the feel of a rural community meeting place, which is exactly what it has been for more than a century. It's musty, dusty and, well, charming. The inventory covers everything from groceries to liquor, souvenirs, antiques, new gift items, clothing, jewelry... even a functioning Post Office. Don't miss the upstairs. The store also sells snacks and cold drinks.

facebook   *4001 Hwy 24, Aladdin WY 82710*   *(307) 896-2226*

Bearlodge Ranger District (1382)

This outdoor recreation jewel includes the north half of the Black Hills on the Wyoming side, and encompasses about 170,000 acres. According to the Sundance

Chamber of Commerce, it "boasts miles and miles of un-crowded trails with breathtaking views for the hiker, mountain biker or horseback rider." Permits are required for motorized vehicles, hunting and fishing. There are Forest Service campgrounds near Sundance at Cook Lake, Reuter, and the Sundance Trailhead. According to trails.com, "the Sundance Trails can be accessed 4 miles north of Sundance from Forest Road 838. Another access point is located 3.5 miles north of Sundance from the Government Valley Road. The loop starts out on good double track road for 1.4 miles and then drops onto a single track constructed specifically for mountain biking. After nearly 4.5 miles, it joins an old double track for approximately 2 miles. The final 1.2 miles are on good double track road." To visit the Forest Service's web page on Bearlodge Ranger District, go to the homepage at fs.usda.gov/blackhills and click on 'Contact Us" (lower left), and then in that same box click on 'Districts". Then click on Bearlodge Ranger District in the main page, at right.

101 S. 21st Street, Sundance, WY 82729   (307) 283-1361   Hours are 8-4:30, M-F
Download off-road guidelines at wyotrails.state.wy.us/pdf/HuntingandATV1.pdf

Vore Buffalo Jump (1383)

This is one of the most important archaeological sites of the late-prehistoric plains Indians. Discovered during the construction of Highway I-90 in the early 1970s, the site is a natural sinkhole that was used as a bison trap from about 1500 to 1800 A.D. Buffalo were driven over the edge as a method for the tribes to procure large quantities of meat and hides needed to survive harsh prairie winters. It was placed on the National Register of Historic Places in 1973.

vorebuffalojump.org   I-90 frontage road between Exits 199 and 205   (307) 266-9530

Inyan Kara Mountain (1384)

This 6,368 foot peak can only be reached by crossing private property with permission. To find out how to gain that, call the Ranger Station (307-283-1361). Inyan Kara (Gatherer of Rocks) has high significance for Lakota culture, and is on the National Register for Historic Places. General Custer stopped here in 1874, the year his party discovered gold in the Black Hills. It's on your right, halfway between Sundance and Four Corners, just west of Hwy 585.

Crook County Museum and the 1875 Art Gallery (1385)

Located in historic downtown Sundance, visitors can have a seat at the Sundance Kid's trial (this was the only place he ever did time – 18 months for hoss thievin'). There is an impressive gun collection, a well-stocked bookstore, and fabulous dioramas featuring Devils Tower, the Custer Expedition, the Vore Buffalo Jump, and America's first experimental nuclear power plant. The site also houses the 1875 Art gallery, which focuses on local art, pottery and custom jewelry. Admission to both is free.

crookcountymuseum.com   309 Cleveland, Sundance WY 82729   (307) 283-3666

The Golf Club at Devils Tower (1386)

"Known for its scenic beauty, awesome changes in elevations, lush fairways, and smooth putting greens, the golf course presents a challenge of skill and strategy.

Recognized as one of America's Top Facilities by the National Golf Foundation and in 2007, honored as Golf Digest's 'Best New Courses', guests find themselves met with all the challenges of a world class course." Full service restaurant, accommodations.
devilstowergolf.com   *75 Tower View Dr., Hulett, WY 82720*   *(307) 467-5773*

Keyhole State Park (1387)

Known for its birds, both migratory and native (about 225 species), the park centers on a 14,720 acre reservoir with a marina and a public boat launch. There are walleye, Northern pike, smallmouth bass and even catfish in the lake. The park also has nine campgrounds with 170+ sites, and the map shows a motel which is probably run by the marina (307-756-9529) although there doesn't seem to be a website for it. The easiest way to get there is to go north at Exit 165 on I-90. There's a playground, some camping cabins, a store and even a bar that serves burgers. Great fishing and swimming.
wyoparks.state.wy.us   *22 Marina Road, Moorcroft WY 82721*   *(307) 756-3591*

Hulett Museum and Art Gallery (1388)

Featuring both prehistoric and historic artifacts, the museum and art gallery is home to "highly regarded local talent, well-known Western artists, archeological finds, paleontology pieces and Native American culture". This is a vibrant, eclectic collection and a wonderful window on the disparate elements that make Wyoming what it is. Admission is free and donations are accepted. A surprising gem in a small town (pop 400), this venue is recommended by the Wyoming Tourism Board.
hulettmuseum.org   *115 Hwy 24, Hulett WY 82720*   *(307) 467-5292*

The West Texas Trail Museum (1389)

The heart and soul of this cattle trail community, the museum tells the stories of ranchers, settlers, trains and teepees. Originally a railway depot, the town took off in the early 1890s with the establishment of a saloon on what was the Texas cattle trail. Ranching still drives the culture, but oil, gas and coal have made a huge impact in recent decades. Teddy Roosevelt stopped here on a whistle stop tour, and tourists have been dropping by for over a century on their way to Yellowstone and the Black Hills.
westtexastrailmuseum.com   *100 E Weston St, Moorcroft WY 82721*   *(307) 756-9300*

The Anna Miller Museum (1390)

Relive the old west in this museum that was built in the 1930s as a WPA project for the 115th Cavalry of the Wyoming National Guard. The hand-hewn sandstone blocks were quarried in nearby Salt Creek. This building originally had a tack room, stables and the sergeant's quarters, which all now house exhibits. The museum was named after Anna Cecelia McMoran Miller, the widow of Sheriff Billy Miller who was killed in the last Indian battle in this area. She was Newcastle's first librarian, a pioneer schoolteacher and school superintendent. The complex also houses a rural one-room schoolhouse and a homesteader's house plus the 1875 Jenney Stockade cabin, 'the oldest existing building of the Black Hills gold rush', which was also a stage station along the Cheyenne to Deadwood trail.
westoncountywyo-museum.org   *401 Delaware, Newcastle WY 82701*   *(307) 746-4188*

The Red Onion Museum (1391)

Walter "Jarbo" Poulson owned and operated the Red Onion Saloon in Upton for many years, and during prohibition he moved it to the barn on his property, which he named the Red Onion Ranch. The museum exhibits photos of the saloon and Jarbo, plus many other artifacts from the Upton area including items associated with Native Americans, early homesteaders, local military personnel – and prints of the renowned artist Dave Paulley. A fixture in Western art, Paulley works in nearby Osage and his Western Wings Gallery can be visited online at theartofdavepaulley.com.

westoncountywyo-museum.org   *729 Birch St, Upton WY 82730*   *(307) 468-2672*

Newcastle Country Club (1392)

The 9-hole course runs 3,167 from the longest tees and is par 36. The course rating is 35.6 and it has a slope rating of 113. It opened in 1966.

facebook   *2302 W Main St, Newcastle, WY 82701*   *(307) 746-2639*

Cedar Pines Golf Course (1393)

This 9-hole course is 26 miles south of Upton on Hwy 116. The clubhouse has a full bar and restaurant, and the course runs 2,995 yards from the longest tees. It's a par 36. There's a driving range and putting area. Fees are minimal: call for tee times.

facebook.com/cedarpines   *2579 Hwy 116, Upton WY 82730*   *(307)   468-2847*

Upton Old Town (1394)

On the northwest corner of the town on Hwy 16, Old Town is a collection of log cabins and outbuildings, a sod house, sheep wagons and farm wagons that give one a very realistic feel for what life was like here more than a century ago. Also included are a blacksmith's shop, the old fire hall, an ice house... and even a brothel.

ghosttowns.com/states/wy/oldupton.html   *Highway 16, Upton, WY 82730*

Rogues Gallery Old West Antiques (1395)

This gallery, art studio and museum features "the Black Hills largest selection of 19th century Plains Indian Beadwork and Old West collectables. The museum displays and sells hundreds of items like rare American Indian weapons, old cowboy spurs, guns and relics from the battle of Little Big Horn". Artwork by Bob Coronato includes oil paintings and original Chine Colle (a special printmaking technique) etchings featuring cowboys, ranching and American Indian life.

bobcoronato.com   *155 Main St, Hulett WY 82720*   *(307) 467-5849*

Devils Tower Climbing (1396)

Located at Devils Tower Lodge B&B, this is an expertly staffed, certified and insured guide service and climbing school with a low 1:1 or 1:2 student to instructor ratio.

devilstowerclimbing.com   *34 Hwy 110, Devils Tower, WY 82714*   *(307) 467-5267*

Devils Tower Trading Post (1397)

Hot air balloon rides, Post Office, general store, souvenirs, lunch and dinner.
devilstowertradingpost.com   *57 Hwy 110, Devils Tower, WY 82714*   *307-467-5295*

Devils Tower KOA (1398)

Rated 'the best campground between Chicago and Yellowstone" by the Chicago Tribune, this really is a unique place. It's located almost at the base of the tower, along the banks of the Belle Fourche river. There are two types of cabins – larger ones that sleep six and have a full kitchen, bathe and deck, and one-room cabins that sit right on the river and have fire rings and picnic tables. There is a 40-acre tent site, plus pull-through sites and full hook-ups for RVs too. There's a pool, playground, nightly hayride, huge gift shop, and a game room among other amenities. Plus, they play the movie *Close Encounters of the Third Kind* outdoors every night, as some of it was filmed here. There's a full restaurant, free WiFi, an ATM and propane, and the grocery store sells wine, beer and spirits.
devilstowerkoa.com   *60 Hwy 110, Devils Tower, WY 82714*   *(307) 467-5395*

Coffee Cup Fuel Stop (1399)

This is a full service truck stop with a large convenience store that has a nice gift/souvenir section. It's about halfway between Sundance and Gillette (and we're mentioning it because bikers might not make it on reserve without stopping!)
coffeecupfuelstops.com   *506 E Converse, Moorcroft, WY 82721*   *(307) 756-3493*

Country Cottage Gifts (1400)

This flower and gift shop has gourmet and fruit baskets, cards, candles and chocolates.
countrycottageflowershop.com   *423 E Cleveland, Sundance WY 82729*   *(307) 283-2450*

Devils Tower View (1401)

This family-owned campground, gift shop and affordable restaurant (with buffalo burgers and beer) is located 3 miles from Devils Tower and offers spectacular views of the monument. Day camping and outdoor dining overlook Campstool Canyon: there's breakfast all day plus broasted chicken and locally famous strawberry-rhubarb pie. The gift shop features work by local artisans, and also Wyoming-made products.
devilstowerview.com   *476 Why 24, Devils Tower WY 82714*   *(307) 467-5737*

Hulett Festivals (1402)

- The Hulett Rodeo is the second weekend in June.
- There's a fireworks show at Devils Tower KOA on July 4th.
- The Duck Derby is in July.
- The Ham 'N Jam festival is the Wednesday of the Sturgis rally.
- Ride a Horse, Feed a Cowboy is held in September: locals ride their horses into town, and there's live music, branding, a poker tournament and a rodeo.

hulett-wyoming.com   *219 Why 24, Hulett WY 82720*   *(307) 467-5771*

Stateline Station (1403)

This convenience store and gas station with a Post Office has a nice selection of souvenirs. It's a pretty spot with picnic tables, just over the border in Wyoming, and the last gas for a while.

5930 Hwy 14, Beulah WY 82712   *(307) 643-2185*

Ranch A Education Center (1404)

This is an historic lodge built by Finnish craftsmen in the 1930s that is currently used as a group retreat. There's a meeting area, kitchen and accommodation for 48 and botanical gardens. The drive there south from Beulah is spectacular (gravel, 5 miles).

rancha.com   *(307) 643-3101*

Buffalo Jump Steakhouse (1405)

The original part of the building was a general store dating back to the late 1890s. Today, the chef is a graduate of Le Cordon Bleu College of Culinary Arts, who spent several years working at Delmonico Steakhouse for Emeril Lagasse of the Food Network

buffalojumpsteak.com   *5877 Old Hwy 14, Beulah, WY 82712*   *(307) 643-7173*

Mae Mae's Place (1406)

Reasonably priced gifts, décor, jewelry and souvenirs. There are wonderful items in every nook and cranny! The coffee pot is always on and there's a small table for children to draw while parents shop

maemaesplace@rangeweb.net   *205 East Main St, Sundance WY 82729*   *(307) 283-3655*

Beulah Testicle Festival (1407)

This happens around Memorial Day weekend (June) and it's a community branding celebration in Beulah. There's live Bluegrass music and Rocky Mountain Oysters (look them up…). The contact person is Sully Simon.

facebook.com/Sullys-Outfitting-156080326445   *(307) 283-2634*

Sand Creek Fishing (1408)

This is one of the better spots for brown trout. There are brook and rainbow, too. Visit the site below for details. Turn south at Exit 205 and look for signs indicating public access and Game and Fish ownership.

wgfd.wyo.gov, click on Fishing and Boating, then Places To Fish in Wyoming.

(307) 672-7418

The Mill on Sand Creek (1409)

A historic 3-level vacation home for rent, located near Beulah on the river banks. 2 bedrooms, sleeps 10, catered or cook yourself. Strong positive reviews.

vrbo.com/160537   *(605) 722-4522*

Zone 4: Rapid City & Environs

Rapid City is South Dakota's major hub for tourism and recreation, and about 70,000 people make their homes here. Another 65,000 are close by, including armed service personnel who live on or close to Ellsworth Air Force Base. In 2014, the US Census Bureau estimated the metro area population at 135,193.

The city is a regional center of commerce, healthcare services and manufacturing. Ranching and mining are still very important to the local economy, as is education. The city is home to the nationally renowned South Dakota School of Mines & Technology; the He Sapa campus of the Oglala Lakota College; an SDSU Regional Center; the USD's University Center Rapid City; a National American University campus; and Western Dakota Technical Institute. Archeology is thriving in the Black Hills: the Archaeological Research Center at 217 Kansas City Street is a program of the South Dakota State Historical Society, and it maintains records on more than 23,000 archaeological sites and 12,000 projects. The Center (*history.sd.gov/Archaeology*) has also been a long-term partner with the Journey Museum in Rapid City (*journeymuseum.org*), which hosts archaeological exhibits based on artifacts from its collections.

Originally known as The City of Presidents because of its proximity to Mount Rushmore, that title has now been firmly reinforced with the addition of bronze, life-size statues of every U.S. chief executive – all of them placed outdoors on downtown streets where visitors can cozy up and take photos (above, some of my own family members pose with George Washington). The city was founded by gold rush miners in 1876, and was at first known as Hay Camp. But it was quickly renamed for the fast-flowing creek that runs through the valley. On the 9th of June, 1972, Rapid Creek became a raging torrent and the ensuing flood – South Dakota's worst natural disaster – took the lives of more than 250 people. Since then, major engineering works have been put in place to prevent flooding.

The downtown area is vibrant, welcoming, and full of great shopping, galleries, museums and dining. The city has done a great job preserving its heritage while also developing new facilities such as Rushmore Plaza Civic Center, and Main Street Square. The latter, located in the heart of downtown, is described as "a fun-filled public space that features special events, arts and culture, live concerts, seasonal ice skating and interactive fountains".

There is an excellent website, downtownrapidcity.com, where visitors can go to find out everything that's happening during their stay.

Things To See and Do – in or near Rapid City

Badlands National Park (1425)

While not exactly part of the Black Hills, the Badlands are conveniently placed on the best route into the Hills (I-90). They bear mentioning because many visitors drive past them on their way here, and wonder whether they should stop. The answer is a resounding YES. The bizarre sedimentary formations in the park's 244,000 acres are home to one of the world's largest fossil deposits. Most of the soft rock is more than 28 million years old, but it only started eroding a few hundred thousand years ago. Today, 39 mammal species, 9 reptile, 6 amphibian, 69 butterfly and more than 200 bird species call this fantasyland home. From bugs to bison, prairie dogs to pronghorn, they all contribute to a vibrant ecosystem. This was also the scene of human involvement – everything from Lakota Ghost Dance rituals to US Air Force bombing ranges. It has been hunted by Native Americans for 11,000 years. There are two campgrounds in the park, and a visitor center that hosts a quarter of a million tourists each year. Most of the more spectacular features are accessible via boardwalks and paths. A few of them involve climbing steps. Hikers must carry water: there are no potable sources. In 2016, some of the admission fees are $15/car, $10 motorcycle, $30 annual pass. There are some discounts available. The park is on the south side of I-90 at Wall. There's a loop road between Exit 131, where the Ben Reifel Visitor Center sits near the Northeast gate, and Exit 110 in Wall, about five miles north of the Pinnacles Entrance. Near the latter, one can follow Sage Creek Rim Road to view a prairie dog town. On the way out (or in), stop at the National Grasslands Visitor Center at 708 Main Street in Wall, and see displays of wildlife and plants, grazing management, and a history of the twenty National Grasslands and the Midewin National Tallgrass Prairie. There's even a natural mixed-grass prairie landscape behind the Center.

nps.gov/badl   *25214 Ben Reifel Pl, Interior, SD 57750*   *(605) 433-5361*

Badlands Petrified Gardens (1426)

If you're planning a stop at the Badlands, you might also wish to schedule an hour or two at this attraction about twenty miles east of the park. Petrified wood is essentially timber where the organic structure has slowly been completely replaced by minerals (rock). It still looks like wood, but it has turned to stone. The Gardens also include a large collection of fossils such as ammonites, saber tooth tiger and dinosaurs, plus rock formations from sand crystals to fluorescent rocks. Begun in 1938 near Piedmont, the Gardens moved to their current location in 1956, and are still a family-run concern. Adult admission is $6, and kids 6 through 16 are just $3. There's even a $1-off printable coupon on the website. Children under 6 are free. Open mid-April through mid-October, and high summer hours in June, July and August are from 7 AM to 7 PM. It's right by I-90 Exit 152, on the south frontage road. There are a couple of acres of displays outdoors, and a large building housing the fossil collection.

badlandspetrifiedgardens.net   *23104 Hwy 248, Kadoka SD 57543*   *(605) 837-2448*

Bear Country USA (1427)

Located about halfway between Rapid City and Mount Rushmore on Hwy 16, Bear Country U.S.A. is "a unique drive-thru wildlife park featuring North American wildlife. Encounter bears, wolves, elk, buffalo, and other wildlife on your three mile drive. Enjoy the playful antics of bear cubs and other park offspring in the walk through Babyland. See where the animals roam free!" Built on the Safari park model, this is a 200-acre privately owned park where you drive your own vehicle through several enclosures and encounter black bear, elk, reindeer, deer, cougars, bobcats, rocky mountain goats, bighorn sheep, dall sheep, pronghorn and buffalo.

bearcountryusa.com   *13820 S Hwy 16, Rapid City, SD 57702*   *(605) 343-2290*

Black Hills & Badlands Visitor Center (1428)

As you pull into Rapid City from the east, stop for a few minutes at Exit 61 and visit this wonderful facility. Here you will find "brochures and free travel guides, free reservation phones, road reports, weather radar, snow conditions and a list of today's events… a retail shop with a great selection of regional books, jewelry, pottery and one-of-a-kind gifts. Pick up state park passes, fishing licenses and free maps – area, state and region. Have a question or need detailed directions? Our travel experts have all the answers – and if they don't, they'll find the person who does." They're not kidding: these people really know the area and can answer just about any questions you might have. The Center also has a number of displays showing major features of the Hills, plus it has "sparkling clean restrooms, pet exercise areas and plenty of free parking". Go north at Exit 61 for a couple of blocks past the Flying J, and take a left on East Mall Drive. The Visitor Center is on your left, on Discovery Circle.

blackhillsbadlands.com/business/black-hills-visitor-information-center
                          1851 Discovery Cir, Rapid City, SD 57701   *(605) 355-3700*

Black Hills Bluegrass Festival (1429)

If you're in the Hills the last week of June, you're in for a treat. There's a huge traditional bluegrass and acoustic 3-day festival at the Elkview Campground in Sturgis (elkviewcampground.com). The campground has full hookup campsites, tent camping and unlimited parking close to the concert area. Food and beverages will be available (no alcohol). On Saturday and Sunday mornings,  there will be biscuits and gravy for breakfast. Make reservations early, and come on Wednesday or Thursday to get a great start on the weekend. Jamming will be encouraged and the festival is a family event. To see who is playing, you can view or download a brochure on the website: go to the 'Festival' pull-down menu at the top of the page and click on 'Brochure' for the PDF. The venue is located 5 minutes from Sturgis. Take I-90 Exit 37 and go east on Pleasant Valley Road (that's a right if you were in the westbound lane, or a left if you were heading toward Rapid City). The campground is about a mile up the road on the left.

blackhillsbluegrass.com   *13014 Pleasant Valley Rd, Sturgis SD 57785*   *(605) 348-1198*

Black Hills Caverns (1430)

Visitors to this cave system can see a number of rock formations including logomites, stalagmites, stalactites, helictites, rare frost crystal, flowstone, dogtooth spar crystal, box-work, cave flower, soda straw stalactites, columns, draperies, popcorn crystals and nail-head spar crystal. There are two different tours. The Crystal Tour is "an easy, 1/2 hour, 1500-ft walking tour in the first level of the cave. See millions of Calcite Crystals and hear about the cave's process of formation. Moderate walking is required." The Adventure option is "the complete tour of the Black Hills Caverns. It usually takes 1 hour to complete. It includes all 3 levels of the cave, approximately 3/4 of a mile. See the best variety of cave formations on this tour." From downtown Rapid City take Omaha Street, which turns into Hwy 44 west. After about fifteen minutes you'll pass Elkhart Road and then the Johnson Siding fire station. The next right is Cavern Road. *blackhillscaverns.com*   *2600 Cavern Rd, Rapid City, SD 57702*   *(605) 343-0542*

Black Hills Maze (1431)

This is actually a pretty extensive family activities park that is centered on a giant maze (1.2 miles of it!) with wooden walls and lots of decks and towers. There's also bank-shot basketball; a batting cage; a large climbing wall; kid-powered go-carts (no engines); a water balloon slingshot duel; and even mini golf. Located just 3 miles south of Rapid City on Highway 16, on the way to Mt. Rushmore. You can pick and choose which activities to do, and pay accordingly. The Deluxe Package (2016) includes everything and runs $19.81. There are picnic tables and snacks (hotdogs, chips etc.) available. *blackhillsmaze.com*   *6400 Hwy 16, Rapid City, SD 57701*   *(605) 343-5439*

Chapel In The Hills (1432)

In 1180 in the remote village of Borgund, Norway, a new 'Viking' style stave church was built. The Black Hills chapel is an exact reproduction of that ancient Stavkirke, which is the best preserved of Norway's twenty-eight extant stave churches. The original building is part of the Borgund parish in the Indre Sogn deanery in the Diocese of Bjørgvin, and although it is no longer used regularly for church functions, it is used as a museum run by the Society for the Preservation of Ancient Norwegian Monuments. The Black Hills chapel was built in 1969 as a home for the Lutheran Vespers radio ministry. "Arriving visitors are greeted at the 'Stabbur', which is an authentic grass-roofed storehouse, built in Norway and assembled on site. It serves as the visitor center and gift shop. Literature about the chapel and its ministry is available at the gift shop, along with an extensive assortment of items of a Scandinavian theme. Also on the grounds is an authentic log cabin museum. Built by a Norwegian prospector who came to the Black Hills during the gold rush, it houses articles brought over from Norway or made by Scandinavians in this country during the 1800s. Visitors are welcome and encouraged to wander the chapel grounds, taking their time as they experience the presence of God in this beautiful natural setting." Worship services are conducted each evening at 7:30 in the chapel during the summer months, to which everyone is invited. Dress is informal. Admission is free, donations are welcome. *chapel-in-the-hills.org*   *788 Chapel Ln, Rapid City, SD 57702*   *(605) 342-8281*

City of Presidents (1433)

Life-sized bronze statues of our nation's past Presidents greet visitors to downtown Rapid City and "give those who are shopping, dining or walking a historic reminder of the legacy our nation's presidents have created." Meticulously sculpted by nationally renowned artists, these lifelike figures really bring a sense of reality to history. Kids can learn a lot while they have fun posing for pictures. There's a President on every corner in the historic downtown district. You can enjoy and view these remarkable statues and tour the City of Presidents visitor center for free – it's a one-room museum on Main Street that's open from June to October.

downtownrapidcity.com/city-of-presidents.html   *631 Main St, Rapid City*   *(800) 487-3223*

Cosmos Mystery Area (1434)

This is a great place to take kids from about 5 to 10 years old. Teenagers might get a kick out of it, and older adults with weak stomachs will probably want to wait in the gift shop. It's a series of experiences where level and plumb are thrown to the wind, and your mind is tricked into a strange sense of gravity bending. The walls and floors are out of kilter, and even though you know a ball can't roll uphill, you'll watch one do it. Tours run about 20 minutes, adults are $11 and 5-11 year-olds are $6 (2016).

cosmosmysteryarea.com   *24040 Cosmos Rd, Rapid City, SD 57702*   *(605) 343-9802*

Dinosaur Park (1435)

This is a free attraction on top of a hill with magnificent views over the city. The seven dinosaurs are concrete, and were built in 1936 by the WPA. It's a strenuous walk up a long stairway from the parking lot to the summit, but absolutely worth the effort for the views. There's a café (it's pretty good) and gift shop at the edge of the parking lot, and a large deck out back that overlooks the eastern half of the city. Even if you don't want to tackle the stairs, the drive up there is worth doing. Listed on the National Register of Historic Places. From I-90 Exit 57 (Mount Rushmore Hwy 16), go south until you cross Omaha and the street becomes West Boulevard. Go five blocks to Quincy Street, hang a right and after about seven blocks the road becomes a paved switchback (ok for motorcycles). Drive carefully to the top. The parking lot is on your left, the dinosaurs are on the right.

940 Skyline Dr., Rapid City, SD 57701   *(605) 343-8687*

Flags & Wheels Indoor Racing (1436)

Indoor go-cart racing, bumper cars, laser tag, paintball, batting cages and arcade. If go-carts aren't macho enough, try racing around their 27,000 square foot track in an Extreme Racing Kart. These American-made karts are Flags & Wheels' premier indoor attraction, and can reach speeds of over 40 mph! They require a U.S. driver's license and parental waiver signature if under the age of 18. Driver weight limit is 250 lbs. Helmets are provided.

flagsandwheels.com   *405 12th St, Rapid City, SD 57701*   *(605) 341-7585*

Fort Hays Chuck-wagon & Tours (1437)

This is a reconstruction of an Old West town where every morning from Mother's Day through mid-October the cowboys and cowgirls rise with the sun and start cooking breakfast for their visitors. Their Mount Rushmore tour package is "the most popular tour in the Black Hills because it's such a good deal. We leave every morning after breakfast for the whole day and come back for our famous Chuck-wagon Supper & Show. All admissions and two meals are included!" The facility is open all day, every day, and you can stop in for a Cowboy Breakfast every morning and make Reservations for the tour or a chuck-wagon supper and cowboy music variety show. There is no admission fee to browse the *Dances With Wolves* film set, and see the original buildings used in the Oscar-winning movie. Plus, kids can make a brick at the brick factory, a plate at the tin shop, a rope at the rope shop, or buy a knife at the blacksmith's shop. In 2016, the chuck-wagon supper starts at $29 (kids 5-12 are half price and under 4 are $5), breakfast begins at 99¢ for all-you-can-eat pancakes, and the guided bus tours run from $80.

mountrushmoretours.com   *2255 Fort Hayes Rd, Rapid City SD 57702*   *(605) 394-9653*

Ivan's Hunting and Fishing B&B (1438)

This is an interesting set-up: Ivan Burandt has a suburban home in Black Hawk, just west of Rapid City at I-90 Exit 48, where he provides guided deer hunting on private land (he'll help you get the deer out and process it); unguided but inexpensive turkey hunting during the 7-week season in April and May; and walleye fishing: "Enjoy a relaxing fun day on the lake. Just bring your lunch… and everything is supplied for fishing in my custom 20 foot Lake Assault fishing boat, plus your fish are cleaned. We fish Orman Dam near Belle Fourche." It's not just a B&B: all meals are included., and a washer and dryer are available.

blackhillshuntingandfishing.com   *12800 Larene Dr. Black Hawk SD 57718* *(605) 791-3273*

John Lopez Sculptures (1439)

This world renowned sculptor is celebrated for his metal 'found parts' creations that recycle farm and ranch metals into breathtaking art forms. He is "a product of a place. His people's ranches are scattered along the Grand River in South Dakota, not far from where Sitting Bull was born and died." Lopez has several pieces on public display throughout the Black Hills. Click on MAPS on his website for details. His 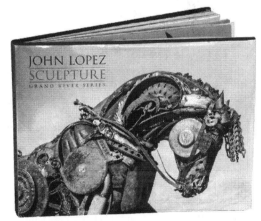 coffee table book (shown) is also available through the website, and it in itself is a magnificent work of art.

johnlopezstudio.com   *19493 Railway Street, Lemmon SD 57638*   *(605) 209-0954*

Journey Museum, The (1440)

The Journey Museum & Learning Center brings together four major prehistoric and historic collections to tell the complete story of the Western Great Plains - from the perspective of the Lakota people and the pioneers who shaped its past, to the scientists who now study it. Interactive learning experiences such as the Wells Fargo Theater, Paleontology Tent and Learning Lab give you the chance to learn and play every day.
journeymuseum.org   222 New York St, Rapid City SD 57701   (605) 394-6923

La Grand Station/Call of the Wild (1474)

This is a small, free, taxidermy museum of wild animals from North America, Africa and Asia. "The taxidermy mounts are skillfully crafted to show each animal in its truest sense, depicting a realistic pose and expression within the habitat diorama."
callofthewildmuseum.com   3851 Eglin St, Rapid City SD 57703   (605) 791-1947

Museum of Geology (1441)

Magnificent small museum on the campus of the South Dakota School of Mines & Technology. It's on the upper floor of the Administration Building, and admission is free. Kids will really enjoy the large mounted skeletons of dinosaurs, mammals, marine reptiles, and fish. There are rare fossils from the White River Badlands, all arranged in time-specific dioramas, and mineral displays including the Hall of South Dakota Minerals, plus meteorites and a fluorescent mineral room. The gift shop toys, books, models and more, and the prices are very reasonable. This is one of the best family attractions in the Hills, especially for kids with a love of learning. There are some hands-on displays that will captivate younger students, and dramatic items that teens and adults will enjoy. We are privileged to have this resource in our community.
museum.sdsmt.edu   501 E Saint Joseph St, Rapid City SD 57701   (605) 394-2467

Old McDonald's Petting Farm (1442)

Meet over 100 popular farm animals in a clean, relaxed hands-on environment. This beautiful farm on the road to Mount Rushmore is a great place to play with, feed and even bottle feed some of the many friendly animals. Kids can play with baby animals, hug a rabbit, go for pony rides and hold a brand new chick. 2016 rates (for a three-day consecutive pass) are $13.50 for adults, $11.50 for seniors and $10.50 for children. Bring some quarters, too, to feed pigs, goats, fish, lambs…
oldmacdonaldsfarmrc.com   23691 Busted Five Ct, Rapid City SD 57702   (605) 737-4815

Petrified Forest of the Black Hills (1443)

Open since1929, this is one of the largest outcroppings of fossilized petrified wood in the area. There's a short video, and outdoor hike, and a visit to the museum which houses petrified wood, rocks and fossils that are 120 to 130 million years old. I-90 Exit 46, then go 1 mile east.
Elkcreekresort.net   8228 Elk Creek Rd. Piedmont SD 57769   (605) 787-4884

Putz N Glo (1444)

This attraction offers three family attractions: indoor Black Light Mini Golf, Gemstone Panning, and the Human Maze Adventure.

putznglo.com   *23694 Strato Rim Dr., Rapid City SD 57702*   *(605) 716-1230*

Rapid City Rush Professional Hockey (1445)

Hockey fans visiting the Hills between early October and early April can book tickets to watch the Rush play at Rushmore Plaza Civic Center's ice arena. This is a professional ice hockey team in the ECHL, which is currently affiliated with the National Hockey League's Arizona Coyotes and the American Hockey League's Springfield Falcons.

rapidcityrush.com   *444 Mt Rushmore Road, Rapid City SD 57701*   *(605) 716-7825*

Reptile Gardens (1446)

Founded in 1937, this is one of the most popular attractions in the Hills. It is "the largest reptile zoo in the world, housing more species of reptiles than any other zoo or wild animal park". Visitors can enjoy a chance encounter with a notorious saltwater crocodile, visit the legendary collection of venomous snakes, or pet gentle giant Galapagos and Aldabra tortoises. There are also a few non-reptilian residents, including a majestic bald eagle named Cheyenne and a prairie dog village. The gardens are beautiful, there are shows all day long: watch the alligators and crocodiles do their thing, learn about snakes, or meet birds from around the world. There's some food available. This is a very clean, upbeat facility and the staff are professional and caring. There's a huge gift shop, too.

reptilegardens.com   *8955 S Highway 16, Rapid City SD 57702 (605) 342-5873*

Rushmore Plaza Civic Center (1447)

This is the largest (150,000-square-foot) exhibition center in the Black Hills and it offers a constant stream of national and regional top-notch entertainment – from music concerts to magic shows, circus events, comedians, monster truck demos, dance, rodeos, endure bikes and more. From Disney to Dunham, BB King to Taylor Swift, this is the place to be. To see what's happening while you're here, go to *gotmine.com* and click on 'Tickets'. You'll be pleasantly surprised.

gotmine.com   *444 N Mount Rushmore Rd, Rapid City SD 57701*   *(605) 394-4115*

South Dakota Air & Space Museum (1448)

This free attraction showcases over 30 vintage military aircraft ranging from World War II bombers to the modern-day B-1. The indoor galleries are filled with aerospace exhibits that showcase engineering, innovation, science, and history. Outside, you can walk around and touch everything from the B1B Lancer to an H-13 Helicopter. A bus tour of Ellsworth Air Force Base includes a visit to a Minuteman II missile silo.

sdairandspacemuseum.com   *2890 Davis Dr., Rapid City SD 57706*   *(605) 385-5189*

Storybook Island (1449)

This is an admission-free children's theme park that is open Memorial Day through Labor Day from 9 AM to 7 PM daily, weather permitting. The park allows kids to run, explore, slide, hang out with life-size statues of their favorite storybook characters and even ride a little train. There are castles and bridges and ponds and it's perfect for kids under ten. From downtown, take Omaha or Main and go west to Mountain View Road. Take a left and go south until this meets Hwy 44. Take a right and go to Sheridan Lake Road. Go right (north) and the park is on your left. (facebook.com/storybookisland)
storybookisland.org   1301 Sheridan Lake Rd, Rapid City SD 57702   (605) 342-6357

Wall Drug Store (1451)

Visitors traveling to the Hills on westbound I-90 absolutely MUST stop at Wall Drug! This is kitsch gone wild, a marvelous mayhem that is one of the world's best tourist traps. The food is good: there are the famous homemade donuts and hot beef sandwiches, buffalo burgers and 5 cent coffee! The complex houses several specialty stores and a few pretty cool surprises, such as a water show and lots of crazy photo opportunities in the Backyard. In the shops you'll find trinkets, art, clothing, Christmas ornaments, leather goods, jewelry, cowboy boots, buckles and belts, lots of books – and truckloads of souvenirs.
walldrug.com   510 Main St, Wall SD 57790   (605) 279-2175

WaTiki Indoor Waterpark (1452)

This is a 30,000 square foot indoor facility with 3 slides, an activity pool, a lazy river, a kiddie pool with a tip bucket and mini slide, and a hot tub. There's also a bar & grill. Admission (2016): 7- $24.99 plus taxes and fees. 3-6 - $17.99 plus taxes and fees. Parents and grandparents can buy an all-day spectator pass that includes the hot tub, for $9.99 plus taxes. If you stay in the adjoining hotels, there are good discounts.
watikiwaterpark.com   1314 N Elk Vale Rd, Rapid City SD 57703   (877) 545-2897

City View Trolley (1453)

This service operates from June through the end of August and offers passengers "informative tours filled with recent and historical information about Rapid City and the surrounding area". It begins and ends at the downtown bus transfer facility, with the last trip beginning at 4 PM. It makes 15 stops during each tour including stops at popular Rapid City attractions such as the Journey Museum, Storybook Island, Dinosaur Park, and the Dahl Arts Center. You may board the City View Trolley at any of the stops along its route. In 2016, adults are $2 and kids $1.
rapidride.org/ city-view-trolley   333 6ᵗʰ St Rapid City SD 57701   (605) 394-6631

Main Street Square (1454)

Located in the heart of Downtown Rapid City, Main Street Square is "a fun-filled public space that features special events, arts and culture, live concerts, seasonal ice skating and interactive fountains". For a schedule of events during a date range you can specify, go to mainstreetsquarerc.com/calendar.html. The fountains are an all-day highlight that light up after dark. Visitors can enjoy and touch the water features without entering the cascade area, except the interactive fountain, which is for public use. (Kids, bring your swimsuits!)

mainstreetsquarerc.com   *512 Main St, Rapid City SD 57701*   *(605) 716-7979*

Rapid City Bicycle Sharing Program (1455)

This is an automated bike sharing system designed for short trips around town. There are currently two stations: at Main Street Square in downtown, and on the campus of the South Dakota School of Mines & Technology. Bike rental costs $5 for 24 hours and includes unlimited 60-minute bike checkouts. However, you will be charged an extra fee for checking out any one bike for longer than 60 minutes ($3 an hour). To avoid that, just return your bike to any station within 60 minutes and get another one. (It's just designed to prevent theft.)

RapidCity.BCycle.com   *512 Main St., Ste. 980, Rapid City SD 57701*   *(605) 716-7979*

Black Hills Community Theatre (1456)

BHCT's season includes five main stage productions, a Dinner Theatre fundraiser, shows by the Cherry Street Players (the BHCT children's troupe), and the Well Done Players (BHCT's troupe of well seasoned actors), and a number of other special projects, classes and workshops throughout the year. Black Hills Community Theatre also operates a Costume Shop, which is open to the public for costume rentals throughout the year. All shows are staged at the Performing Arts Center of Rapid City, located at 601 Columbus St., unless otherwise noted on the website. Tickets are quite reasonable and the production values are high.

bhct.org   *713 7th St, Rapid City SD 57701*   *(605) 394-1786*

Canvas 2 Paint (1457)

This business offers "crazy, fun, creative classes for both the artistic and well… the not so artistic". Show up for a little bit of paint, a little bit of wine, and whole lot of fun. They're bridging the gap between fine art and fun art. Learn the basics of acrylic canvas painting while enjoying the company of friends, and go home with a one of a kind painting that you created. In 2016, the cost is $25 - $40 (kids and adults), which includes studio time, a 16x20 canvas, use of their paints and brushes, an apron to wear, and lots of inspiration. Reservations are not required.

canvas2paint.com   *632 St. Joseph St., Rapid City SD 57701*   *(605) 716-3325*

Rapid City Walking Tours (1458)

These are guided 90-minute tours downtown with local historian Holly Kennedy. You can explore the City of Presidents on the Presidential Trivia Tour or embrace your inner adrenaline junky with ghastly tales on the Strange and Ghostly Tour. Adults

(2016) are $15, seniors and 7+ are $10. Cash only. It's a leisurely walk.
rapidcitywalkingtour.com   *500 St Joseph St, Rapid City SD 57701*   *(605) 430-6445*

Performing Arts Center of Rapid City (1459)

This venue is based in Rapid City High School and is home to Black Hills Community Theatre, Black Hills Symphony Orchestra, Rapid City Children's Chorus, and Black Hills Showcase Chorus. There are two stages: two venues: the 830-seat Historic Theater, or the more intimate 175 seat Studio Theater.
performingartsrc.org   *601 Columbus St., Rapid City SD 57701*   *(605) 394-1786*

The Potter Family Theatre (1460)

This is a very talented family group that performs music from the 30s through today. Check the website for venues: they are moving from their current location in 2016.
the-potter-family.com   *632 1/2 St. Joseph St., Rapid City SD 57701*   *(605) 415-5593*

Meadowbrook Golf Course (1461)

This is an 18 hole championship facility, voted "Black Hills Best" golf course by the Rapid City Journal Reader's Choice Award in 2012 and 2013. This David Gill designed course features a classic parkland-style layout with cottonwood, spruce, pine and apple trees. It runs over 6,900 yards, with Rapid Creek winding through the course and water coming into play on 9 holes. Meadowbrook was honored to host the 1984 USGA Women's Public Links Championship, and the 2009 and 2010 NAIA College Women's National Golf Championships. 2016 course rates are $44/18, $27/9. Carts run $17 per rider. Various discounts and punch cards are shown on the website. Call for a tee time.
golfatmeadowbrook.com   *3625 Jackson Blvd, Rapid City SD 57702*   *(605) 394-4191*

Executive Golf Course (1462)

Centrally located near downtown, this course is designed to accommodate every level of player from beginner to single-digit handicappers. It is a nine-hole facility with seven par threes and two par fours among giant cottonwoods, with Rapid Creek running along two of the nine holes, it's an excellent opportunity to hone your iron game.
golfatmeadowbrook.com/junior-golf/executive-golf-course
200 Founders Park Drive, Rapid City, SD 57701   *(605) 394-4124*

Rapid River Art Gallery (1463)

This is a free museum-like gallery where owner Patrick Roseland's collection is not for sale, but other local artists showcase and sell. The beautifully restored space exhibits a fine collection of historic Rapid City-related art.
rapidrivergallery.com   *910 Main St., Rapid City, SD 57701*   *(605) 721-7555*

Rapid City Summer Nights (1464)

This is a free, very popular event (average attendance is about 8,000) that occurs every Thursday during the summer from 6-9 PM. The stage is located at 7th Street and St.

Joseph. Must have ID to purchase alcohol. The event is kid-friendly and there are lots of food vendors. Service animals only (no pets). The bands are classic rock, '80s, modern country and more! Click on each band's link on the Schedule page to learn more about the performers.

rapidcitysummernights.com   *700 St. Joseph St., Rapid City, SD 57701*   *(605) 343-1823*

Memorial Park Promenade & Legacy Commons Playground (1465)

The promenade is a wide walkway that was designed to be "a fun place, a destination and a convenient and identifiable connection between Downtown and the Rushmore Plaza Civic Center". It wanders through a truly beautiful city park, located north of Omaha Street near the Rushmore Plaza Civic Center. The park and promenade link the downtown area to Rushmore Plaza Civic Center, Rapid City Central High School and the Journey Museum. The park is 27.5 acres and includes Memorial Pond, the Flood Memorial fountain, picnic areas, a formal rose garden, the Legacy Statue, the Leonard Swanson Memorial Pathway, restrooms, the Berlin Wall Memorial, the Veterans Memorial and a band shell. Legacy Commons is adjacent to the park and was designed for people to spend some time there, rather than just stroll through. It includes a climbing area with an art garden, an accessible and inclusive play area with an elevated accessible garden, a nature climbing area with adjacent Black Hills prairie and medicinal gardens, an age 2-5 play area with a children's garden , and an active play area with an adjacent sustainable landscape.

301 N. Fifth St., Rapid City SD 57701   *(605) 716-7979*

Pirate's Cove Miniature Golf (1466)

"Come and see why this facility received the Rapid City, SD Beautification Award and was voted Best in the State for miniature golf courses. Putt your way through the world of 18th century pirates, carousing buccaneers, sunken ships, cascading waterfalls, dreaded pirate dungeons and romantic pirate lore from the 1700s." As much fun for adults as it is for kids, this feature is on the left as you go south on LaCrosse from I-90 Exit 59. In 2016, adults were $8.50, Children 4-12 $7.50, 3 and under free.

piratescove.net/rapid-city   *1500 N Lacrosse St, Rapid City SD 57701*   *(605) 343-8540*

Art Alley (1467)

Located between 6th and 7th Avenues, and Main and Saint Joseph Streets, this is an unusual feature in a well-ordered city. Artists paint directly on the building walls, and there is a large following: many people make it a must-do stop when they visit the Hills. The Arts Council not only tolerates it, but actively encourages this mode of expression, and even issues permits to artists. Who knew you'd find government-sponsored graffiti in such a well-behaved town… The quality of some of the artwork is quite impressive.

artalleyrc.com   *599 7th St, Rapid City, SD 57701*   *(605) 394-4101*

APEX Gallery (1468)

The gallery is located at the South Dakota School of Mines and Technology in classroom building 211, and hosts a new exhibit every four to six weeks. It was established in 1989 and is open to the public, offering educational arts and science exhibitions for both enjoyment and enrichment. One catch: it's only open during the school year, M-F from 10 AM to 5 PM. It's closed all summer, and on holidays and long weekends.

sdsmt.edu/ApexGallery   *501 E. Saint Joseph St., Rapid City SD 57701*   *(605) 394-2511*

Black Hills Symphony Orchestra (1469)

With an 80-year pedigree, this magnificent orchestra employs about 90 musicians, including some 60 strings. In addition to a concert season that , the orchestra works with the Dakota Choral Union, Music in the Schools, Black Hills Dance Theatre, Black Hills Community Theater, and numerous individual musician outreaches. Click on 'Concerts' on the website to see the current schedule. Tickets are usually in the $12 to $30 range. The season runs October through April.

bhsymphony.org   *601 Columbus St, Rapid City SD 57701*   *(605) 348-4676*

Historic Elks Movie Theater (1470)

Cinema Treasures says that "the main screen is huge and the sound quality fabulous". Now more than a century old, the Elks is an iconic feature in Rapid City, beloved by generations of movie-goers. Designed by Sioux City architect John P. Eisentraut, it began in 1912 as an opera house and the stage is still used for functions today – including private parties/screenings, concerts, corporate training seminars and other presentations. To see what's playing tonight, click 'Movies" at the top of the homepage. General admission (2016) is $5 adult, $4 children 3-12, under 2 free.

elkstheatre.com   *512 6th St, Rapid City SD 57701*   *(605) 341-4149*

Suzie Cappa Art Gallery (1471)

This is an art gallery downtown that sells very reasonably priced works, and offers a lot of the pieces as prints, canvas wraps, greeting cards and so on, making them even more affordable. It's a nonprofit Art Center that believes disability is not a boundary, and all people can be creative in a supportive environment. Judging by the work on exhibit, they're onto something. A lot of the pieces express the simple joy of living, while others offer a very personal glimpse into the artist's view of life. The gallery underlines the fact that 'creative expression fosters personal growth and self-esteem'. It was founded in 2001 and named in memory of artist Suzie Cappa. It began with the vision of providing a supportive, inspiring environment for artists of all abilities. The downtown location opened in March of 2013 with 20 full-time artists. Since opening, that has grown to 24 full-time and 4 part-time artists who work in a wide variety of media. If you can't make it to the downtown gallery, a lot of the artists' work is available online: just click on 'Catalog'. Some of the pieces that caught our eye were Nancy Weiss's 'Goat' and 'Moonlight', Heather Morris's hauntingly beautiful 'Paris', and Hoksila Long's 'Horse'.

suziecappaart.com   *722 Saint Joseph St, Rapid City SD 57701*   *(605) 791-3578*

The Sculpture Project (1472)

The Sculpture Project, *Passage of Wind and Water*, is a massive and magnificent public art project underway in the heart of downtown. It features twenty-one large granite rocks being hewn into depictions of the Badlands and Black Hills, exploring "a vast expanse of the region's history of continuous and often rapid transformation". A selection committee of arts and community leaders chose stone sculptor Masayuki Nagase to be the project's artist from an international pool of 88 artists. Nagase trained in Japan, is based in Berkeley and has a long career as a stone sculptor and public artist. Using traditional stone carving tools, he began the five-year project in 2013, carving by hand on-site during the summer months. The $2-million endeavor is entirely privately funded through a partnership between Destination Rapid City and the John T. Vucurevich Foundation. Photo by author.

rcsculptureproject.com   *600 Main St, Rapid City SD 57701*   *(605) 716-7979*

Hiking in Rapid City (1473)

If you like to hike, visit the AllTrails website for listings of both Rapid City and general Black Hills reader-recommended routes with notes and comments.

alltrails.com/us/south-dakota/rapid-city

The Dinosaur Museum (1474)

Travel 90 million years in just a few miles. The Dinosaur Museum is conveniently located adjacent to Reptile Gardens. Also has a Mirror Maze and Mini Golf.

Facebook   *8973 S Highway 16*   *(605) 342-8140*

Where To Stay – Rapid City

Hotels • Motels • Cabins • Bed & Breakfasts

Audrie's Cottages & B&B (1500)
23029 Thunderhead Falls Rd, Rapid City SD 57702   (605) 342-7788

Americas Best Value Inn (1502)
620 Howard St, Rapid City SD 57701   (605) 343-5434

AmericInn (1503)
1632 Rapp St, Rapid City SD 57701   (605) 343-8424

Amie St. Jean B&B (1504)
624 Adams St, Rapid City SD 57701   (605) 858-0043

Avanti Motel (1505)
102 N Maple Ave, Rapid City SD 57701   (605) 348-1112

Silver Mountain Inn & Cabins (1506)
13350 Silver Mountain Rd, Rapid City SD 57702   (605) 342-2246

Baymont Inn & Suites (1507)
4040 Cheyenne Blvd, Rapid City SD 57703   (605) 791-5151

Best Western Ramkota Hotel (1508)
2111 N Lacrosse St, Rapid City SD 57701   (605) 343-8550

Big Sky Lodge (1509)
4080 Tower Rd, Rapid City SD 57701   (605) 348-3200

Black Forest Inn (1510)
23191 Hwy 385, Rapid City SD 57702   (605) 574-2000

Black Hills Cabins & Motel (1511)
24060 Hwy 385, Rapid City SD 57702   (605) 391-3217

Black Hills Mile Hi Motel (1512)
6406 Cog Hill Ln, Rapid City SD 57702   (605) 673-4048

Budget Inn Motel (1513)
610 E North St, Rapid City SD 57701   (605) 342-8594

Cambria Hotel & Suites (1514)
3333 Outfitter Rd, Rapid City SD 57701   *(605) 341-0101*

Canyon Lake Resort (1515)
4510 Shore Dr., Rapid City SD 57702   *(605) 343-0234*

Colonial Motel (1518)
511 E North St, Rapid City SD 57701   *(605) 342-1417*

Comfort Inns & Suites (1519)
915 Fairmont Blvd, Rapid City SD 57701   *(605) 415-4572*

Comfort Suites (1520)
1333 N Elk Vale Rd, Rapid City SD 57703   *(605) 791-2345*

Corral Motel (1521)
210 E North St, Rapid City SD 57701   *(605) 342-7511*

Country Inns & Suites (1522)
2321 N Lacrosse St, Rapid City SD 57701   *(605) 394-0017*

Coyote Blues Village B&B (1523)
23165 Horsemans Ranch Rd, Rapid City, SD 57702   *(605) 574-4477*

Days Inn – Jackson (1524)
725 Jackson Blvd, Rapid City SD 57702   *(605) 343-6040*

Days Inn – LaCrosse (1525)
1570 N Lacrosse St, Rapid City SD 57701   *(605) 348-8410*

Double Diamond Ranch (1526)
23818 Hwy 385, Rapid City SD 57702   *(605) 574-4560*

Econo Lodge (1527)
625 E Disk Dr., Rapid City SD 57701   *(605) 342-6400*

Edelweiss Mountain Lodging (1528)
12780 Black Forest Rd, Rapid City SD 57702   *(605) 574-2430*

Elk Creek Resort (1529)
8220 Elk Creek Rd, Piedmont, SD 57769   *(605) 787-4884*

Fair Value Inn (1531)
1607 N Lacrosse St, Rapid City SD 57701   *(605) 342-8118*

Fairfield Inn & Suites (1532)
1314 N Elk Vale Rd, Rapid City SD 57703   *(605) 718-9600*

Family Inn (1533)
3737 Sturgis Rd, Rapid City SD 57702   *(605) 342-2892*

Foothills Inn (1534)
1625 N Lacrosse St, Rapid City SD 57701   *(605) 348-5640*

Garden Cottages Motel (1535)
4030 Jackson Blvd, Rapid City SD 57702   *(605) 342-6922*

Gold Star Motel (1536)
801 E North St, Rapid City SD 57701   *(605) 341-7051*

Grand Gateway Hotel (1537)
1721 N Lacrosse St, Rapid City SD 57701   *(605) 342-1300*

Grandstay Residential Suites (1538)
660 Disk Dr., Rapid City SD 57701   *(605) 341-5100*

Hampton Inn (1539)
1720 Rapp St, Rapid City SD 57701   *(605) 348-1911*

Happy Holiday Motel (1540)
9008 S Hwy 16, Rapid City SD 57702   *(605) 342-8101*

Hillside Country Cabins (1541)
13315 S Hwy 16, Rapid City SD 57702   *(605) 342-4121*

Hilton Garden Inn (1542)
815 E Mall Dr., Rapid City SD 57701   *(605) 791-9000*

Hisega Lodge B&B (1543)
23101 Triangle Trail, Rapid City SD 57702   *(605) 342-8444*

Holiday Inn (1544)
505 N 5th St, Rapid City SD 57701   *(605) 348-4000*

Quality Inn (1545)
750 Cathedral Dr., Rapid City SD 57701   *(605) 341-9300*

Holiday Inn Express & Suites (1546)
645 E Disk Dr., Rapid City SD 57701   *(605) 355-9090*

Hotel Alex Johnson (1547)
523 6th St., Rapid City SD 57701   *(605) 342-1210*

Howard Johnson (1548)
950 North St, Rapid City SD 57701   *(605) 737-4656*

La Quinta/Watiki (1550)
1416 N Elk Vale Rd, Rapid City SD 57703 (605) 718-7000

Lazy U Motel (1551)
2215 Mt Rushmore Rd, Rapid City SD 57701 (605) 343-4242

M-Star Motel (1552)
2401 Mt Rushmore Rd, Rapid City SD 57701 (605) 348-1453

Madison Ranch B&B (1553)
8800 Nemo Rd, Rapid City SD 57702 (605) 342-6997

Mainstay Suites (1554)
3231 E Mall Dr., Rapid City SD 57701 (605) 719-5151

Microtel Inn & Suites by Wyndham (1556)
1740 Rapp St, Rapid City SD 57701 (605) 348-2523

Motel 6 (1557)
620 Latrobe Ave, Rapid City SD 57701 (605) 221-0166

Motel Rapid (1558)
3515 Sturgis Rd, Rapid City SD 57702 (605) 342-5834

My Place Hotel (1559)
1612 Discovery Cir, Rapid City SD 57701 (605) 791-5800

Mystery Mountain Resort (1560)
13752 S Hwy 16, Rapid City SD 57702 (605) 342-5368

Peregrine Pointe B&B (1561)
23451 Peregrine Point, Rapid City SD 57702 (605) 348-3987

Price Motel (1562)
401 E North St, Rapid City SD 57701 (605) 343-1806

Quality Inn (1563)
750 Cathedral Dr., Rapid City SD 57701 (605) 341-9300

Ramada Rapid City (1564)
1902 N Lacrosse St, Rapid City SD 57701 (605) 342-3322

Ranch House Motel (1565)
202 E North St, Rapid City SD 57701 (605) 341-0785

Rodeway Inn – LaCrosse (1567)
1313 N Lacrosse St, Rapid City SD 57701 (605) 348-3313

Sleep Inn & Suites (1569)
4031 Cheyenne Blvd, Rapid City SD 57703   *(605) 791-5678*

South Dakota Rose Inn (1570)
212 East Blvd N, Rapid City SD 57701   *(605) 343-8232*

Summer Creek Inn (1572)
23204 Summer Creek Dr., Rapid City SD 57702   *(605) 574-4408*

Super 8 – Tower Rd (1573)
2520 Tower Rd, Rapid City SD 57701   *(605) 342-4911*

Super 8 – LaCrosse (1574)
2124 N Lacrosse St, Rapid City SD 57701   *(605) 348-8070*

Sweetgrass Inn (1575)
9356 Neck Yoke Rd, Rapid City SD 57702   *(605) 343-5351*

The Rushmore Hotel and Suites (1576)
445 Mt Rushmore Rd, Rapid City SD 57701   *(605) 348-8300*

Time Inn Motel (1578)
601 E North St, Rapid City SD 57701   *(605) 343-5565*

Town House Motel (1579)
210 Saint Joseph St, Rapid City SD 57701   *(605) 791-3987*

Trails End Cabins & Motel (1580)
320 Park St., Hill City, SD 57745   *(605) 574-4900*

Travelodge (1581)
2505 Mt Rushmore Rd, Rapid City SD 57701   *(605) 343-5383*

Western Thrifty Inn (1582)
621 E North St, Rapid City SD 57701   *(605) 791-1133*

Whispering Wind Cottages (1583)
12720 S Hwy 16, Rapid City SD 57702   *(605) 574-9533*

Willow Springs Cabins B&B (1584)
11515 Sheridan Lake Rd, Rapid City SD 57702   *(605) 342-3665*

Yak Ridge Cabins & Farmstead (1585)
24041 Cosmos Road   Rapid City SD 57702   *(605) 390 7627*

Campgrounds

After The Ride Campground (1609)
13121 Lincoln Tarken Ln, Piedmont, SD 57769   *(605) 393-7340*

Central States Fairgrounds (1610)
800 San Francisco Street Rapid City, South Dakota 57701   *(605) 355-3861*

Covered Wagon Resort (1611)
14189 Sturgis Rd, Piedmont, SD 57769   *(605) 787-4440*

Elk Creek Resort (1612)
8220 Elk Creek Rd, Piedmont, SD 57769   *(605) 787-4884*

Happy Holliday Resort (1613)
9008 S Hwy 16, Rapid City, SD 57701   *(605) 342-8101*

Hart Ranch Camping Resort (1614)
23756 Arena Dr., Rapid City, SD 57702   *(605) 399-2582*

Heartland Resort (1615)
24743 S Highway 79, Hermosa, SD 57744   *(605) 255-5460*

Horse Creek Inn Campground (1616)
23570 Highway 385, Rapid City, SD 57702   *(605) 574-2908*

Lake Park Campground (1617)
2850 Chapel Ln, Rapid City, SD 57702   *(605) 341-5320*

Mystery Mountain Resort (1618)
13752 S Highway 16, Rapid City, SD 57702   *(605) 342-5368*

Rapid City KOA (1619)
3010 East Hwy 44, Rapid City, SD 57709   *(605) 348-2111*

Rapid City RV Park and Campground (1620) – *[Privately owned, not a municipal facility]*
4110 S Highway 16, Rapid City, SD 57701   *(605) 342-2751*

Rushmore Shadows Resort (1621)
23680 Busted Five Ct, Rapid City, SD 57702   *(605) 343-4544*

Silver Mountain Cabins (1622)
13350 Silver Mtn Rd, Rapid City, SD 57702   *(605) 342-2246*

Spur Campground (1623)
2305 Elk Creek Rd, Piedmont, SD 57769   *(605) 787-6082*

Tee Pee Campground (1624)
2200 Fort Hayes Road, Rapid City, SD 57702   *(605) 343-6319*

Three Flags RV Park (1625)
9484 Three Flags Ln, Black Hawk, SD 57718   *(605) 787-7898*

Tilford Gulch Campground (1626)
13157 Deer Meadow Rd, Piedmont, SD 57769   *(605) 787-5573*

Whispering Pines (1627)
22700 Silver City Rd, Rapid City, SD 57702   *(605) 341-3667*

Whispering Wind Campground (1628)
12720 S Highway 16, Rapid City, SD 57702   *(605) 574-9533*

Cabela's (1629) reportedly allows customers with RVs to park overnight with no hookups, but provides potable water and a dump station. Call for details.
3231 E Mall Dr., Rapid City, SD 57701   *(605) 388-5600*

Where To Eat – Rapid City

- **Family Dining**
- **Pizza**
- **Fast Food**
- **Ethnic Restaurants**
- **Coffee, Sandwiches and Deli**
- **Bars, Grills, Pubs & Steakhouses**
- **Desserts & Treats**
- **Fraternal Organizations**

Family Dining

Cambell Street Café (1652)
211 N Cambell St　　Rapid City 57701　　(605) 348-5344

Colonial House Restaurant (1653)
2315 Mt. Rushmore Rd　　Rapid City 57701　　(605) 342-4640

Connie's Place (1654)
8000 Black Hawk Rd　　Black Hawk 57718　　(605) 716-7002

Country Corner (1655)
15000 Sturgis Rd　　Piedmont 57769　　(605) 787-5758

Denny's (1656)
2206 N LaCrosse　　Rapid City 57701　　(605) 716-7272

Dickey's Barbecue (1657)
1565 Haines Ave　　Rapid City 57701　　(605) 791-5400

Fairmont Diner (1658)
402 East Fairmont Blvd　　Rapid City 57701　　(605) 791-4151

Famous Dave's (1659)
1718 Eglin St　　Rapid City 57701　　(605) 341-2115

Firehouse Brewing Company (1660)
610 Main St　　Rapid City 57701　　(605) 348-1915

~Family Dining~

Five Guys Burgers (1661)
1329 Eglin   *Rapid City 57701*   *(605) 342-4897*

Flying J Buffet, Exit 61 (1662)
4200 N I-90 Service Rd   *Rapid City 57701*   *(605) 342-5450*

Fort Hays Chuckwagon (1663)
2255 Fort Hayes Rd   *Rapid City 57702*   *(605) 394-9653*

Fuddruckers at Rushmore Mall (1664)
2200 N Maple Ave   *Rapid City 57701*   *(605) 348-9990*

Garden Bar & Grill at the Hilton (1665)
815 E Mall Dr.   *Rapid City 57701*   *(605) 791-9000*

IHOP (1666)
550 Disk Dr.   *Rapid City 57701*   *(605) 341-4467*

Kōl (1667)
504 Mt. Rushmore Rd.   *Rapid City 57701*   *(605) 791-1600*

Marlin's Roadhouse Grill (1668)
2803 Deadwood Ave   *Rapid City 57702*   *(605) 342-9456*

Millstone Family Restaurant (1669)
1520 N Lacrosse St   *Rapid City 57701*   *(605) 348-9022*

Millstone Family Restaurant (1670)
2010 W Main St   *Rapid City 57702*   *(605) 343-5824*

Morningside Café (1671)
710 N Lacrosse St   *Rapid City 57701*   *(605) 348-2233*

Perkins Restaurant & Bakery (1672)
1715 N Lacrosse St   *Rapid City 57701*   *(605) 341-3810*

Perkins Restaurant & Bakery (1673)
2305 Mount Rushmore   *Rapid City 57701*   *(605) 341-5225*

Perkins Restaurant & Bakery (1674)
1300 North Elk Vale Rd   *Rapid City 57703*   *(605) 348-4301*

Philly Ted's Cheesesteak & Pizza (1675)
1415 N Lacrosse St   *Rapid City 57701*   *(605) 348-6113*

Red Lobster (1676)
120 Disk Dr.   *Rapid City 57701*   *(605) 348-9717*

~Family Dining~

Ron's Café (1677)
2332 W Main St *Rapid City 57702* *(605) 791-2484*

Ruby Tuesday (1678)
821 Fairmont Blvd *Rapid City 57701* *(605) 343-1700*

Sandwich Shop (1679)
201 Main St *Rapid City 57701* *(605) 791-2939*

Historic Freighthouse (1680)
306 Seventh St. *Rapid City 57701* *(605) 721-1463*

Tally's Silver Spoon (1681)
530 Sixth St. *Rapid City 57701* *(605) 342-7621*

TGI Friday's (1682)
2205 N Lacrosse St *Rapid City 57701* *(605) 343-8443*

Z'Mariks Noodle Café (1683)
2335 W Main St *Rapid City 57702* *(605) 721-3333*

Pizza

Blaze Pizza (1700)
1325 Eglin St *Rapid City 57701* *(605) 348-2101*

Chuck E. Cheese – it's a kids' place **(1701)**
30 Knollwood Dr. *Rapid City 57701* *(605) 341-6193*

Domino's Pizza (1702)
128 E North St *Rapid City 57701* *(605) 341-2401*

Domino's Pizza (1703)
5509 Bendy Drive *Rapid City 57702* *(605) 791-5411*

Domino's Pizza (1704)
219 Main Gate Rd *Box Elder 57719* *(605) 923-1491*

Independent Ale House (1705)
625 St Joseph Street *Rapid City 57701* *(605) 718-9492*

Lintz Bros. Pizza (1706)
811 E Disk Dr. *Rapid City 57701* *(605) 791-3773*

Little Caesars (1707)
1601 Mount Rushmore Rd *Rapid City 57701* *(605) 341-0808*

~Pizza~

Little Caesars (1708)
    2120 W Main St   *Rapid City 57701*   *(605) 342-2120*

Little Caesars (1709)
    685 N Lacrosse St   *Rapid City 57701*   *(605) 399-1040*

Marco's Pizza (1710)
    3625 Jackson Blvd   *Rapid City 57702*   *(605) 791-4949*

Marco's Pizza (1711)
    4040 Cheyenne Blvd   *Rapid City 57703*   *(605) 791-4744*

Papa John's (1712)
    1011 Mount Rushmore Rd,   *Rapid City 57701*   *(605) 388-9999*

Papa John's (1713)
    1520 Haines Ave   *Rapid City 57701*   *(605) 348-7272*

Papa Murphy's Take 'N' Bake Pizza (1714)
    606 E North St   *Rapid City 57701*   *(605) 341-3252*

Papa Murphy's Take 'N' Bake Pizza (1715)
    741 Mountain View Rd   *Rapid City 57702*   *(605) 341-7979*

Pauly's Pizzeria & Sub Co. (1716)
    1624 E. St. Patrick   *Rapid City 57703*   *(605) 348-7827*

Peppy's Pizza Arcade & Lazer (1717)
    937 E North St   *Rapid City 57701*   *(605) 399-1494*

Piesano's Pacchia (1718)
    3618 Canyon Lake Dr.   *Rapid City 57702*   *(605) 341-6941*

Pizza Hut (1719)
    1402 E Saint Patrick St   *Rapid City 57701*   *(605) 342-4200*

Pizza Hut (1720)
    2005 Mount Rushmore Rd   *Rapid City 57701*   *(605) 342-1542*

Pizza Ranch (1721)
    1556 Luna Ave   *Rapid City 57701*   *(605) 348-9114*

Pizza Ranch (1722)
    405 E Stumer Rd   *Rapid City 57701*   *(605) 791-5255*

Rodaro's Pizza & More (1723)
    2200 N Maple Ave   *Rapid City 57701*   *(605) 348-1456*

Fast Food

A&W (1750)
501 Deadwood Ave.   *Rapid City 57702*   *(605) 388-0588*

Arby's (1751)
2400 Mount Rushmore Rd   *Rapid City 57701*   *(605) 348-8605*

Arby's (1752)
1620 Cambell St   *Rapid City 57701*   *(605) 341-3811*

Arby's (1753)
326 East Stumer   *Rapid City 57701*   *(605) 342-0848*

Arby's (1754)
2410 W Main St   *Rapid City 57702*   *(605) 341-2049*

Arby's (1755)
3920 Cheyenne Blvd   *Rapid City 57703*   *(605) 342-8370*

Armadillo's Ice Cream Shoppe (1756)
202 Main Street   *Rapid City 57701*   *(605) 355-0507*

Burger King (1757)
2110 N Lacrosse St   *Rapid City 57701*   *(605) 348-2448*

Burger King (1758)
1002 E North St   *Rapid City 57701*   *(605) 348-2450*

Burger King (1759)
711 Jackson Blvd   *Rapid City 57702*   *(605) 341-5777*

Culver's (1760)
1015 Eglin St   *Rapid City 57701*   *(605) 718-8665*

Culver's (1761)
2121 W Main St   *Rapid City 57702*   *(605) 348-6218*

Dairy Queen (1762)
1601 Campbell St   *Rapid City 57701*   *(605) 343-6142*

Dairy Queen (1763)
1702 Mt Rushmore Rd   *Rapid City 57701*   *(605) 342-4874*

Dairy Queen (1764)
2200 N Maple Ave   *Rapid City 57701*   *(605) 348-3186*

~Fast Food~

Dairy Queen (1765)
    5224 Ridgeview Rd   *Rapid City 57701*   *(605) 673-5556*

Dairy Queen (1766)
    3535 Canyon Lake Dr.   *Rapid City 57702*   *(605) 343-9282*

Dairy Queen (1767)
    504 N Ellsworth Rd   *Box Elder 57719*   *(605) 923-9700*

Hardee's (1768)
    604 5th St   *Rapid City 57701*   *(605) 348-5692*

Hardee's (1769)
    2250 Haines Ave   *Rapid City 57701*   *(605) 341-3056*

Hardee's (1770)
    1001 E North St   *Rapid City 57701*   *(605) 342-6864*

Hardee's (1771)
    679 Reagan Ave   *Box Elder 57719*   *(605) 923-4306*

Jimmy John's (1772)
    36 Stumer Rd   *Rapid City 57701*   *(605) 791-5646*

Jimmy John's (1773)
    1565 Haines Ave   *Rapid City 57701*   *(605) 718-2210*

Jimmy John's (1774)
    615 Mountain View Rd,   *Rapid City 57702*   *(605) 718-0600*

KFC (1775)
    515 Mountain View Rd   *Rapid City 57702*   *(605) 342-1515*

KFC/Long John Silver's (1776)
    817 E North   *Rapid City 57701*   *(605) 342-2515*

McDonald's (1777)
    720 Cleveland St   *Rapid City 57701*   *(605) 343-6984*

McDonald's (1778)
    804 E North St   *Rapid City 57701*   *(605) 342-3772*

McDonald's (1779)
    1200 N Lacrosse St   *Rapid City 57701*   *(605) 342-5442*

McDonald's (1780)
    2223 W Main St   *Rapid City 57702*   *(605) 342-3483*

~Fast Food~

McDonald's (1781)
    3919 Cheyenne Blvd   *Rapid City 57703*   *(605) 923-5951*

Pita Pit (1782)
    725 Main St   *Rapid City 57701*   *(605) 718-7482*

Popeye's Louisiana Kitchen (1783)
    1323 E North St   *Rapid City 57701*   *(605) 791-5444*

Sonic Drive-In (1784)
    2316 Mount Rushmore Rd   *Rapid City 57701*   *(605) 716-3663*

Sonic Drive-In (1785)
    815 Jackson Blvd   *Rapid City 57702*   *(605) 716-3668*

Subway (1786)
    800 Mountain View Rd   *Rapid City 57701*   *(605) 342-7827*

Subway (1787)
    532 E Anamosa St   *Rapid City 57701*   *(605) 343-4256*

Subway (1788)
    918 E North St   *Rapid City 57701*   *(605) 342-2847*

Subway (1789)
    2415 Mount Rushmore Rd   *Rapid City 57701*   *(605) 341-0387*

Subway at the Pilot Truck-stop (1790)
    2783 Deadwood Ave   *Rapid City 57702*   *(605) 348-7070*

Subway - Rushmore Mall (1791)
    2200 North Maple Avenue   *Rapid City 57701*   *(605) 348-2847*

Taco Bell (1792)
    902 E North St   *Rapid City 57701*   *(605) 341-7564*

Taco Bell (1793)
    2700 Mount Rushmore Rd   *Rapid City 57701*   *(605) 388-0212*

Taco Bell (1794)
    2323 W Main St   *Rapid City 57702*   *(605) 341-5202*

Taco Bell (1803)
    1024 Endeavour Blvd   *Rapid City 57703*   *(605) 341-7808*

Taco John's (1795)
    1828 Haines Ave   *Rapid City 57701*   *(605) 343-3119*

~Fast Food~

Taco John's (1796)
    1710 Cambell St   *Rapid City 57701*   *(605) 343-6778*

Taco John's (1797)
    3020 W Main St   *Rapid City 57701*   *(605) 343-6432*

Taco John's - Rushmore Mall (1798)
    2200 N Maple Ave   *Rapid City 57701*   *(605) 342-6996*

Wendy's (1799)
    701 E North St   *Rapid City 57701*   *(605) 342-3142*

Wendy's (1800)
    751 Cathedral Dr.   *Rapid City 57701*   *(605) 343-8557*

Wendy's (1801)
    1911 Haines Ave   *Rapid City 57701*   *(605) 342-9410*

Wendy's (1802)
    520 Mountain View Rd   *Rapid City 57702*   *(605) 348-8549*

Ethnic Restaurants

Baan Thai (1851)
    114 Box Elder Rd W   *Box Elder 57719*   *(605) 791-5130*

Botticelli Ristorante Italiano (1852)
    523 Main Street   *Rapid City 57701*   *(605) 348-0089*

China Luck (1853)
    740 Mountain View Rd   *Rapid City 57702*   *(605) 399-1859*

China Pantry in Rushmore Mall (1854)
    2200 N Maple Ave   *Rapid City 57701*   *(605) 737-0888*

China Wok (1855)
    1575 N Lacrosse St   *Rapid City 57701*   *(605) 716-9965*

Ciao! Italian Eatery (1856)
    512 Main St. Ste. 130   *Rapid City 57701*   *(605) 716-4323*

Coco Palace (1857)
    1900 N Maple Ave   *Rapid City 57701*   *(605) 718-2678*

Curry Masala (1858)
  510 St. Joseph Street   *Rapid City 57701*   *(605) 716-7783*

El Mariachi Mexican Restaurant (1859)
  1012 E. North St   *Rapid City 57701*   *(605) 791-4788*

Everest Cuisine (1860)
  2328 West Main St   *Rapid City 57702*   *(605) 343-4444*

Fuji Japanese Steakhouse & Sushi Bar (1861)
  1731 Eglin St   *Rapid City 57701*   *(605) 721-8886*

Fuji Sushi & Sake Bar, Rushmore Mall (1862)
  2200 N Maple Ave   *Rapid City 57701*   *(605) 343-1819*

Golden Corral (1863)
  1180 N Lacrosse St   *Rapid City 57701*   *(605) 399-2195*

Golden Fortune Restaurant (1864)
  1118 E North St   *Rapid City 57701*   *(605) 343-3496*

Golden Phoenix (1865)
  2421 W Main   *Rapid City 57702*   *(605) 348-4195*

Great Wall Chinese Restaurant (1866)
  315 E North St   *Rapid City 57701*   *(605) 348-1060*

Gyro Hub (1867)
  1301 W. Omaha St.   *Rapid City 57701*   *(605) 348-2877*

Hana Korean Grill & Sushi Bar (1869)
  3550 Sturgis Rd   *Rapid City 57702*   *(605) 348-0299*

Hong Kong Buffet (1870)
  927 E North St   *Rapid City 57701*   *(605) 716-4664*

Huhot Mongolian Grill (1871)
  1745 Eglin St   *Rapid City 57701*   *(605) 791-5555*

Hunan Chinese Restaurant (1872)
  1720 Mt. Rushmore Rd   *Rapid City 57701*   *(605) 341-3888*

Ichiban (1873)
  1109 W Omaha St   *Rapid City 57701*   *(605) 341-7178*

Imperial Chinese Restaurant (1874)
  702 E North St   *Rapid City 57701*   *(605) 394-8888*

Ixtapa Mexican Restaurant (1875)
603 Omaha St   Rapid City 57701   (605) 343-3585

Kang San (1876)
520 N Ellsworth Rd   Box Elder 57719   (605) 923-9993

Kathmandu Bistro (1877)
727 Main St   Rapid City 57701   (605) 343-5070

Mongolian Grill (1878)
1415 N Lacrosse St   Rapid City 57701   (605) 388-3187

Olive Garden (1879)
160 Disk D   Rapid City 57701   (605) 348-4640

On the Border (1880)
1331 E North St   Rapid City 57701   (605) 791-5791

Pacific Rim Café (1881)
1375 N Lacrosse St   Rapid City 57701   (605) 791-4148

Panchero's Mexican Grill (1882)
1221 W Omaha St   Rapid City 57701   (605) 718-2251

Qdoba Mexican Grill (1883)
1745 Eglin St   Rapid City 57701   (605) 791-1555

Qdoba Mexican Grill (1884)
741 Mountain View Rd   Rapid City 57702   (605) 341-9900

Qué Pasa (1885)
502 Main St   Rapid City 57701   (605) 716-9800

Sabor A Mexico (1886)
208 E North St   Rapid City 57701   (605) 343-1581

Saigon Restaurant (1887)
221 E North St   Rapid City 57701   (605) 348-8523

Sumo Japanese Kitchen (1888)
214 E Saint Joseph St   Rapid City 57701   (605) 791-4401

Coffee, Sandwiches & Deli

Alternative Fuel Coffee House (1925)
512 Main St., Suite 110   Rapid City 57701   (605) 791-3791

Black Hills Bagels (1926)
913 Mount Rushmore Rd   Rapid City 57701   (605) 399-1277

Cherry Bean, The (1927)
1576 E. St. Patrick St   Rapid City 57703   (605) 593-3390

Dark Canyon Coffee Co. (1928)
1141 Deadwood Ave.   Rapid City 57702   (605) 394-9090

Dixon Coffee Co. (1929)
915 Omaha St   Rapid City 57701   (605) 939-8958

Dunn Brothers Coffee (1930)
719 Omaha St.   Rapid City 57701   (605) 721-0600

Einstein Bros Bagels at the School of Mines (1931)
501 E Saint Joseph St   Rapid City 57701   (605) 394-1953

Essence of Coffee (1032)
908 Main St   Rapid City 57701   (605) 342-3559

Gizzi's Coffee (1933)
234 Main Gate Rd   Box Elder 57719   (605) 923-1617

Glazed & Dazed/Daylight Donuts (1934)
2120 West Main St   Rapid City 57702   (605) 348-9890

Great Harvest Bread Co. (1935)
721 Omaha St.   Rapid City 57701   (605) 791-5623

Hippo Steve Pastiche (1936)
628 Sixth St.   Rapid City 57701   (605) 389-2503

Jerry's Cakes & Donuts (1937)
109 E Omaha   Rapid City 57701   (605) 341-4814

Perk It Up Downtown (1938)
909 St Joseph St   Rapid City 57701   (605) 545-4538

Pretzel Place - Rushmore Mall (1939)
2200 N Maple   Rapid City 57701   (605) 348-3581

Pure Bean Roasted Coffee (1940)
201 Main St   Rapid City 57701   (605) 716-7894

Rumours (1941)
5509 Bendt Dr.   Rapid City 57702   (605) 791-5558

Smiling Moose Deli Rapid City (1942)
1745 Eglin St   Rapid City 57701   (605) 791-5500

Starbucks at Alex Johnson (1943)
523 Sixth St.   Rapid City 57701   (605) 342-1210

Starbucks (1945)
1734 Eglin St (I-90 Exit 60)   Rapid City 57701   (605) 341-3101

The Depot Deli at Johnson Siding (1944)
12300 West Hwy 44   Rapid City 57702   (605) 342-4803

Bars, Grills, Pubs & Steakhouses

Applebee's (1975)
2160 Haines Ave   Rapid City 57701   (605) 394-0338

Boston's Restaurant & Sports Bar (1976)
620 E Disk Dr.   Rapid City 57701   (605) 348-7200

Brass Rail Lounge (1977)
624 Saint Joseph St   Rapid City 57701   (605) 341-1768

Buffalo Wild Wings (1978)
715 Mountain View Rd   Rapid City 57702   (605) 721-9464

Buffalo Wings and Rings (1979)
5622 Sheridan Lake Rd   Rapid City 57702   (605) 791-9464

Cheers Sports Bar & Casino (1980)
1721 N Lacrosse St   Rapid City 57701   (605) 342-2273

Chili's Grill & Bar (1981)
2125 Haines Ave   Rapid City 57701   (605) 388-8100

Clocktower Lounge (1982)
2525 W Main St   Rapid City 57702   (605) 342-8876

Dakotah Steakhouse (1983)
1325 N Elk Vale Rd   Rapid City 57703   (605) 791-1800

~Bars, Grills, Pubs & Steakhouses~

Delmonico Grill (1984)
    609 Main St.   *Rapid City 57701*   *(605) 791-1664*

Elk Creek Steakhouse & Lounge (1985)
    9408 Elk Creek Rd   *Piedmont   57769*   *(605) 787-6349*

Enigma Restaurant, The (1986)
    445 Mt Rushmore Rd   *Rapid City 57701*   *(605) 348-8300*

Gold Bison Grill, Holiday Inn (1987)
    505 N Fifth Street   *Rapid City 57701*   *(605) 399-7043*

Grill at Rimrock Canyon, The (1988)
    23021 Hisega Rd   *Rapid City 57702*   *(605) 391-8102*

Horse Creek Inn Restaurant (1990)
    23570 Hwy 385   *Rapid City 57702*   *(605) 574-2908*

Joe's Place (1991)
    4302 Pendleton Drive   *Rapid City 57701*   *(605) 394-7716*

Juniper (1992)
    5734 Sheridan Lake Rd   *Rapid City 57702*   *(605) 484-8593*

Kelly's Sports Lounge (1993)
    825 Jackson Blvd   *Rapid City 57702*   *(605) 348-1213*

LongHorn Steakhouse (1994)
    1510 Eglin St   *Rapid City 57701*   *(605) 342-2321*

Minerva's Restaurant and Bar (1995)
    2111 N Lacrosse St   *Rapid City 57701*   *(605) 394-9505*

Murphy's Pub & Grill (1996)
    510 Ninth St.   *Rapid City 57701*   *(605) 791-2244*

Musekamp's at Black Forest Inn (1997)
    23191 Highway 385   *Rapid City 57702*   *(605) 574-2000*

Native Grill and Wings (1998)
    1756 Eglin St   *Rapid City 57703*   *(605) 519-5117*

Oasis Lounge (1999)
    711 Main St   *Rapid City 57701*   *(605) 342-9809*

Outback Steakhouse (2000)
    665 E Disk Dr.   *Rapid City 57701*   *(605) 341-1192*

Paddy O'Neill's Irish Pub at Alex Johnson (2001)
    523 Sixth St.   *Rapid City 57701*   *(605) 342-1210*

Reflect Bistro and Bar at Cambria (2002)
    3333 Outfitter's Rd   *Rapid City 57701*   *(605) 721-7143*

Rimrock Happy Tavern (2003)
    12300 W Highway 44   *Rapid City 57702*   *605-348-9733*

Robbinsdale Lounge (2004)
    803 E Saint Patrick St   *Rapid City 57701*   *(605) 342-7271*

Sacora Station Bar & Grill (2005)
    14200 Sturgis Rd   *Piedmont   57769*   *(605) 787-9797*

Sally O'Mally's Pub and Casino (2006)
    3064 Covington St   *Rapid City 57703*   *(605) 721-8636*

Shipwreck Lee's Bar and Grill (2007)
    9356 Neck Yoke Rd   *Rapid City 57702*   *(605) 341-3515*

Shooters Wood Fire Grill (2008)
    2424 W Main St   *Rapid City 57702*   *(605) 348-3348*

Slash J Saloon (2009)
    105 N 1st St   *Piedmont   57769*   *(605) 787-6940*

Sliders Bar & Grill at WaTiki Waterpark (2010)
    1314 N Elk Vale Rd   *Rapid City 57703*   *(877) 545-2897*

Stonewall's Kitchen (2011)
    5955 S Hwy 16   *Rapid City 57702*   *(605) 342-6100*

Texas Roadhouse (2012)
    2106 N Maple Ave   *Rapid City 57701*   *(605) 341-2901*

Thirsty's (2013)
    819 Main St   *Rapid City 57701*   *(605) 343-3104*

Time Out Lounge (2014)
    615 E North St   *Rapid City 57701*   *(605) 341-9753*

Valley Sports Bar (2015)
    1865 S Valley Drive   *Rapid City 57703*   *(605) 343-2528*

Vertex Sky Bar at Alex Johnson (2016)
    523 Sixth St., Ste. 400   *Rapid City 57701*   *(605) 716-4530*

Wine Cellar Restaurant (2017)
    513 Sixth St.   *Rapid City 57701*   *(605) 718-2675*

Wobbly Bobby British Pub (2018)
    510 Main St   *Rapid City 57701*   *(605) 721-7468*

Desserts & Treats

CherryBerry (2050)
    1520 Haines Ave   *Rapid City 57701*   *(605) 856-5816*

Chubby Chipmunk at Alex Johnson (2051)
    523 6th St.   *Rapid City 57701*   *(605) 348-8515*

Kelly's Frozen Yogurt, BH Chocolates (2052)
    1919 Mount Rushmore Rd   *Rapid City 57701*   *(605) 343-5961*

Orange Julius, Rushmore Mall (2053)
    2200 N Maple Ave   *Rapid City 57701*   *(605) 348-3186*

Rocky Mountain Chocolate Factory (2054)
    507 Sixth St.   *Rapid City 57701*   *(605) 716-4700*

Silver Lining Creamery, The (2055)
    512 Main St., Ste. 100   *Rapid City 57701*   *(605) 791-1141*

Smallcakes (2056)
    1745 Eglin St   *Rapid City 57701*   *(605) 791-5577*

Sugar Sweet Candy Store (2057)
    524 Seventh St.   *Rapid City 57701*   *(605) 721-3252*

Yoyo Berri (2058)
    36 Stumer Rd   *Rapid City 57701*   *(605) 388-5546*

Zoom Soda & Candy (2059)
    515 Main St.   *Rapid City 57701*   *(605) 718-2693*

Fraternal Organizations

Eagle's Lodge (2075)
1410 East Centre Street   *Rapid City 57703*   *(605) 343-2321*

Loyal Order of Moose Lodges (2076)
841 E Saint Patrick St   *Rapid City 57701*   *(605) 342-2760*

Rapid City Elks Lodge No 1187 (2077)
3333 Jolly Lane   *Rapid City 57703*   *(605) 393-1187*

VFW Post 1273 (2078)
420 Main St.   *Rapid City 57701*   *(605) 342-9804*

Where To Shop – Rapid City

There are several major shopping areas in the Rapid City metro area, among which are…
- *The historic downtown*
- *The Rushmore Mall (rushmoremall.com)*
- *Rushmore Crossing (shoprushmorecrossing.com).*

In addition, some gift/souvenir stores are listed below…

Alex Johnson Mercantile (2100)
    608 St. Joseph St.   *Rapid City 57701*   *(605) 343-2383*
Badlands Trading Post (2101)
    21290 Hwy 240   *Philip 57567*   *(605) 433-5411*
BW Ramkota Gift Shop (2102)
    2111 N LaCrosse St   *Rapid City 57701*   *(605) 343-8550*
Dakota's Best (2103)
    818 Main St   *Rapid City 57701*   *(605) 355-0900*
Gold Diggers (2104)
    2017 Mount Rushmore Rd   *Rapid City 57701*   *(605) 341-9655*
Mitzi's Books (2105)
    510 Main St   *Rapid City 57701*   *(605) 721-2665*
Perfect Hanging Gallery (2106)
    512 Main St   *Rapid City 57701*   *(605) 348-7761*
Prairie Edge (2107)
    606 Main Street   *Rapid City 57701*   *(605) 342-3086*
Prairie Harvest Mercantile and Gifts (2108)
    14603 Sturgis Rd   *Piedmont 57769*   *(605) 791-5445*
Reflections Fine Art Gallery (2109)
    605 Main St   *Rapid City 57701*   *(605) 341-3234*
Roam'n Around (2110)
    512 Main   *Rapid City 57701*   *(605) 716-1660*
Shaviq Studio & Gallery (2111)
    626 Saint Joseph St   *Rapid City 57701*   *(605) 394-0020*
The Weathered Vane (2112)
    2255 Haines Ave   *Rapid City 57701*   *(605) 348-8154*
Vita Sana Olive Oil Company (2113)
    627 St. Joseph St   *Rapid City 57701*   *(605) 721-6555*

The Black Hills Visitor Information Center,
located at I-90 Exit 61, also has a really nice gift/souvenir/book shop.
1851 Discovery Circle, Rapid City SD 57701 - (605) 355-3700
blackhillsbadlands.com/business/black-hills-visitor-information-center

Lakota Culture

Interpretive Centers, Sites & Museums

Akta Lakota Museum & Cultural Center (2150)

Located at the St. Joseph's Indian School in Chamberlain on the banks of the Missouri River, the Center tells the unique history of the Northern Plains tribes as no other museum can. It's an opportunity to connect personally with the culture and traditions of the Lakota, Dakota and Nakota people through exhibits and programs. Expect to be profoundly changed and as you discover something new about the tribes and their rich history, culture and traditions. Admission is free, a donation of $5 per person or $15 per family is suggested. 8 – 6 M – S and 9-5 Sunday during the summer, 8 – 5 M – F in winter. Guided tours are available, there is a museum gift shop, and you can spend a reflective few minutes in the outdoor Medicine Wheel Garden overlooking the river.
aktalakota.stjo.org   *1301 N Main St, Chamberlain SD 57325*   *(800) 798-3452*

Buechel Memorial Lakota Museum (2151)

Open Memorial Day through Labor Day (call for hours), the collection "demonstrates the Mission's enduring respect for the traditions, culture, and history of the Lakota of the Rosebud Reservation. Named after Father Eugene Buechel, S.J., a noted missionary, linguist, and ethnologist who came to St. Francis Mission in 1902, the museum contains many unique artifacts, images, and documents. [It] is an important resource for historians, ethnographers, anthropologists, and artists. Today there are over two thousand items in the ethnographic collection, as well as an extensive photographic collection that exceeds 42,000 items." Articles for purchase in the Museum Gift Shop are made locally by the Lakota people. The local vendors, in negotiation with the museum director, receive a fair price for their work. Profits from the gift shop support the work of preserving and displaying Lakota artifacts.
From I-90 at Murdo go south on Hwy 83 through White River to Hwy 18. Take a right and go past Lakeview Road to Rosebud Road (Hwy 1). Go through the town of Rosebud, past two Strike to St. Francis.
groups.creighton.edu/sfmission/museum   350 S Oak, Saint Francis SD 57572   (605) 747-2745

Vore Buffalo Jump (1383)

This is one of the most important archaeological sites of the late-prehistoric plains Indians. Discovered during the construction of Highway I-90 in the early 1970s, the site is a natural sinkhole that was used as a bison trap from about 1500 to 1800 A.D. Buffalo were driven over the edge as a method for the tribes to procure large quantities of meat and hides needed to survive harsh prairie winters. It was placed on the National Register of Historic Places in 1973.
vorebuffalojump.org   I-90 frontage road between Exits 199 and 205   (307) 266-9530

Buffalo Interpretive Center (2152)

This facility is located 7 miles East of Fort Pierre on Hwy 1806, on the western edge of a large pasture. It is oriented so that the tribe's buffalo (American bison) graze in close viewing range. Call ahead to confirm that the center is open, as staff sometimes have to attend to other herd-related tasks. In the building, exhibits illustrate the importance of the buffalo to Native Americans, while large windows look out on the herd and some magnificent landscape. The Lower Brule Sioux Tribe has three bison pastures (units); the Buffalo Center overlooks the Cherry Ranch unit. The Tribe maintains a herd of 300 bison on 6200 acres, and members of the Tribe operate the Interpretive Center. Items in the gift shop are made by Native American artisans. The exhibits include tools and toys made from bison, and kids are encouraged to touch. Admission is free, donations welcome.

lbst.org   *29349 Hwy 1806, Fort Pierre SD 57532*   *(605) 223-2260*

Heritage Center of Red Cloud Indian School (2153)

"One of the earliest cultural centers and museums located on an Indian reservation in the United States (it's on the Pine Ridge), the Heritage Center represents the rich and storied heritage of North America's Native community and the skill and creativity that remain mainstays of the local Lakota and other Native American cultures. We take special pride in our work to strengthen cultural pride and celebrate, as well as preserve, the local Lakota culture and artistic tradition. We are more than just a museum or art gallery. We are also an economic engine on the Pine Ridge Reservation. With rates of up to 80 percent unemployment here, the Lakota community faces challenging economic and social conditions in southwestern South Dakota. Through the Center's renowned gift shop and online store, our local artists are empowered to increase their own economic self-sufficiency by making their incredible work available to a wider community… and in doing so, preserve their skills and extend appreciation for their artistry to all corners of the globe."

The Heritage Center collection began with the purchase of three prize-winning pieces from the Red Cloud Indian Art Show in 1969, and has grown today to include nearly 10,000 pieces of Native American contemporary and historical Lakota art (all recently catalogued thanks to generous funding from the Institute for Museum and Library Services and the Bush Foundation). The collection includes paintings, textiles, traditional art, historical items, pottery and sculpture, as well as a library and historical archives. To get there, take Hwy 40 south from Hermosa, or Hwy 18 south from Hot Springs. It's about an hour from either town, and absolutely worth it. Call for hours.

redcloudschool.org   *100 Mission Dr., Pine Ridge SD 57770*   *(605) 867-5888*

Oglala Lakota College Historical Center (2154)

Located within the Pine Ridge Indian Reservation of the Oglala Lakota, this is an impressive endeavor. "As you walk through the historical center, you will hear, see and feel the history of the Oglala Lakota people. See historical photographs and artwork displays that chronicle the history of the Oglala Lakota from the early 1800s to the Wounded Knee Massacre in 1890. An audiotape of this history provides greater meaning to the displays that you will see. The Oglala Lakota College Historical Center honors the struggles of those who have come before us and have lost their lives to protect the Lakota way of life. The college hopes that your visit to the Historical Center will result in a better understanding of Native American people."

The Center is located on the campus of Oglala Lakota College, which is chartered by the Oglala Sioux Tribe. The college's mission is to provide educational opportunities that enhance Lakota life, including community services, certificates, GEDs, associate, bachelor, and graduate degrees. The Center is open Monday through Saturday 9-5 from June through August. The Lakota name for Kyle, phežúta ȟaká, translates as 'Branched Medicine'. The town's population is about 900, but combined enrollment in the Little Wound Schools (elementary, middle, and high) usually exceeds that number. The Reservation is vast, but resources are very scarce. About 30 minutes southwest of Kyle is Wounded Knee, where a mass grave contains the remains of 146 Native Americans who were killed by U.S. soldiers on Dec. 29, 1890. Estimates are that about 300 Native people lost their lives that day. There is a small museum there: call (605) 407-0243 or (605) 867-5684 for more info, or visit facebook.com/themuseumatwoundedknee. A visit to the gravesite is a profound experience.

olc.edu/about/historical_center.htm   490 Piya Wiconi Rd, Kyle SD 57752   (605) 455-6000

Bear Butte
State Park (605)

This unique mountain is seen by many Native Americans as a place where the

Creator has chosen to communicate with them through visions and prayer. If you visit the park and/or hike to the summit (just under two miles), you'll notice colorful pieces of cloth and small bundles or pouches hanging from trees. These prayer cloths and tobacco ties represent prayers offered by individuals during their worship. Please respect these and leave them undisturbed.

The mountain is an igneous (fire, as in volcano) eruption. The Bear Butte Education Center highlights the mountain's geology, history and the cultural beliefs of the Northern Plains Indians. An on-site interpreter is available during the summer months. Across the highway, there is a fishing lake with crappies and northern pike that has a dock, a campground, a horse camp and a picnic shelter. A bison herd roams the base of the butte, and visitors should not get close as these are dangerous wild animals. Alcohol is illegal in the park, as are uncased firearms and bows. Bear Butte was added to the National Register of Historic Places in 1973. Daily fees are $4 per person or $6 per vehicle, or a SD State Park sticker. Campsites (23 of them) are non-electric and run $11 ($13 for horse sites).

gfp.sd.gov/state-parks/directory/bear-butte   20250 Hwy 79 N   (605) 347-5240

Wounded Knee Museum, Wall (2155)

This is a major cultural asset that will, unfortunately, be closed for the 2016 season. After a fire in September 2012, the exhibits were reconstructed and displayed at a temporary location, but will be returning to their original location in Wall with an expected opening date of May 2017. The museum will be expanding its displays and exhibits. It originally opened in 2003, with the purpose of sharing the events leading to the massacre at Wounded Knee in 1890.

woundedkneemuseum.org   *600 Main St, Wall SD 57790*   *(605) 279-2573*

Appendices

Appendix 1:
Museums in and around the Black Hills

Tri-State Museum (001)	Belle Fourche
South Dakota Air and Space Museum	Box Elder
Buffalo Historical Museum	Buffalo
Akta Lakota Museum	Chamberlain
Crazy Horse Memorial	Crazy Horse
National Museum of Woodcarving	Custer
1881 Courthouse Museum	Custer
Custer State Park	Custer
Four Mile Old West Town	Custer
Days of '76 Museum (120)	Deadwood
Historic Adams House (121)	Deadwood
Adams Museum (121)	Deadwood
Celebrity Hotel Memorabilia Display (145)	Deadwood
Trails, Trains & Pioneers Museum	Edgemont
Buffalo Interpretive Center	Fort Pierre
Casey Tibbs South Dakota Rodeo Center	Fort Pierre
Hermosa Arts and History Museum	Hermosa
Civilian Conservation Corps Museum of South Dakota	Hill City
Wade's Gold Mill	Hill City
Black Hills Museum of Natural History	Hill City
South Dakota State Railroad Museum	Hill City
Pioneer Historical Museum of South Dakota	Hot Springs
Mammoth Site of Hot Springs	Hot Springs
Wind Cave National Park	Hot Springs
Badlands National Park	Interior
Minuteman Missile National Historic Site	Jackson County
Badlands Petrified Garden	Kadoka
Mount Rushmore	Keystone

Borglum Historical Center	Keystone
Keystone Historical Museum	Keystone
Big Thunder Gold Mine	Keystone
National Presidential Wax Museum	Keystone
Oglala Lakota College Historical Center	Kyle
Black Hills Mining Museum (341)	Lead
Grand River Museum	Lemmon
Petrified Wood Park	Lemmon
Major James McLaughlin Heritage Center	McLaughlin
Pioneer Auto Show	Murdo
South Dakota's Original 1880 Town	Murdo
Newell Museum	Newell
Heritage Center of Red Cloud Indian School	Pine Ridge
Dahl Arts Center	Rapid City
South Dakota School of Mines APEX Gallery	Rapid City
Chapel in the Hills	Rapid City
Journey Museum and Gardens	Rapid City
Museum of Geology	Rapid City
High Plains Western Heritage Center	Spearfish
D.C. Booth Historic National Fish Hatchery	Spearfish
Buechel Memorial Lakota Museum	St. Francis
Fort Meade Museum	Sturgis
Sturgis Motorcycle Museum & Hall of Fame	Sturgis
Wounded Knee Museum	Wall
Armed Forces Military Display and Gifts	Wasta

Appendix 2:
ZIP CODES in the Black Hills

Belle Fourche	57717
Box Elder	57719
Custer	57730
Deadwood	57732
Devils Tower	82714
Ellsworth AFB	57706
Hill City	57745
Hot Springs	57747
Keystone	57751
Lead	57754
Moorcroft	82721
Newcastle	82701, 82715
Rapid City	57701, 57702, 57703
Spearfish	57783
Sturgis	57785
Sundance	82729

Appendix 3:
Airfields in the Black Hills

Belle Fourche Municipal Airport	airnav.com/airport/KEFC	(605) 892-6345
Clyde Ice Field, Spearfish	airnav.com/airport/KSPF	(605) 642-4112
Ellsworth Air Force Base	airnav.com/airport/KRCA	(605) 385-1000
Rapid City Regional Airport	airnav.com/airport/KRAP	(605) 394-4195
Hulett Municipal Airport	hulett.org/Airport.htm	(307) 467-5771

Appendix 4:
Art Galleries in the Black Hills

Elk Park Antiques & Art	12140 Upper Elk Pk. Rd	Custer	(605) 673-3365
Annie's Emporium	325 Mt Rushmore Rd	Custer	(605) 673-5600
Art Expressions	36 South 6th St	Custer	(605) 673-3467
A Walk in the Woods	506 Mt Rushmore Rd	Custer	(605) 673-6400
American West Gallery	134 Sherman St	Deadwood	(605) 571-0105
Black Hills Bronze	23942 Thompson Dr.	Hill City	(605) 574-3200
Warrior's Work	277 Main St	Hill City	(605) 574-4954
ArtForms Gallery	280 Main St	Hill City	(605) 574-4894
Hill City Mercantile	227 Main St	Hill City	(605) 574-2001
Jon Crane Gallery	256 Main St	Hill City	(605) 574-4440
Sandy Swallow Gallery	280 Main Street	Hill City	(605) 574-9505
Dakota Nature & Art	216 Main Street	Hill City	(605) 574-2868
Shaman Gallery	405 North River St	Hot Springs	(605) 745-6602
Blue Horn Gallery	631 North River St	Hot Springs	(605) 745-3717
Prairie Edge	606 Main St	Rapid City	(605) 342-3086
Dahl Arts Center	713 7th St	Rapid City	(605) 394-4101
Flat Earth Studio	3123 E Fairgrounds	Spearfish	(605) 642-5794
Matthews Art Center	612 Main St	Spearfish	(605) 642-7973
Termesphere Gallery	1920 Christensen Dr.	Spearfish	(605) 642-4805
West River Studio	611 Main St	Spearfish	(605) 559-2787

Appendix 5:
Lakes in the Black Hills

Fishing regulations can be a bit confusing for locals, let alone visitors. The following two links should be able to answer all your questions about limits and licenses…

- **Dakota Angler & Outfitter**
  flyfishsd.com/black-hills-fishing   *513 7th St., Rapid City SD 57701*   *(605) 341-2450*

- **South Dakota Game, Fish & Parks**
  gfp.sd.gov   *4130 Adventure Trail, Rapid City, SD 57702*   *(605) 394-2391*

Angostura	10 miles southeast of Hot Springs, off U.S. 385-18.
Bear Butte	6 miles NE of Sturgis off SD 79.
Belle Fourche Reservoir	8 miles E of Belle Fourche off SD 212.
Bismarck Lake	5 miles east of Custer on Hwy 16A.
Center Lake	9 miles east of Custer off Hwy 87 North.
Cold Brook Reservoir	1 mile north of Hot Springs.
Cottonwood Springs Lake	5 miles west of Hot Springs just off Highway 18.
Dalton Lake	From Nemo, go north on FSR 26 for 4 miles, and then east on FSR 224 for 5 miles.
Horsethief Lake	From Hill City, go 3 miles south on Hwy 16/385 and then left on Rt. 244 for 6 miles.
Iron Creek Lake	From I-90 Exit 8 in Spearfish, go south 13 miles on McGuigan, which becomes Tinton Rd (gravel), then right on Beaver Creek Rd ½ mile, then left.
Legion Lake	8 miles east of Custer on 16A.
Major Lake	Small lake in Hill City – fishing and osprey watching.
Mirror Lakes	I-90 Exit 2 west of Spearfish (home to McNenny Hatchery).
Pactola Reservoir	14 miles north of Hill City on Hwy 385.
Roubaix Lake	16 miles south of Deadwood on Hwy 385.
Sheridan Lake	8 miles northeast of Hill City on Hwy 385.
Stockade Lake	4 miles east of Custer on Hwy 16A.
Sylvan Lake	7 miles north of Custer on Hwy 89.

Appendix 6:
Radio Stations in the Black Hills

KBHU	89.1 FM	Spearfish	Alternative
KZMX	580 AM	Hot Springs	Classic country
KRKI	99.5 FM	Keystone	Classic country
KIMM	1150 AM	Rapid City	Classic country
KQRQ	92.3 FM	Rapid City	Classic hits
KKLS	920 AM	Rapid City	Classic hits (80s)
KVAR	93.7 FM	Pine Ridge	Classic rock
KVKR	88.7 FM	Pine Ridge	Classic rock
KFXS	100.3 FM	Rapid City	Classic rock
KZZI	95.9 FM	Belle Fourche	Country
KZMX	96.7 FM	Hot Springs	Country
KMLO	100.7 FM	Lowry	Country
KIQK	104.1 FM	Rapid City	Country
KOUT	98.7 FM	Rapid City	Country
KJKT	90.7 FM	Spearfish	Edu: Black Hills State University
KTEQ	91.3 FM	Rapid City	Edu: SD School of Mines & Tech.
KILI	90.1 FM	Porcupine	Ethnic: Lakota
KOYA	88.1 FM	Rosebud	Ethnic: Rosebud Sioux Tribe
KXMZ	102.7 FM	Box Elder	Hot adult contemporary
KKMK	93.9 FM	Rapid City	Hot adult contemporary
KBFS	1450 AM	Belle Fourche	News Talk Information
KOTA	1380 AM	Rapid City	News Talk Information
KBHB	810 AM	Sturgis	News Talk Information
KFMH	101.9 FM	Belle Fourche	Oldies
KDSJ	980 AM	Deadwood	Oldies
KRCS	93.1 FM	Sturgis	Pop contemporary hit radio
KPSD	97.1 FM	Faith	Public radio
KQSD	91.9 FM	Lowry	Public radio
KZSD	102.5 FM	Martin	Public radio
KBHE	89.3 FM	Rapid City	Public radio
KYSD	91.9 FM	Spearfish	Public radio
KWRC	90.9 FM	Hermosa	Religious
KASD	90.3 FM	Rapid City	Religious
KTPT	97.9 FM	Rapid City	Religious
KSLT	107.1 FM	Spearfish	Religious
KLMP	88.3 FM	Rapid City	Religious
KJFP	92.7 FM	Hot Springs	Religious
KFND	97.1 FM	Rapid City	Religious
KJRC	89.9 FM	Rapid City	Religious
KDDX	101.1 FM	Spearfish	Rock
KZLK	106.3 FM	Rapid City	Rock
KSQY	95.1 FM	Deadwood	Rock
KTOQ	1340 AM	Rapid City	Sports
KLND	89.5 FM	Little Eagle	Variety

Appendix 7:
A Few of the Great Drives/Rides in the Black Hills

Iron Mountain Road

Pigtail bridges and tunnels from Custer State Park to Mount Rushmore. Fantastic!

Devils Tower Loop

An all-day adventure that can begin at Beulah on the WY/SD state line, or in Belle Fourche (take Hwy 34 west at the gold course), or in Sundance. The circle is Sundance to Devils Tower on 14, to Hulett, to Aladdin on 24, and from there back to Belle Fourche or Beulah. It's a bit over 100 miles, so bikers will need to top up their tanks in one of the towns.

Needles Highway

Fourteen miles of 'impossible' road winds through some of the most startling geological formations in the Hills, with lots of sharp turns and low tunnels. An inexpensive daily park sticker is required (available when the road enters Custer State Park).

Peter Norbeck Scenic Driveway

A loop from Custer to Keystone, this is 68 miles of winding roads with absolutely magnificent scenery.

Spearfish Canyon Scenic Byway

Starting between I-90 Exits 12 and 14 on the south frontage road, the canyon winds through 19 miles of spectacular cliffs and waterfalls (Bridal, Roughlock and Spearfish) and ends up at Cheyenne Crossing which is one of the best little restaurants in the Hills. Go left from there through Lead and Deadwood and back to Exit 17.

Vanocker Canyon Road

A beautiful canyon ride, this is one of the best quiet motorcycle roads in America, with lots of curves and awesome scenery. Follow it to Nemo, and from there go to Rapid City on another great biking road, or go to Brownsville and over to Hwy 385 and the southern Hills.

Quick Navigation Guide

Zone 3: Wyoming's Black Hills

Zone 4: Rapid City & Environs

Lakota Culture - Interpretive Centers, Sites & Museums

INDEX

Applebee's (520)	Spearfish	53
Arby's (1751)	Rapid City	147
Arby's (1752)	Rapid City	147
Arby's (1753)	Rapid City	147
Arby's (1754)	Rapid City	147
Arby's (1755)	Rapid City	147
Arby's (490)	Spearfish	52
Arby's (660)	Sturgis	60
Armadillo's Ice Cream Shoppe (1756)	Rapid City	147
Arnold's Classic Diner (1650)	Rapid City	143
Arriba Mexican Grill (1285)	Keystone	110
Art Alley (1467)	Rapid City	133
Art Expressions Gallery of Custer (891)	Custer	77
ArtForms Gallery (937)	Hill City	82
Aspire Boutique (410)	Lead	45
ATV Rentals at Custer Crossing (187)	Deadwood	26
Audrie's Cottages & B&B (1500)	Rapid City	136
Avanti Motel (1505)	Rapid City	136
B & B Lounge (531)	Spearfish	53
Baan Thai (1851)	Box Elder	150
Back Roads Inn & Cabins (1506)	Rapid City	136
Backroads Inn & Cabins (1301)	Keystone	112
BackRoads Inn and Cabins (1021)	Hill City	89
Badlands National Park (1425)	Interior	123
Badlands Petrified Gardens (1426)	Kadoka	123
Badlands Trading Post (2101)	Philip	159
Baker's Bakery & Café (791)	Custer	72
Barbacoa's Burritos & Wraps (470)	Spearfish	52
Barefoot Resort (380)	Lead	45
Barlee's (1286)	Keystone	110
Battle Creek Lodge (1302)	Keystone	112
Battle Mountain Lookout (1119)	Hot Springs	100
Bavarian Inn (835)	Custer	76
Bay Leaf Café - Mediterranean (476)	Spearfish	52
Baymont Inn & Suites (1182)	Hot Springs	103
Baymont Inn & Suites (1507)	Rapid City	136
Bear Butte Creek Campground (695)	Sturgis	61
Bear Butte State Park (605)	Sturgis	57
Bear Country USA (1427)	Rapid City	124
Bear Rock Cabins (836)	Custer	76
Bearlodge Ranger District (1382)	Sundance	117
Beaver Bar (625)	Sturgis	59
Beaver Lake Camp & Cabins (837)	Custer	76
Beaver Lake Water Slide (769)	Custer	70
Begging Burro Mexican Bistro (792)	Custer	73
Bell's Motor Lodge (561)	Spearfish	54

Belle Flowers & Gifts (74)	Belle Fourche	19
Belle Fourche Country Club (39)	Belle Fourche	17
Belle Fourche Country Club (6)	Belle Fourche	11
Belle Inn Restaurant (24)	Belle Fourche	15
Belle Joli Winery (626)	Sturgis	60
Berg Jewelry (300)	Deadwood	36
Beseler's Cadillac Ranch (63)	Belle Fourche	18
Best Western (1183)	Hot Springs	103
Best Western (567)	Spearfish	54
Best Western Buffalo Ridge Inn (838)	Custer	76
Best Western Golden Spike Inn & Suites (1022)	Hill City	89
Best Western Hickok House (240)	Deadwood	32
Best Western Hickok House Restaurant (200)	Deadwood	28
Best Western Ramkota Hotel (1508)	Rapid City	136
Best Western Sturgis Inn (680)	Sturgis	61
BH Gold Jewelry by Coleman (301)	Deadwood	36
BHSU Bookstore (590)	Spearfish	55
Big Hill X-Country Skiing (440)	Spearfish	51
Big Pine Camp & Cabins (839)	Custer	76
Big Rig RV Park (696)	Sturgis	61
Big Sky Lodge (1509)	Rapid City	136
Big Thunder Gold Mine (1251)	Keystone	106
Big Thunder Gold Mine (1288)	Keystone	110
Big Thunder Gold Mine Co. Store (1340)	Keystone	114
Big Time Pizza (1289)	Keystone	110
Bike Deadwood (171)	Deadwood	23
Bison Express Tours (1118)	Hot Springs	100
Bitter Esters Brewhouse (793)	Custer	73
Black Forest Inn (1510)	Rapid City	136
Black Hill National Cemetery (608)	Sturgis	58
Black Hills & Badlands Visitor Center (1428)	Rapid City	124
Black Hills Bagels (1926)	Rapid City	153
Black Hills Balloons (761)	Custer	69
Black Hills Barbeque (1651)	Rapid City	143
Black Hills Bluegrass Festival (1429)	Sturgis	124
Black Hills Books & Treasures (1230)	Hot Springs	104
Black Hills Bungalows (841)	Custer	76
Black Hills Burger and Bun Co. (794)	Custer	73
Black Hills Cabins & Motel (1511)	Rapid City	136
Black Hills Caverns (1430)	Rapid City	125
Black Hills Central Railroad – Keystone (1252)	Keystone	106
Black Hills Community Theatre (1456)	Rapid City	131
Black Hills Gifts & Gold (1341)	Keystone	114
Black Hills Gifts & Souvenirs (70)	Belle Fourche	19
Black Hills Glass Blowers (1342)	Keystone	114
Black Hills Inn & Suites (241)	Deadwood	32

Black Hills Maze (1431)	Rapid City	125
Black Hills Mickelson Trail (350)	Lead	42
Black Hills Mile Hi Motel (1512)	Rapid City	136
Black Hills Mile Hi Motel (840)	Custer	76
Black Hills Mining Museum (341)	Lead	40
Black Hills Off-Road Rentals (172)	Deadwood	23
Black Hills Open-Top Tours (950)	Hill City	85
Black Hills Parks & Forest Association (1101)	Hot Springs	96
Black Hills Playhouse (755)	Custer	67
Black Hills Ponderosa Place (842)	Custer	76
Black Hills Rally And Gold (720)	Sturgis	62
Black Hills Souvenirs & Gifts (1343)	Keystone	114
Black Hills State University Theater (441)	Spearfish	51
Black Hills Symphony Orchestra (1469)	Rapid City	134
Black Hills Taco & Tortilla	Custer	73
Black Hills Trailside Park Resort (1023)	Hill City	89
Black Hills Veterans' MARCH (188)	Hill City	26
Black Hills Wild Horse Sanctuary (1102)	Hot Springs	96
Blackbird Espresso (450)	Spearfish	52
Blackstone Lodge & Suites (383)	Lead	45
Blacktail Horseback Tours (191)	Deadwood	27
Blaze Pizza (1700)	Rapid City	145
Bloomers Flowers and Gifts (411)	Lead	45
Blue Bell Lodge (785)	Custer	72
Blue Bell Lodge Cabins (843)	Custer	76
Blue Bell Stables (762)	Custer	69
Boar's Nest (368)	Lead	44
Bob's Café (27)	Belle Fourche	16
Bob's Silver Star Lounge (360)	Lead	44
Bobkat's Purple Pie Place (796)	Custer	73
Bobs Family Restaurant (627)	Sturgis	60
Bodega Casino (141)	Deadwood	23
Boondock's Diner & Amusements (201)	Deadwood	28
Boot Hill Tours (175)	Deadwood	24
Boothill Emporium (303)	Deadwood	36
Boston's Restaurant & Sports Bar (1976)	Rapid City	154
Botticelli Ristorante Italiano (1852)	Rapid City	150
Boulder Canyon Country Club (609)	Sturgis	58
Brass Rail Lounge (1977)	Rapid City	154
Braun Historic Hotel (1184)	Hot Springs	103
BrGr 61 (1287)	Keystone	110
Broken Arrow - Horse & RV (844)	Custer	76
Broken Arrow Trading Co. (1053)	Hill City	93
Broken Arrow Trading Co. (304)	Deadwood	36
Broken Arrow Trading Company (1344)	Keystone	114
Broken Boot Gold Mine (123)	Deadwood	21

Broken Spoke Saloon (628)	Sturgis	60
Brookside Motel (1304)	Keystone	112
Brown Rock Sports Café (202)	Deadwood	28
Budget Inn Motel (1513)	Rapid City	137
Buechel Memorial Lakota Museum (2151)	Saint Francis	160
Buen Dia (1142)	Hot Springs	102
BuffalBobs (1054)	Hill City	93
Buffalo Bodega Saloon & Steakhouse (203)	Deadwood	28
Buffalo Chip Campground (697)	Sturgis	61
Buffalo Interpretive Center (2152)	Fort Pierre	161
Buffalo Jump Steakhouse (1405)	Beulah	121
Buffalo Ridge Camp Resort (845)	Custer	76
Buffalo Rock Lodge (1303)	Keystone	112
Buffalo Wild Wings (1978)	Rapid City	154
Buffalo Wings and Rings (1979)	Rapid City	154
Buglin' Bull Restaurant and Sports Bar (797)	Custer	73
Bullock Casino (142)	Deadwood	23
Bullock Hotel (242)	Deadwood	32
Bully's Restaurant (204)	Deadwood	28
Bumpin Buffal(972)	Hill City	87
Bunkhouse and Gambling Hall (143)	Deadwood	23
Bunkhouse Motel (55)	Belle Fourche	18
Burger King (1757)	Rapid City	147
Burger King (1758)	Rapid City	147
Burger King (1759)	Rapid City	147
Burger King (491)	Spearfish	52
Burger King (661)	Sturgis	60
Butch Cassidy Suites (243)	Deadwood	32
BW Ramkota Gift Shop (2102)	Rapid City	159
Cabela's- RV overnight parking (1629)	Rapid City	142
Cadillac Jack's (244)	Deadwood	32
Cadillac Jack's Gaming Resort (144)	Deadwood	23
Cafe 608 (479)	Spearfish	52
Café 808 (370)	Lead	44
Calamity Peak Lodge (846)	Custer	76
Cambell Street Café (1652)	Rapid City	143
Cambria Hotel & Suites (1514)	Rapid City	137
Camp Harley (545)	Spearfish	54
Candlelight B&B (59)	Belle Fourche	18
Canvas 2 Paint (1457)	Rapid City	131
Canyon Lake Resort (1515)	Rapid City	137
Canyon View Amish (305)	Deadwood	36
Captain's Table (798)	Custer	73
Carson Drug (896)	Custer	78
Carver's Café (1265)	Keystone	110
Cascade Falls (1103)	Hot Springs	97

Castle Inn (1516)	Rapid City	137
CBH Travel Center (81)	Belle Fourche	19
CCC Museum of South Dakota (948)	Hill City	85
Cedar Feathers (1055)	Hill City	93
Cedar Pines Golf Course (1393)	Upton	119
Cedar Wood Inn (245)	Deadwood	32
Celebrity Casinos (145)	Deadwood	23
Celebrity Hotel (246)	Deadwood	32
Center of the Nation AMC Car Collection (7)	Belle Fourche	11
Center of the Nation Monument & Visitor Center (3)	Belle Fourche	10
Central States Fairgrounds (1610)	Rapid City	141
Chamber of Commerce (721)	Sturgis	62
Chapel In The Hills (1432)	Rapid City	125
Chateau Le Funk (1517)	Rapid City	137
Cheers Sports Bar & Casino (1980)	Rapid City	154
Cherry Bean, The (1927)	Rapid City	153
CherryBerry (2050)	Rapid City	157
CherryBerry (460)	Spearfish	52
Cheyenne Crossing (361)	Lead	44
Chief Motel (847)	Custer	76
Chili's Grill & Bar (1981)	Rapid City	154
China Buffet (1143)	Hot Springs	102
China Garden (25)	Belle Fourche	15
China Luck (1853)	Rapid City	150
China Pantry in Rushmore Mall (1854)	Rapid City	150
China Wok (1855)	Rapid City	150
Chinatown Tour (132)	Deadwood	22
Chops & Hops (1144)	Hot Springs	102
Chris' Camp (546)	Spearfish	54
Chubby Chipmunk at Alex Johnson (2051)	Rapid City	157
Chubby Chipmunk Chocolates (306)	Deadwood	36
Chuck E. Cheese (1701)	Rapid City	145
Chute Roosters (973)	Hill City	87
Ciao! Italian Eatery (1856)	Rapid City	150
City of Presidents (1433)	Rapid City	126
City View Trolley (1453)	Rapid City	130
Claw, Antler and Hide Co. (902)	Custer	79
Clocktower Lounge (1982)	Rapid City	154
Coco Palace (1857)	Rapid City	150
Coffee Cup Fuel Stop (1399)	Moorcroft	120
Cold Brook Lake (1104)	Hot Springs	97
Cold Brook Lake Campground (1219)	Hot Springs	103
Cole Cabins (270)	Deadwood	34
Colonial House Restaurant (1653)	Rapid City	143
Colonial Motel (1518)	Rapid City	137
Comfort Inn & Suites (247)	Deadwood	32

Comfort Inn & Suites (848)	Custer	76
Comfort Inn Gift Shop (307)	Deadwood	36
Comfort Inns & Suites (1519)	Rapid City	137
Comfort Suites (1520)	Rapid City	137
Common Grounds Restaurant (451)	Spearfish	52
Community Center and Indoor Pool (5)	Belle Fourche	11
CON Visitor Info Center's Gift Shop (72)	Belle Fourche	19
Connie's Place (1654)	Black Hawk	143
Copper Mountain Resort (384)	Lead	45
Corral Motel (1521)	Rapid City	137
Cosmos Mystery Area (1434)	Rapid City	126
Cottonwood Springs (1223)	Hot Springs	103
Cottonwood Springs Lake (1105)	Hot Springs	97
Country Corner (1655)	Piedmont	143
Country Cottage Gifts (1400)	Sundance	121
Country Inn Bar & Casin(974)	Hill City	87
Country Inns & Suites (1522)	Rapid City	137
Country Store At The Forks (1056)	Hill City	93
Covered Wagon Resort (1611)	Piedmont	141
Cowboy Back Bar (37)	Belle Fourche	17
Coyote Blues Village B&B (1523)	Rapid City	137
Crazy Horse Camp & Cabins(850)	Custer	76
Crazy Horse Memorial (756)	Crazy Horse	67
Creekside Campground (291)	Deadwood	35
Creekside Campground (698)	Sturgis	61
Creekside Country Resort (1024)	Hill City	89
Creekside Lodge (849)	Custer	76
Creekside Restaurant at Deadwood Gulch (205)	Deadwood	28
Crook County Museum, 1875 Art Gallery (1385)	Sundance	118
Crooked Creek Resort and RV Park (1025)	Hill City	89
Crow Peak Brewing Company (530)	Spearfish	53
Crow Peak Lodge (562)	Spearfish	54
Cruizzers (1266)	Keystone	110
Culver's (1760)	Rapid City	147
Culver's (1761)	Rapid City	147
Culver's (492)	Spearfish	52
Curry Masala (1858)	Rapid City	150
Custer County Candy Company (799)	Custer	73
Custer Crossing Campground (292)	Deadwood	35
Custer Farmers' Market (763)	Custer	69
Custer State Park 750-64	Custer	64
Custer State Park Gift Shop (890)	Custer	77
Custer-Mt. Rushmore KOA (851)	Custer	76
Custer's Gulch RV & Camp (852)	Custer	76
Daarthe's Eats & Treats Food Truck (975)	Hill City	87
Dahl's Chainsaw Art (1345)	Keystone	114

Daily Bread Bakery & Café (1145)	Hot Springs	102
Dairy Queen (1146)	Hot Springs	102
Dairy Queen (1267)	Keystone	110
Dairy Queen (1762)	Rapid City	147
Dairy Queen (1763)	Rapid City	147
Dairy Queen (1764)	Rapid City	147
Dairy Queen (1765)	Rapid City	148
Dairy Queen (1766)	Rapid City	148
Dairy Queen (1767)	Box Elder	148
Dairy Queen (233)	Deadwood	31
Dairy Queen (33)	Belle Fourche	16
Dairy Queen (493)	Spearfish	52
Dairy Queen (662)	Sturgis	60
Dairy Queen (800)	Custer	73
Dairy Queen (976)	Hill City	87
Dairy Twist (977)	Hill City	87
Dakota Coin & Collectibles (308)	Deadwood	36
Dakota Cowboy Inn (853)	Custer	76
Dakota Cowboy Inn Restaurant (801)	Custer	73
Dakota Dream B&B & Horse (854)	Custer	76
Dakota Nature & Art Gallery (938)	Hill City	82
Dakota Shivers Brewing (362)	Lead	44
Dakota Spur Hotel (385)	Lead	45
Dakota Stone Rock Shop (1057)	Hill City	93
Dakota Stone's Rock Shop (933)	Hill City	81
Dakota's Best Gifts (1058)	Hill City	93
Dakota's Best (2103)	Rapid City	159
Dakota's Best Wine & Gifts (899)	Custer	78
Dakotah Steakhouse (1983)	Rapid City	154
Dale's Family Restaurant (1147)	Hot Springs	102
Dark Canyon Coffee Co. (1928)	Rapid City	153
David Harding (586)	Spearfish	55
Day's Inn (687)	Sturgis	61
Days End Campground (699)	Sturgis	61
Days Inn – Jackson (1524)	Rapid City	137
Days Inn – LaCrosse (1525)	Rapid City	137
Days Inn (568)	Spearfish	54
Days Inn of Custer (855)	Custer	76
Days of 76 Campground (290)	Deadwood	35
Days of 76 Museum (120)	Deadwood	20
Days of 76 Museum Gift Shop (309)	Deadwood	36
Days of 76 Rodeo (181)	Deadwood	25
DC Booth Hatchery & City Park (425)	Spearfish	46
Deadweird (186)	Deadwood	26
Deadwood Chamber & Visitor Center (179)	Deadwood	25
Deadwood Dick's Gift Shop (310)	Deadwood	36

Deadwood Dick's Saloon and Eatery (206)	Deadwood	28
Deadwood Dick`s (248)	Deadwood	32
Deadwood Gift Shoppe (311)	Deadwood	36
Deadwood Grille (207)	Deadwood	28
Deadwood Gulch (146)	Deadwood	23
Deadwood Gulch (249)	Deadwood	32
Deadwood Harley-Davidson (312)	Deadwood	36
Deadwood Jam (183)	Deadwood	25
Deadwood KOA (293)	Deadwood	35
Deadwood KOA (313)	Deadwood	37
Deadwood Legends Steakhouse (208)	Deadwood	29
Deadwood Mickelson Trail Marathon (189)	Hill City	27
Deadwood Mini Golf (124)	Deadwood	21
Deadwood Mountain Grand (147)	Deadwood	23
Deadwood Mountain Grand (250)	Deadwood	32
Deadwood Mountain Grand Coffee Kiosk (209)	Deadwood	29
Deadwood Mtn Grand Co. Store (314)	Deadwood	37
Deadwood Recreation Center (174)	Deadwood	24
Deadwood Social Club (210)	Deadwood	29
Deadwood Stage Coach Tours (128)	Deadwood	22
Deadwood Station (251)	Deadwood	32
Deadwood Station Bunkhouse & Gambling Hall (211)	Deadwood	29
Deadwood Super 8 (148)	Deadwood	23
Deadwood Tobacco Co. (316)	Deadwood	37
Deadwood Trolleys (184)	Deadwood	26
Dee'zz Inn (1305)	Keystone	112
Deer Mountain Ski Mystic (349)	Lead	42
Delmonico Grill (1984)	Rapid City	155
Denny's (1656)	Rapid City	143
Depot Gift Shop -1880 Train (1079)	Hill City	95
Derby Elk Resort (1026)	Hill City	89
Designs by Delise (1237)	Hot Springs	104
Desperados Cowboy Cuisine (978)	Hill City	87
Devils Tower Climbing (1396)	Devils Tower	120
Devils Tower KOA (1398)	Devils Tower	120
Devils Tower National Monument (1380)	Devils Tower	116
Devils Tower Trading Post (1397)	Devils Tower	120
Devils Tower View (1401)	Devils Tower	121
Dew Drop Inn (1148)	Hot Springs	102
Diamond Lil's Bar & Grill (212)	Deadwood	29
Diamond M Ranch B&B (541)	Spearfish	54
Dickey's Barbecue (1657)	Rapid City	143
Dinosaur Park (1435)	Rapid City	126
Dixon Coffee Co. (1929)	Rapid City	153
DJ Saddlery Leather Goods (76)	Belle Fourche	19
Dollar Inn (1185)	Hot Springs	103

Domino's Pizza (1702)	Rapid City	145
Domino's Pizza (1703)	Rapid City	145
Domino's Pizza (1704)	Box Elder	145
Domino's Pizza (510)	Spearfish	53
Domino's Pizza (663)	Sturgis	60
Double D Bed & Breakfast (1205)	Hot Springs	103
Double Diamond Ranch (1027)	Hill City	89
Double Diamond Ranch (1526)	Rapid City	137
Double Diamond Ranch B&B (856)	Custer	76
Dough Trader (511)	Spearfish	53
Dry Creek Coffee (979)	Hill City	87
Dungeon Bar (629)	Sturgis	60
Dunn Brothers Coffee (1930)	Rapid City	153
Eagle's Lodge (2075)	Rapid City	158
Eagles Landing Campground (700)	Sturgis	61
Earth Goods Natural Foods (1233)	Hot Springs	104
Earth Treasures Rock Shop (1346)	Keystone	114
Easyriders Saloon & Steakhouse (630)	Sturgis	60
Econo Lodge (1527)	Rapid City	137
Econo Lodge (53)	Belle Fourche	18
Econo Lodge (857)	Custer	76
Econo Lodge Near Mt. Rushmore Memorial (1306)	Keystone	112
Edelweiss Mountain Lodging (1528)	Rapid City	137
Einstein Bros Bagels at the School of Mines (1931)	Rapid City	153
El Mariachi Mexican Restaurant (1859)	Rapid City	151
Elk Creek Resort (1529)	Piedmont	138
Elk Creek Resort (1612)	Piedmont	141
Elk Creek Steakhouse & Lounge (1985)	Piedmont	155
Elk Mountain/Wind Cave (1222)	Hot Springs	103
Elk Park Antiques & Art (908)	Custer	79
Elk Ridge Bed & Breakfast (1307)	Keystone	112
Elkhorn Ridge Golf Club (426)	Spearfish	46
Elkhorn Ridge RV Park (547)	Spearfish	54
Emporium (1347)	Keystone	114
Enigma Restaurant, The (1986)	Rapid City	155
Eno's Pizza (1268)	Keystone	110
Espresso and More (802)	Custer	74
Essence of Coffee (1032)	Rapid City	153
Evan's Plunge (1107)	Hot Springs	98
Everest Cuisine (1860)	Rapid City	151
Everything Prehistoric (1059)	Hill City	93
Everything Prehistoric & The Geological Museum (932)	Hill City	81
Executive Golf Course (1462)	Rapid City	132
Executive Suites Inc. (1530)	Rapid City	138
Fabric Junction Quilt Shop (722)	Sturgis	62
Fair Value Inn (1531)	Rapid City	138

Fairfield Inn & Suites (1532)	Rapid City	138
Fairfield Inn by Marriott (569)	Spearfish	54
Fairmont Diner (1658)	Rapid City	143
Fall River Fibers (1234)	Hot Springs	104
False Bottom Bar (532)	Spearfish	53
Family Inn (1533)	Rapid City	138
Famous Dave's (1659)	Rapid City	143
Firehouse Brewing Company (1660)	Rapid City	143
First Deadwood Cottages (272)	Deadwood	34
First Deadwood Souvenirs (317)	Deadwood	37
First Gold Hotel & Gaming (149)	Deadwood	23
First Gold Hotel & Gaming (252)	Deadwood	33
First Gold Nugget Buffet (217)	Deadwood	30
Fish 'N Fry Campground (294)	Deadwood	35
Fish N Fry (125)	Deadwood	21
Five Guys Burgers (1661)	Rapid City	144
Flags & Wheels Indoor Racing (1436)	Rapid City	126
Flanagan's Irish Pub (472)	Spearfish	52
FlatIron Historic Inn (1186)	Hot Springs	103
Flora's Jewelry & Western Wear (900)	Custer	78
Flying E (585)	Spearfish	55
Flying J Buffet, Exit 61 (1662)	Rapid City	144
Foothills Inn (1534)	Rapid City	138
Fort Hays Chuck-wagon & Tours (1437)	Rapid City	127
Fort Hays Chuckwagon (1663)	Rapid City	144
Fort Welikit Family Camp (858)	Custer	76
Four Mile Old West Town (764)	Custer	70
Franklin Hotel/Silverado (152)	Deadwood	23
Franklin Motor Lodge (253)	Deadwood	33
French Creek RV Park (859)	Custer	76
Frontier Grill (803)	Custer	74
Frontier Photo (765)	Custer	70
Fuddruckers at Rushmore Mall (1664)	Rapid City	144
Fuji Japanese Steakhouse & Sushi Bar (1861)	Rapid City	151
Fuji Sushi & Sake Bar, Rushmore Mall (1862)	Rapid City	151
Full Throttle Saloon (631)	Sturgis	60
Garden Bar & Grill at the Hilton (1665)	Rapid City	144
Garden Cottages Motel (1535)	Rapid City	138
Gem Steakhouse & Saloon (214)	Deadwood	29
GeoFunTrek Tours (1116)	Hot Springs	100
George S Mickelson Trailhead (182)	Deadwood	25
Gizzi's Coffee (1933)	Box Elder	153
Glazed & Dazed/Daylight Donuts (1934)	Rapid City	153
Gold Bison Grill, Holiday Inn (1987)	Rapid City	155
Gold Camp Cabins (860)	Custer	76
Gold Country Inn (254)	Deadwood	33

Gold Diggers (1060)	Hill City	93
Gold Diggers (2104)	Rapid City	159
Gold Dust C-Store (318)	Deadwood	37
Gold Dust Casino (150)	Deadwood	23
Gold Nugget Restaurant (215)	Deadwood	29
Gold Nugget Trading Post (319)	Deadwood	37
Gold Pan Pizza (632)	Sturgis	60
Gold Pan Saloon (804)	Custer	74
Gold Star Motel (1536)	Rapid City	138
Golden Corral (1863)	Rapid City	151
Golden Dragon - Chinese (471)	Spearfish	52
Golden Fortune Restaurant (1864)	Rapid City	151
Golden Phoenix (1865)	Rapid City	151
Golden Spike -Best Western (980)	Hill City	87
Grand Gateway Hotel (1537)	Rapid City	138
Grand Magic (772)	Custer	71
Grandstay Residential Suites (1538)	Rapid City	138
Granite Sports (1061)	Hill City	93
Grap's Burgers & Brews (40)	Belle Fourche	17
Grapes & Grinds (1269)	Keystone	110
Great Harvest Bread Co. (1935)	Rapid City	153
Great Wall Chinese Restaurant (1866)	Rapid City	151
Grill at Rimrock Canyon, The (1988)	Rapid City	155
Grizzly Creek (1270)	Keystone	110
Grizzly Creek Gifts (1349)	Keystone	114
Grizzly Gulch Adventure Golf (766)	Custer	70
Guadalajara's – Mexican (474)	Spearfish	52
Gunslinger Coffee (320)	Deadwood	37
Gus' Best Ice Cream (1149)	Hot Springs	102
Gypsy Vintage Cycle (603)	Sturgis	57
Gyro Hub (1867)	Rapid City	151
Gyro Hub (1868)	Box Elder	151
Halley's 1880 Store (1350)	Keystone	114
Hamilton's Patio & Grille (1989)	Rapid City	155
Hampton Inn (1539)	Rapid City	138
Hampton Inn (570)	Spearfish	54
Hampton Inn/Tin Lizzie (255)	Deadwood	33
Hana Korean Grill & Sushi Bar (1869)	Rapid City	151
Handley Recreation Center (351)	Lead	43
Happy Days Gift Shop (321)	Deadwood	37
Happy Holliday Motel (1540)	Rapid City	138
Happy Holliday Resort (1613)	Rapid City	141
Happy Trails Cabins (1028)	Hill City	90
Hardee's (30)	Belle Fourche	16
Hardee's (1768)	Rapid City	148
Hardee's (1769)	Rapid City	148

Hardee's (1770)	Rapid City	148
Hardee's (1771)	Box Elder	148
Harley Davidson Plaza (601)	Sturgis	56
Harney Peak (1255)	Keystone	107
Harney Peak Inn (1029)	Hill City	90
Hart Ranch Camping Resort (1614)	Rapid City	141
Heart of the Hills Antiques (1062)	Hill City	94
Heart of the Hills Vacation Homes (1030)	Hill City	90
Heartland Resort (1615)	Hermosa	142
Heartsong Quilts (1232)	Hot Springs	104
Helicopter Tours (760)	Custer	68
Heritage Center of Red Cloud Indian School (2153)	Pine Ridge	161
Heritage Village Campground (861)	Custer	76
Hickok's Hotel (151)	Deadwood	23
Hickok's Hotel & Gaming (256)	Deadwood	33
Hickok's Pizza (216)	Deadwood	29
Hidden Valley Campground (295)	Deadwood	35
Hide-A-Way Cabins (1187)	Hot Springs	103
High Country Guest Ranch (930)	Hill City	80
High Country Guest Ranch Cabins & Camping (1031)	Hill City	90
High Mountain Outfitters (416)	Lead	45
High Plains Western Heritage Center (428)	Spearfish	47
Hike Crow Peak (438)	Spearfish	50
Hike Lookout Mountain (437)	Spearfish	50
Hill City CafŽ (981)	Hill City	87
Hill City Harley-Davidson (1063)	Hill City	94
Hill City Mercantile & Quilt Co. (1064)	Hill City	94
Hill City Visitor Information Center (951)	Hill City	86
Hills Inn (1188)	Hot Springs	103
Hillside Country Cabins (1032)	Hill City	90
Hillside Country Cabins (1541)	Rapid City	138
Hilton Garden Inn (1542)	Rapid City	138
Himalayan Indian Cuisine (1271)	Keystone	110
Hippo Steve Pastiche (1936)	Rapid City	153
Hisega Lodge B&B (1543)	Rapid City	138
Historic Black Hills Studios (190)	Deadwood	27
Historic Elks Movie Theater (1470)	Rapid City	134
Historic Franklin Hotel/Silverado (257)	Deadwood	33
Historic Homestake Opera House (342)	Lead	40
Historic Log Cabin Motel (1189)	Hot Springs	103
Holiday Inn (1544)	Rapid City	138
Holiday Inn (571)	Spearfish	54
Holiday Inn & Suites (1033)	Hill City	90
Holiday Inn Express (1545)	Rapid City	139
Holiday Inn Express (258)	Deadwood	33
Holiday Inn Express (681)	Sturgis	61

Holiday Inn Express (862)	Custer	76
Holiday Inn Express & Suites (1308)	Keystone	112
Holiday Inn Express & Suites (1546)	Rapid City	139
Holly House B&B (1034)	Hill City	90
Holy Smoke Resort (1309)	Keystone	112
Holy Smoke Trail Rides (1256)	Keystone	107
Holy Terror Antique Mall (1351)	Keystone	114
Holy Terror Coffee Co. (1272)	Keystone	110
Holy Terror Mini Golf (1257)	Keystone	107
Homestake Gold Mine Visitor Center (340)	Lead	39
Homestake Visitor Center (340)	Lead	45
Hong Kong Buffet (1870)	Rapid City	151
Horse Creek Inn at Sheridan Lake (982)	Hill City	87
Horse Creek Inn Campground (1616)	Rapid City	142
Horse Creek Inn Restaurant (1990)	Rapid City	155
Horse Thief Lake (1263)	Keystone	109
Hot Brook Canyon (1120)	Hot Springs	101
Hot Springs Coffee Kiosk (1150)	Hot Springs	102
Hot Springs Vault (1151)	Hot Springs	102
Hotel Alex Johnson (1547)	Rapid City	139
Hotel by Gold Dust (259)	Deadwood	33
Howard Johnson (1548)	Rapid City	139
Howard Johnson (572)	Spearfish	54
Howdy's Whitewood Plaza (723)	Sturgis	62
Hub Cap Diner (983)	Hill City	87
Huhot Mongolian Grill (1871)	Rapid City	151
Hulett Festivals (1402)	Hulett	121
Hulett Museum and Art Gallery (1388)	Hulett	118
Hunan Chinese Restaurant (1872)	Rapid City	151
Ichiban (1873)	Rapid City	151
IHOP (1666)	Rapid City	144
Imperial Chinese Restaurant (1874)	Rapid City	151
Imperial Hotel (1549)	Rapid City	139
Independent Ale House (1705)	Rapid City	145
Indian Motorcycle Sturgis (604)	Sturgis	57
Inyan Kara Mountain (1384)	Sundance	118
Iron Creek Lake (439)	Spearfish	50
Iron Creek Lake Campground (548)	Spearfish	54
Iron Creek Leather & Gifts (1352)	Keystone	114
Iron Horse Campground (701)	Sturgis	61
Iron Horse Inn (260)	Deadwood	33
Iron Horse Inn Casino (153)	Deadwood	23
Iron Horse Inn, Whitewood (682)	Sturgis	61
Iron Horse Saloon (633)	Sturgis	60
Iron Mountain Road Gift Shop (1353)	Keystone	114
Ivan's Hunting and Fishing B&B (1438)	Black Hawk	127

Ixtapa Mexican Restaurant (1875)	Rapid City	152
JacketZone (589)	Spearfish	55
Jade Palace China Buffet (475)	Spearfish	52
Jakes Fine Dining (213)	Deadwood	29
Jambonz Grill & Pub (635)	Sturgis	60
Jane's Boardwalk Pizza (1273)	Keystone	110
Janssen's Lode Stone Motel & Cabins (1035)	Hill City	90
Jenny's Floral (1065)	Hill City	94
Jenny's Floral (901)	Custer	78
Jerry's Cakes & Donuts (1937)	Rapid City	153
Jewel Cave National Monument (774)	Custer	71
Jewels of the West (1066)	Hill City	94
Jimmy John's (1772)	Rapid City	148
Jimmy John's (1773)	Rapid City	148
Jimmy John's (1774)	Rapid City	148
Jimmy John's (495)	Spearfish	52
JJ Davenport's (634)	Sturgis	60
JL's Gift Shop (413)	Lead	45
Joe's Place (1991)	Rapid City	155
John Lopez Sculptures (1439)	Lemmon	127
Johnny Spaulding Cabin (2)	Belle Fourche	10
Jon Crane Gallery (934)	Hill City	81
Jon Crane Gallery & Frame Shop (1080)	Hill City	95
Journey Museum, The (1440)	Rapid City	128
JP's Family Dining (1152)	Hot Springs	102
Jumpin' Jacks (23)	Belle Fourche	15
Juniper (1992)	Rapid City	155
Just Dandy (1067)	Hill City	94
Just For Looks (724)	Sturgis	62
K Bar S Lodge Hotel (1310)	Keystone	112
Kang San – Korean (636)	Sturgis	60
Kang San (1876)	Box Elder	152
Kathmandu Bistro (1877)	Rapid City	152
KDR Unlimited Lodging (386)	Lead	45
Kelly's Frozen Yogurt, BH Chocolates (2052)	Rapid City	157
Kelly's Sports Lounge (1993)	Rapid City	155
Kemo Sabay Campground (1220)	Hot Springs	103
Kemp's Kamp (1311)	Keystone	112
Ken's Minerals & Trading Post (903)	Custer	79
Key Antiques (584)	Spearfish	55
Key Photo (1354)	Keystone	114
Keyhole State Park (1387)	Moorcroft	118
Keystone Boardwalk Inn & Suites (1312)	Keystone	112
Keystone Fun Zone (1254)	Keystone	107
Keystone House/Mijo's	Keystone	111
Keystone Mercantile - Souvenirs (1355)	Keystone	114

Keystone Museum & Walking Tour (1258)	Keystone	108
KFC (1775)	Rapid City	148
KFC/Long John Silver's (1776)	Rapid City	148
KFC/Long John Silver's (494)	Spearfish	52
Kick Start Travel Center (725)	Sturgis	62
Killian's Tavern & Steakhouse(480)	Spearfish	52
King's Inn (56)	Belle Fourche	18
KOA (1216)	Hot Springs	103
KOA (549)	Spearfish	54
Kōl (1667)	Rapid City	144
Kool Deadwood Nights (185)	Deadwood	26
L&J Golden Circle Tours (771)	Custer	71
La Grand Station/Call of the Wild (1441)	Rapid City	128
La Quinta/Watiki (1550)	Rapid City	139
Lake Park Campground (1617)	Rapid City	142
Lamphere Ranch Campground (702)	Sturgis	61
Lantern Inn (1036)	Hill City	90
Lantern Motel (683)	Sturgis	61
Larive Lake Resort (1221)	Hot Springs	103
Laughing Water Restaurant (805)	Custer	74
Lazy U Motel (1551)	Rapid City	139
Lead Country Club (344)	Lead	40
Lead Deadwood Arts Center (414)	Lead	45
Lee Street Station Café (218)	Deadwood	30
Legion Lake Lodge	Custer	76
Legion Lake Lodge (786)	Custer	72
Leones' Creamery (461)	Spearfish	52
Level Wine Bar (533)	Spearfish	53
Lewie's Saloon & Eatery (363)	Lead	44
Lintz Bros. Pizza (1706)	Rapid City	145
Little Caesars (1707)	Rapid City	145
Little Caesars (1708)	Rapid City	146
Little Caesars (1709)	Rapid City	146
Little Caesars (516)	Spearfish	53
Lodge at Palmer Gulch & KOA (1037)	Hill City	91
LongHorn Steakhouse (1994)	Rapid City	155
Lotus Up Espresso & Deli (364)	Lead	44
Loud American Roadhouse (637)	Sturgis	60
Love That Shoppe Antiques (77)	Belle Fourche	19
Loyal Order of Moose Lodges (2076)	Rapid City	158
Lucky's 13 (481)	Spearfish	52
Lucy and the Green Wolf Earth Friendly Goods (1235)	Hot Springs	104
Luigi's Italian Restaurant (26)	Belle Fourche	16
Lynn's Dakotamart (410)	Lead	45
M-Star Motel (1552)	Rapid City	139
Mac's Grub (984)	Hill City	87

Mad Mountain Adventures (173)	Deadwood	24
Madame Peacock's Accessories (322)	Deadwood	37
Madison Ranch B&B (1553)	Rapid City	139
Main Street Manor Hostel (387)	Lead	45
Main Street Market Place Ice Cream (904)	Custer	79
Main Street Square (1454)	Rapid City	131
Mainstay Suites (1554)	Rapid City	139
Man Cave Cigar, Tobacco & Knives (79)	Belle Fourche	19
Mangy Moose Saloon (985)	Hill City	87
Marco's Pizza (1710)	Rapid City	146
Marco's Pizza (1711)	Rapid City	146
Maria's Mexican Food Truck (806)	Custer	74
Marlin's Roadhouse Grill (1668)	Rapid City	144
Marriott Execustay (1555)	Rapid City	139
Martin Mason Hotel (262)	Deadwood	33
Mason's 5th Ave Gas and Gifts (78)	Belle Fourche	19
Matthews Opera House (429)	Spearfish	47
Maurice's (582)	Spearfish	55
Mavericks Steak and Cocktails (219)	Deadwood	30
Maya Jo's B&B (266)	Deadwood	34
McDonald's (1777)	Rapid City	148
McDonald's (1778)	Rapid City	148
McDonald's (1779)	Rapid City	148
McDonald's (1780)	Rapid City	148
McDonald's (1781)	Rapid City	149
McDonald's (496)	Spearfish	52
McDonald's (664)	Sturgis	60
McNenny State Fish Hatchery (435)	Spearfish	49
Meadowbrook Golf Course (1461)	Rapid City	132
Memorial Pk Promenade & Legacy Commons (1465)	Rapid City	133
Microtel Inn & Suites by Wyndham (1556)	Rapid City	139
Midnight Star (154)	Deadwood	23
MidWest Mercantile (1356)	Keystone	114
Millstone Family Restaurant (1669)	Rapid City	144
Millstone Family Restaurant (1670)	Rapid City	144
Millstone Family Restaurant (482)	Spearfish	52
Mind Blown Studio (130)	Deadwood	22
Miner Brewing (941)	Hill City	83
Miner Brewing Co. (986)	Hill City	87
Mineral Palace Casino (155)	Deadwood	23
Mineral Palace Hotel and Gaming (262)	Deadwood	33
Mineral Palace Store (323)	Deadwood	37
Minerva's Restaurant and Bar (1995)	Rapid City	155
Mini-Needles Art Studio (892)	Custer	77
Miss Kitty's Mercantile (324)	Deadwood	37
Mistletoe Ranch Inc. (1068)	Hill City	94

Mitzi's Books (2105)	Rapid City	159
Mongolian Grill (1878)	Rapid City	152
Mornin' Sunshine Coffee Shop (1153)	Hot Springs	102
Morningside Café (1671)	Rapid City	144
Motel 6 (1190)	Hot Springs	103
Motel 6 (1557)	Rapid City	139
Motel Rapid (1558)	Rapid City	139
Mount Coolidge Fire Tower (753)	Custer	66
Mount Mariah Cemetery (122)	Deadwood	21
Mount Roosevelt Monument (170)	Deadwood	23
Mount Rushmore All American (1275)	Keystone	111
Mount Rushmore Memories (1069)	Hill City	94
Mount Rushmore National Memorial (1250)	Keystone	105
Mount Slushmore (1276)	Keystone	111
Mountain Brew Espresso (453)	Spearfish	52
Mountain Eagle Outpost (1357)	Keystone	114
Mountain Treats (987)	Hill City	87
Mountain View Lodge & Cabins (1038)	Hill City	91
Mountains tPrairies B&B (1039)	Hill City	91
Mt. Meadow Cabins & Campground (1040)	Hill City	91
Mt. Moriah Cemetery Gift Shop (325)	Deadwood	37
Mt. Rushmore's White House Resort (1314)	Keystone	113
Murphy's Pub & Grill (1996)	Rapid City	155
Musekamp's at Black Forest Inn (1997)	Rapid City	155
Museum of Geology (1441)	Rapid City	128
Mustang Sally's (220)	Deadwood	30
Mustang Sally's Casino (156)	Deadwood	23
My Place Hotel (1559)	Rapid City	139
Mystery Mountain Resort (1560)	Rapid City	139
Mystery Mountain Resort (1618)	Rapid City	142
Mystic Hills Hideaway (221)	Deadwood	30
Mystic Hills Hideaway (273)	Deadwood	34
Mystic Hills Hideaway (See 172, 221, 273)	Deadwood	35
Mystic Valley Inn (864)	Custer	76
Naked Winery (807)	Custer	74
Naked Winery (943)	Hill City	83
Naked Winery Kitchen (988)	Hill City	87
National Museum of Woodcarving (759)	Custer	68
National Presidential Wax Museum (1259)	Keystone	108
Native Grill and Wings (1998)	Rapid City	155
Newcastle Country Club (1392)	Newcastle	119
Newell Conoco (726)	Sturgis	62
Newton Fork Ranch Cabins (1041)	Hill City	91
No Name City Cabins & RV (703)	Sturgis	61
Northern Hills Fly Fisher (415)	Lead	45
Northern Hills Railway Society (127)	Deadwood	21

Northern Hills Rec. Association (346)	Lead	41
Oasis Bar & Fireside Lounge (638)	Sturgis	60
Oasis Lounge (1999)	Rapid City	155
Office Emporium (73)	Belle Fourche	19
Oggie's Sports Bar (222)	Deadwood	30
Oglala Lakota College Historical Center (2154)	Kyle	162
Old Fort Meade Museum (607)	Sturgis	58
Old McDonald's Petting Farm (1442)	Rapid City	128
Old West Trading Post (315)	Deadwood	37
Olive Garden (1879)	Rapid City	152
On the Border (1880)	Rapid City	152
On The Rocks Chophouse (808)	Custer	74
One-Eyed Jack's Saloon (639)	Sturgis	60
Orange Julius, Rushmore Mall (2053)	Rapid City	157
Orchard Creek Cottages (563)	Spearfish	54
Our Place (809)	Custer	74
Outback Steakhouse (2000)	Rapid City	156
Outlaw Ranch - Lutheran (865)	Custer	76
Outlaw Saloon (36)	Belle Fourche	16
Oyster Bay Bar (223)	Deadwood	30
Pacific Rim Café (1881)	Rapid City	152
Paddy O'Neill's Irish Pub at Alex Johnson (2001)	Rapid City	156
Page's Banana Stand (810)	Custer	74
Panchero's Mexican Grill (1882)	Rapid City	152
Papa John's Pizza (28)	Belle Fourche	16
Papa John's (1712)	Rapid City	146
Papa John's (1713)	Rapid City	146
Papa Murphy's Pizza (512)	Spearfish	53
Papa Murphy's Take 'N' Bake Pizza (1714)	Rapid City	146
Papa Murphy's Take 'N' Bake Pizza (1715)	Rapid City	146
Patty's Place (21)	Belle Fourche	15
Paul Horsted, Dakota Photographic LLC (893)	Custer	77
Pauly's Pizzeria & Sub Co. (1716)	Rapid City	146
Peggy's Place (1277)	Keystone	111
Peppy's Pizza Arcade & Lazer (1717)	Rapid City	146
Peregrine Pointe B&B (1561)	Rapid City	140
Perfect Hanging Gallery (2106)	Rapid City	159
Performing Arts Center of Rapid City (1459)	Rapid City	132
Perk It Up Downtown (1938)	Rapid City	153
Perkins Restaurant (483)	Spearfish	52
Perkins Restaurant & Bakery (1672)	Rapid City	144
Perkins Restaurant & Bakery (1673)	Rapid City	144
Perkins Restaurant & Bakery (1674)	Rapid City	144
Peter Norbeck Outdoor Education Center (754)	Custer	66
Petrified Forest of the Black Hills (1443)	Piedmont	128
Philly Ted's Cheesesteak & Pizza (1675)	Rapid City	144

Philly Ted's Cheezsteaks (497)	Spearfish	52
Piesano's Pacchia (1718)	Rapid City	146
Pine Rest Cabins (1042)	Hill City	91
Pioneer Museum (1109)	Hot Springs	98
Pirate's Cove Miniature Golf (1466)	Rapid City	133
Pita Pit (1782)	Rapid City	149
Pizza Hut (514)	Spearfish	53
Pizza Hut (1154)	Hot Springs	102
Pizza Hut (1719)	Rapid City	146
Pizza Hut (1720)	Rapid City	146
Pizza Hut (29)	Belle Fourche	16
Pizza Hut (665)	Sturgis	60
Pizza Hut (811)	Custer	74
Pizza Lab (365)	Lead	44
Pizza Mill (812)	Custer	75
Pizza Ranch (1721)	Rapid City	146
Pizza Ranch (1722)	Rapid City	146
Pizza Ranch (515)	Spearfish	53
Pizza Ranch (667)	Sturgis	60
Pizza Works (813)	Custer	75
Ponderosa Motor Lodge (388)	Lead	45
Ponderosa Steakhouse (989)	Hill City	87
Ponderosa Trading Co. (326)	Deadwood	37
Popeye's Louisiana Kitchen (1783)	Rapid City	149
Posy Palace Flowers & Gift Baskets (75)	Belle Fourche	19
Powder House Lodge (1278)	Keystone	111
Powder House Lodge Cabins & Motel (1315)	Keystone	113
Prairie Berry Winery (940)	Hill City	83
Prairie Berry Winery (990)	Hill City	87
Prairie Edge (2107)	Rapid City	159
Prairie Harvest Mercantile and Gifts (2108)	Piedmont	159
Presidents View Resort (1313)	Keystone	112
Pretzel Place - Rushmore Mall (1939)	Rapid City	153
Price Motel (1562)	Rapid City	140
Pump House at Mind Blown Studio (224)	Deadwood	30
Pure Bean Roasted Coffee (1940)	Rapid City	154
Putz N Glo (1444)	Rapid City	129
Qdoba Mexican Grill (1883)	Rapid City	152
Qdoba Mexican Grill (1884)	Rapid City	152
Quail's Crossing, Motel and Cabins (1043)	Hill City	91
Quality Inn (1044)	Hill City	91
Quality Inn (1563)	Rapid City	140
Quality Inn (573)	Spearfish	54
Qué Pasa (1885)	Rapid City	152
Queen City Coffee (454)	Spearfish	52
Rabbit Bicycle Shuttle (931)	Hill City	81

Rafter J Bar Ranch Camping (1045)	Hill City	91
Rafter J Bar Ranch Store (1070)	Hill City	94
Railhead Family Restaurant (1279)	Keystone	111
Railroad Roundhouse & Chophouse (343)	Lead	40
Ramada Rapid City (1564)	Rapid City	140
Ramblin' Rangers (1110)	Hot Springs	99
Ranch A Education Center (1404)	Beulah	121
Ranch House Motel (1565)	Rapid City	140
Rapid City Bicycle Sharing Program (1455)	Rapid City	131
Rapid City Elks Lodge No 1187 (2077)	Rapid City	158
Rapid City KOA (1619)	Rapid City	142
Rapid City Rush Professional Hockey (1445)	Rapid City	129
Rapid City RV Park and Campground (1620)	Rapid City	142
Rapid City Summer Nights (1464)	Rapid City	133
Rapid City Walking Tours (1458)	Rapid City	132
Rapid River Art Gallery (1463)	Rapid City	132
Rattlesnake Jake's (1358)	Keystone	114
Recreational Springs ATV (345)	Lead	41
Recreational Springs Resort (389)	Lead	45
Red Garter Saloon (1280)	Keystone	111
Red Lobster (1676)	Rapid City	144
Red Rock River Resort & Spa (1191)	Hot Springs	103
Reflect Bistro and Bar at Cambria (2002)	Rapid City	156
Reflections Fine Art Gallery (2109)	Rapid City	159
Reid Motel (57)	Belle Fourche	18
Reptile Gardens (1446)	Rapid City	129
Restmore Inn & Cabins (1046)	Hill City	92
Richard Tucker, Bronze Sculptor (894)	Custer	78
Rico's (991)	Hill City	88
Ride N Rest Campground (704)	Sturgis	61
Rimrock Happy Tavern (2003)	Rapid City	156
Rimrock Lodge Rustic Cabins (564)	Spearfish	54
Riverside Campground (60)	Belle Fourche	18
Riverside Suites (1192)	Hot Springs	103
Roam'n Around (2110)	Rapid City	159
Robbinsdale Lounge (2004)	Rapid City	156
Robin's Roost Cabins (1047)	Hill City	92
Rock 'n Robin's Biker B&B (1206)	Hot Springs	103
Rock & Pine Adventures, Edgemont (1111)	Edgemont	99
Rock Crest Lodge & Cabins (866)	Custer	76
Rocket Motel (867)	Custer	76
Rockin R Trail Rides (773)	Custer	71
Rocking Tree Floral (727)	Sturgis	62
Rocky Knolls Golf Course - 9 Hole (767)	Custer	70
Rocky Mountain Chocolate Factory (2054)	Rapid City	157
Rocky Point Campground (62)	Belle Fourche	18

Rocky Point Recreation Area (8)	Belle Fourche	12
Rodaro's Pizza & More (1723)	Rapid City	146
Rodeway Inn – LaCrosse (1567)	Rapid City	140
Rodeway Inn – Mount Rushmore Rd (1566)	Rapid City	140
Rodeway Inn and Suites (574)	Spearfish	54
Rogues Gallery Old West Antiques (1395)	Hulett	120
Roma's Ristorante - Italian (473)	Spearfish	52
Ron's Café (1677)	Rapid City	145
Roosevelt Inn Hotel & Restaurant (1316)	Keystone	113
Roost Resort Camp & Cabins (868)	Custer	76
Roscoz Bar (640)	Sturgis	60
Rosestrudel (814)	Custer	75
Roughlock Falls (353)	Lead	43
Roughriders Leather & Gifts (327)	Deadwood	37
Route 16 Diner & Pizzeria (992)	Hill City	88
Ruby House (1281)	Keystone	111
Ruby Tuesday (1678)	Rapid City	145
Rumours (1941)	Rapid City	154
Runs with Wolves Inc. (1071)	Hill City	94
Rush Mountain Park & Rushmore Cave (1261)	Keystone	109
Rush-No-More RV Resort (705)	Sturgis	61
Rushmore Borglum Story (1253)	Keystone	106
Rushmore Express Inn & Family Suites (1317)	Keystone	113
Rushmore Helicopters, Inc. (1262)	Keystone	109
Rushmore Inn (1568)	Rapid City	140
Rushmore Mountain Taffy Shop (1359)	Keystone	114
Rushmore Plaza Civic Center (1447)	Rapid City	129
Rushmore Shadows Resort (1621)	Rapid City	142
Rushmore Tramway Adventures (1260)	Keystone	108
Rushmore View Inn (1318)	Keystone	113
Rustic Country & Candy Store (1236)	Hot Springs	104
Rustic Ridge Guest Cabins (1319)	Keystone	113
Rustic Soul (82)	Belle Fourche	19
Sabor A Mexico (1886)	Rapid City	152
Sacora Station Bar & Grill (2005)	Piedmont	156
Sage Creek Grille (815)	Custer	75
Sage Meadow Ranch (1117)	Hot Springs	100
Saigon Restaurant (1887)	Rapid City	152
Sally O'Mally's Pub and Casino (2006)	Rapid City	156
Saloon #10 (133)	Deadwood	22
Saloon #10 Casino (157)	Deadwood	23
Saloon #10 Outerwear Shop (328)	Deadwood	37
Sandwich Shop (1679)	Rapid City	145
Sandy Swallow Art Gallery (936)	Hill City	82
Sanford's Grub & Pub (1680)	Rapid City	145
Sanford's Grub & Pub (484)	Spearfish	52

Santana's Sports Bar & Grill (225)	Deadwood	30
Scoot Inn B&B (58)	Belle Fourche	18
Secret Garden B&B (542)	Spearfish	54
Shade Valley Camp Resort (706)	Sturgis	61
Shady Rest Motel (869)	Custer	76
Shanghai Garden (641)	Sturgis	60
Shanklin's of South Dakota, Inc. (905)	Custer	79
Shaviq Studio & Gallery (2111)	Rapid City	159
Sheridan Lake (944)	Rapid City	84
Sheridan Lake Marina (945)	Rapid City	84
Sherwood Lodge (565)	Spearfish	54
Shipwreck Lee's Bar and Grill (2007)	Rapid City	156
Shooters Wood Fire Grill (2008)	Rapid City	156
Side Hack Saloon & Grill (642)	Sturgis	60
Silver Dollar Saloon (993)	Hill City	88
Silver Lining Creamery, The (2055)	Rapid City	157
Silver Mountain Cabins (1622)	Rapid City	142
Silverado Franklin's Grand Buffet (226)	Deadwood	31
Ski's Pizzeria (34)	Belle Fourche	16
Skyline Motel (1193)	Hot Springs	103
Slash J Saloon (2009)	Piedmont	156
Slate Creek Grille (994)	Hill City	88
Sleep Inn & Suites (1569)	Rapid City	140
Sliders Bar & Grill at WaTiki Waterpark (2010)	Rapid City	156
Smallcakes (2056)	Rapid City	157
Smiling Moose Deli Rapid City (1942)	Rapid City	154
Smith Fargo Suites (1194)	Hot Springs	103
Smokin' T/D BBQ (1155)	Hot Springs	102
SoDak Honest (906)	Custer	79
Sonic Drive-In (1784)	Rapid City	149
Sonic Drive-In (1785)	Rapid City	149
Soul Food Bistro (456)	Spearfish	52
South Dakota Air & Space Museum (1448)	Rapid City	129
South Dakota Rose Inn (1570)	Rapid City	140
South Pine Motel (686)	Sturgis	61
Southern Hills Community Theatre (1112)	Hot Springs	99
Southern Hills Golf Course (1113)	Hot Springs	99
Spearfish Art Gallery (431)	Spearfish	48
Spearfish B&B (543)	Spearfish	54
Spearfish Canyon Country Club (427)	Spearfish	46
Spearfish Canyon Golf Course (521)	Spearfish	53
Spearfish Canyon Lodge (390)	Lead	45
Spearfish Canyon Scenic Byway (430)	Spearfish	47
Spearfish City Campground (550)	Spearfish	54
Spearfish Creek Inn (566)	Spearfish	54
Spearfish Creek Wine Bar (534)	Spearfish	53

Name	City	Page
Spearfish Falls (352)	Lead	43
Spearfish Regional Hospital 593-55	Spearfish	55
Spearfish Waterpark (432)	Spearfish	48
Spirit of the Hills Wildlife Sanctuary (433)	Spearfish	48
Spokane Cr. Cabins & Camping (1321)	Keystone	113
Spring Creek Inn (1048)	Hill City	92
Springhill Suites/Marriott (263)	Deadwood	33
Spur Campground (1623)	Piedmont	142
Stadium Sports Grill (522)	Spearfish	53
Stage Stop Leather & Gifts (1072)	Hill City	94
Stagecoach Gifts (329)	Deadwood	38
Stampmill Restaurant Saloon (369)	Lead	44
Star-Lite Motel/Knight's Inn (684)	Sturgis	61
Starbucks at Alex Johnson (1943)	Rapid City	154
Starbucks in Safeway (455)	Spearfish	52
Stardust Motel (1571)	Rapid City	140
State Game Lodge (751)	Custer	65
State Game Lodge (787)	Custer	72
State Game Lodge (870)	Custer	76
Stateline Station (1403)	Beulah	121
Stay USA Hotel & Suites (1195)	Hot Springs	103
Steel Wheel Campground (296)	Deadwood	35
Steel Wheel Trading Post (330)	Deadwood	38
Steerfish (485)	Spearfish	52
Stockade (227)	Deadwood	31
Stone Faces Winery (942)	Hill City	83
Stonewall's Kitchen (2011)	Rapid City	156
Storybook Island (1449)	Rapid City	130
Sturgis Coffee Company (643)	Sturgis	60
Sturgis Community Center (600)	Sturgis	56
Sturgis Harley-Davidson (728)	Sturgis	62
Sturgis Motorcycle Museum (606)	Sturgis	57
Sturgis Motorcycle Rally™ (602)	Sturgis	56
Sturgis Photo & Gifts (729)	Sturgis	62
Sturgis RV Park (707)	Sturgis	61
Sturgis Strikers Bowling Alley (611)	Sturgis	58
Sturgis T-Shirt and Gifts (730)	Sturgis	62
Sturgis View Campground (708)	Sturgis	61
Sturgis Wine Co. (644)	Sturgis	60
Subway - Rushmore Mall (1791)	Rapid City	149
Subway (1156)	Hot Springs	102
Subway (1282)	Keystone	111
Subway (1786)	Rapid City	149
Subway (1787)	Rapid City	149
Subway (1788)	Rapid City	149
Subway (1789)	Rapid City	149

Subway (31)	Belle Fourche	16
Subway (32)	Belle Fourche	16
Subway (359)	Lead	44
Subway (668)	Sturgis	60
Subway (816)	Custer	75
Subway (995)	Hill City	88
Subway at the Pilot Truck-stop (1790)	Rapid City	149
Subway by Walmart (499)	Spearfish	53
Subway downtown (498)	Spearfish	53
Sugar Shack (234)	Deadwood	31
Sugar Sweet Candy Store (2057)	Rapid City	157
Summer Creek Inn (1572)	Rapid City	140
Sumo Japanese Kitchen (1888)	Rapid City	152
Sunflower Cottage (581)	Spearfish	55
Sunset Motel (51)	Belle Fourche	18
Sunshine Café – Healthy! (477)	Spearfish	52
Super 8 – LaCrosse (1574)	Rapid City	140
Super 8 – Tower Rd (1573)	Rapid City	140
Super 8 (1049)	Hill City	92
Super 8 (1196)	Hot Springs	103
Super 8 (1320)	Keystone	113
Super 8 (54)	Belle Fourche	18
Super 8 (575)	Spearfish	54
Super 8 (871)	Custer	76
Super 8 Motel (685)	Sturgis	61
Super 8 Pizzeria (228)	Deadwood	31
Super 8-Deadwood (264)	Deadwood	34
Suzie Cappa Art Gallery (1471)	Rapid City	134
Suzie's Camp (709)	Sturgis	61
Swamp Yankee Forge & Mercantile (895)	Custer	78
Swans Organic Discount Market (1073)	Hill City	95
Sweetgrass Inn (1575)	Rapid City	140
Sylvan Lake Lodge (788)	Custer	72
Sylvan Lake Lodge (872)	Custer	76
Sylvan Rocks Climbing School (947)	Hill City	84
T&M Trail Rides (610)	Nemo	58
Taco Bell (1792)	Rapid City	149
Taco Bell (1793)	Rapid City	149
Taco Bell (1794)	Rapid City	149
Taco Bell (500)	Spearfish	53
Taco John's (35)	Belle Fourche	16
Taco John's - Rushmore Mall (1798)	Rapid City	150
Taco John's (1157)	Hot Springs	102
Taco John's (1795)	Rapid City	149
Taco John's (1796)	Rapid City	149
Taco John's (1797)	Rapid City	150

Name	Town	Page
Taco John's (232)	Deadwood	31
Taco John's (501)	Spearfish	53
Taco John's (669)	Sturgis	60
Talking Leaves (1081)	Hill City	95
Tally's Silver Spoon (1681)	Rapid City	145
Tatanka, Story of the Bison (134)	Deadwood	22
Teddy Bear Town (1074)	Hill City	95
Teddy's Deli (1283)	Keystone	111
Tee Pee Campground (1624)	Rapid City	142
Termesphere Gallery (434)	Spearfish	49
Terry Peak (348)	Lead	41
Terry Peak Chalets (391)	Lead	45
Terry Peak Lodge (392)	Lead	45
Texas Roadhouse (2012)	Rapid City	156
TGI Friday's (1682)	Rapid City	145
The Adams House and Museum (121)	Deadwood	20
The Anna Miller Museum (1390)	Newcastle	119
The Branch House (264)	Deadwood	34
The Branding Iron (38)	Belle Fourche	17
The Carriage House (1217)	Hot Springs	103
The Depot Deli at Johnson Siding (1944)	Rapid City	154
The Farmer's Daughter (1075)	Hill City	95
The Freedom Trail & City Parks (1106)	Hot Springs	97
The Golf Club at Devils Tower (1386)	Hulett	118
The Gordon Stockade (752)	Custer	65
The Grand Grille (229)	Deadwood	31
The Green Bean Coffee Shop (20)	Belle Fourche	15
The Green Bean Restaurant (452)	Spearfish	52
The Handbag Store (1076)	Hill City	95
The Indians - Native Art and Crafts (1360)	Keystone	114
The Junk Drawer (591)	Spearfish	55
The Knothole (583)	Spearfish	55
The Knuckle (645)	Sturgis	60
The Knuckle Trading Post (731)	Sturgis	62
The Latchstring Inn (366)	Lead	44
The Lodge at Deadwood (158)	Deadwood	23
The Lodge at Deadwood (261)	Deadwood	33
The Lodge at Mount Rushmore	Keystone	113
The Mammoth Site (1108)	Hot Springs	98
The Old Gringo (230)	Deadwood	31
The Olive Branch Western Store (71)	Belle Fourche	19
The Pink Door Boutique (331)	Deadwood	38
The Potter Family Theatre (1460)	Rapid City	132
The Red Onion Museum (1391)	Upton	119
The River Walk/Bike Path (4)	Belle Fourche	11
The Rock Shed (1361)	Keystone	114

The Rushmore Hotel and Suites (1576)	Rapid City	140
The Sculpture Project (1472)	Rapid City	135
The Sled Haus (367)	Lead	44
The Stables at Palmer Gulch (949)	Hill City	85
The Thoen Stone (436)	Spearfish	50
The Tristate Museum (1)	Belle Fourche	10
The Weathered Vane (2112)	Rapid City	159
The West Texas Trail Museum (1389)	Moorcroft	119
Things That Rock (1077)	Hill City	95
Thirsty's (2013)	Rapid City	156
Three Flags RV Park (1625)	Black Hawk	142
Three Forks Campground (1050)	Hill City	92
Thrifty Motor Inn (1577)	Rapid City	141
Thunder Cove Inn (265)	Deadwood	34
Thunderhead Underground Falls (1450)	Rapid City	130
Tilford Gulch Campground (1626)	Piedmont	142
Time Inn Motel (1578)	Rapid City	141
Time Out Lounge (2014)	Rapid City	156
Tin Lizzie (159)	Deadwood	23
Tin Lizzie Gaming Resort Restaurant (231)	Deadwood	31
Tomahawk Lake Country Club (176)	Deadwood	24
Town Hall Inn (393)	Lead	45
Town House Motel (1579)	Rapid City	141
Trails End Cabins & Motel (1051)	Hill City	92
Trails End Cabins & Motel (1580)	Rapid City	141
Trailshead Lodge (394)	Lead	45
Travelodge (1581)	Rapid City	141
Travelodge Motel (1323)	Keystone	113
Trial of Jack McCall (126)	Deadwood	21
Triple R Ranch Cabins (1324)	Keystone	113
Tristan's New & Used (80)	Belle Fourche	19
Trout Haven Ranch (1114)	Buffalo Gap	99
Trout Haven Resort (192)	Deadwood	27
Tucker Inn B&B (267)	Deadwood	34
Turtle Town (1284)	Keystone	111
Turtle Town (996)	Hill City	88
Twin Pines Lodge (274)	Deadwood	34
Twisted Pine Winery (939)	Hill City	82
UPS Store (588)	Spearfish	55
Upton Old Town (1394)	Upton	120
Valley Sports Bar (2015)	Rapid City	157
Vertex Sky Bar at Alex Johnson (2016)	Rapid City	157
VFW Post 1273 (2078)	Rapid City	158
VFW Post 3442 (818)	Custer	75
VFW Post 5969 (160)	Deadwood	23
Visit Spearfish (592)	Spearfish	55

Vita Sana Olive Oil Company (2113)	Rapid City	159
Vore Buffalo Jump (1383)	Beulah	117
Wade's Gold Mill (946)	Hill City	84
Wall Drug Store (1451)	Wall	130
Wanda's Finds (1231)	Hot Springs	104
Warrior's Work & Ben West Gallery (1078)	Hill City	95
Warrior's Work & Ben West Gallery (935)	Hill City	82
Washington Inn (1325)	Keystone	113
WaTiki Indoor Waterpark (1452)	Rapid City	130
Way Back Inn (873)	Custer	76
Weimer's Diner & Donuts (646)	Sturgis	60
Wendy's (1799)	Rapid City	150
Wendy's (1800)	Rapid City	150
Wendy's (1801)	Rapid City	150
Wendy's (1802)	Rapid City	150
West Main Lodge (395)	Lead	45
Western Thrifty Inn (1582)	Rapid City	141
Whispering Pines (1627)	Rapid City	142
Whispering Wind Campground (1628)	Rapid City	142
Whispering Wind Cottages (1583)	Rapid City	141
Whispering Winds Cottages/Camping (1052)	Hill City	92
Whistlers Gulch Campground (297)	Deadwood	35
White Rocks (180)	Deadwood	25
Whitetail Court Motel (396)	Lead	45
Wild Bill's Trading Post (333)	Deadwood	38
Wild Rose Gifts (580)	Spearfish	55
Wilderness Legends (1362)	Keystone	114
Willow Springs Cabins B&B (1584)	Rapid City	141
Wind Cave National Park (1121)	Hot Springs	101
Windcross Spanish Mustang Conservancy (1115)	Buffalo Gap	100
Windsong Valley Gardens (907)	Custer	79
Wine Cellar Restaurant (2017)	Rapid City	157
Winner's Circle Lanes & Games (1158)	Hot Springs	102
Wobbly Bobby British Pub (2018)	Rapid City	157
Wonderland Cave (612)	Sturgis	59
Wooden Nickel Casino (161)	Deadwood	23
Woody's Wild West (332)	Deadwood	38
Woolly's Grill & Cellar (1159)	Hot Springs	102
Wounded Knee Museum, Wall (2155)	Wall	163
Wrangler Café (817)	Custer	75
Wrinkled Rock (1264)	Keystone	109
Wyatt's Campground (61)	Belle Fourche	18
Xanterra Gift Shop, Mt Rushmore (1348)	Keystone	114
Yak Ridge Cabins & Farmstead (1585)	Rapid City	141
Yoyo Berri (2058)	Rapid City	157
Z Bar & Nightclub (535)	Spearfish	53

Made in the USA
Las Vegas, NV
26 February 2021